Ruth, Esther, Song of Songs, and Judith

Ruth, Esther, Song of Songs, and Judith

Lisa M. Wolfe

CASCADE *Books* · Eugene, Oregon

RUTH, ESTHER, SONG OF SONGS, AND JUDITH

Cascade Books
An Imprint of Wipf and Stock Publishers
199 W. 8th Ave., Suite 3
Eugene, OR 97401

www.wipfandstock.com

ISBN 13: 978-1-60608-520-2

Cataloging-in-Publication data:

Wolfe, Lisa M.

   Ruth, Esther, Song of Songs, and Judith / Lisa M. Wolfe.

   xiv + 264 p. ; 23 cm. Includes bibliographical references and index.

   ISBN 13: 978-1-60608-520-2

   1. Bible. O. T. Ruth—Commentaries. 2. Bible. O. T. Esther—Commentaries. 3. Bible—O. T. Song of Solomon—Commentaries. 4. Bible—O.T. Apocrypha—Judith—Commentaries.

BS1315.3 .W20 2011

Manufactured in the U.S.A.

For Kathy, who got me started
Fred, who saw me through
And Abraham and Phoebe, who joined me at the end

Contents

Preface

Four women's stories: A Moabite widow, a Jewish queen, a young lover, and a pious warrior. Their presence in the Bible is unusual if not astounding. Ruth, Esther, Song of Songs, and Judith still charm, delight, and intrigue us. They also challenge us to reflect on a huge array of issues still relevant to people of faith, from the presence and absence of God to the place of passion and sexuality to the ways we all suffer and impose both oppression and liberation.

These "Uppity Women of the Bible," as I dubbed this project early on, have kept my interest and monopolized my time for the past seven years. It began with an invitation from my mentor, friend, and colleague, Dr. Kathleen A. Farmer to write the volume for a Chalice Press series. When Chalice canceled the series, I was fortunate and grateful to find that K. C. Hanson at Cascade Books of Wipf and Stock Publishers was willing to take on the project.

Like that of all authors, my social location absolutely affects my reading of these texts. So, please keep in mind that what follows is the work of a Bible professor, an ordained Christian minister (United Church of Christ), who is upper-middle-class, white, American, forty-something, married with two young children, and arguably an uppity woman. You may wish to know more; for that the Internet will suffice.

I have tried to read these texts in the way I teach my students, by taking them on their own terms. That of course is more difficult than it sounds in many ways. Nonetheless, the bulk of the commentary consists of my efforts to translate and interpret the texts in their original languages, with an eye toward what they likely meant to their earliest audiences. To that end, the biblical quotations throughout are my translations unless otherwise specified. For the book of Judith I cite the NRSV. In the Conclusion sections at the end of each chapter I reflect on how each biblical book might intersect with the lives of contemporary readers. At certain points in those sections I do lean toward homiletics; at least I intend for them to provide ideas toward that end.

This book is directed largely to clergy and laypersons, though not without interest to the concerns of the scholarly community. To that end, it is particularly appropriate for university and seminary class-rooms, and will be especially useful for courses addressing women in the Bible. I have tried to keep technical language minimal enough that most laypersons could read and comprehend the commentary, even if not understanding all the details. Though I have tried to keep in-depth analysis of issues such as textual or translation problems to a minimum, in most cases I at least address them and provide footnotes and bibliography so that the reader can find further explanation elsewhere.

Because I learn from teaching, I taught widely about the "Uppity Women of the Bible" throughout the writing process. One result of that is the DVD Bible Study series of the same name, published in January 2010 by Living the Questions (www.livingthequestions.com). This book was the starting point of that process, and now it is a companion piece to the DVDs. I hope "Uppity Women of the Bible" study group leaders and participants will find this book a helpful clarification for their learning from the DVDs; those who read this commentary will find the DVDs a concise introduction to the material.

My-cup-runneth-over in gratitude first to all my friends and family who suffered many years of hearing "when I finish the book . . ." Thanks to my mom and sister, who are real-life uppity-women role models for me; thanks to Kathy Farmer, who taught me to be an uppity-woman Bible scholar and professor, and who originally got me started on this project. Thanks to my children, Abraham and Phoebe, who cuddled and nursed with me at the computer from their earliest days. And above all thanks to Fred, who couldn't have been a better partner for this Uppity Woman if I'd written the story myself.

I am grateful to all the students and parishioners over the years who have taught and learned with me about the "Uppity Women of the Bible." Though I cannot name them all, I especially thank the groups at David's UCC (Dayton, Ohio), Christ Episcopal Church (Dayton, Ohio), Pleasant Hill UCC (Ohio), the Sisters of the Precious Blood in Dayton, the Esther Women group (Oklahoma City), and the Kiva Class (Oklahoma City). Thanks also for the insights and patience of my many students at Oklahoma City University, and seminarians at United Theological Seminary (Dayton, Ohio) and Saint Paul School of Theology at Oklahoma City University, some of whom surely grew weary of hearing about these four books.

In addition to my family, a number of people and groups helped to financially support this project. A real-life beauty queen, Jane Jayroe Gamble, and her husband, Jerry Gamble, helped support the final stages of work by funding a research assistant, along with the Esther Women and Ann Wilson. Thanks also to United Theological Seminary and Oklahoma City University for helpful library staff, and for teaching loads that allowed me some writing time.

I owe a debt of gratitude to Andy Nelms, my able and hard-working research assistant. You did great work. Thanks also to Shannon Rodenberg for helping proofread the Greek. The book is better because of your work, but the mistakes that remain are my own.

Finally, thanks to Christina Young, Liz Donnelly, Helene Harpman, Jo Wheeler, and Pam Norton for babysitting assistance so I could have additional writing time.

Lisa M. Wolfe
Oklahoma City, OK
Christmas 2010

Abbreviations

Hebrew Bible / Old Testament

Gen	Judg	Neh	Song	Hos	Nah
Exod	Ruth	Esth	Isa	Joel	Hab
Lev	1–2 Sam	Job	Jer	Amos	Zeph
Num	1–2 Kgs	Ps (*pl.* Pss)	Lam	Obad	Hag
Deut	1–2 Chr	Prov	Ezek	Jonah	Zech
Josh	Ezra	Eccl (or Qoh)	Dan	Mic	Mal

New Testament

Matt	Acts	Eph	1–2 Tim	Heb	1–2–3 John
Mark	Rom	Phil	Titus	Jas	Jude
Luke	1–2 Cor	Col	Phlm	1–2 Pet	Rev
John		Gal		1–2 Thess	

Apocryphal / Deuterocanonical Books

Tob	Wis	1–3 Esd	Sg Three	Bel	3–4 Macc
Jdt	Sir	Ep Jer	Sus	1–2 Macc	Pr Man
Add Esth			Bar		

Other Ancient Sources

Ant.	Josephus, *Antiquities*
AT	Alpha Text of Esther
Hist.	Herodotus, *The Histories*
Jos. Asen.	*Joseph and Aseneth*
LXX	Septuagint
MT	Masoretic Text
War	Josephus, *Jewish War*

Modern Sources

AB	Anchor Bible
ABD	*The Anchor Bible Dictionary.* 6 vols. Edited by David Noel Freedman. New York: Doubleday, 1992
AOTC	Abingdon Old Testament Commentaries
BDB	Francis Brown, S. R. Driver, and Charles A. Briggs. *Hebrew and English Lexicon of the Old Testament.* Oxford: Clarendon, 1907
BibInt	*Biblical Interpretation*
CBQ	*Catholic Biblical Quarterly*
CBR	*Currents in Biblical Research*
CC	Continental Commentaries
CEV	Contemporary English Version
FCB	The Feminist Companion to the Bible
HDR	Harvard Dissertations in Religion
HSM	Harvard Semitic Monographs
JBL	*Journal of Biblical Literature*
JHNES	Johns Hopkins Near Eastern Studies
LSJ	Henry George Liddell, Robert Scott, and Henry Stuart Jones. *A Greek-English Lexicon.* 9th ed. Oxford: Clarenfdon, 1996. BibleWorks v. 8
NIB	*The New Interpreter's Bible.* 12 vols. Edited by Leander E. Keck et al. Nashville: Abingdon, 2003
NIDB	*The New Interpreter's Dictionary of the Bible.* 5 vols. Edited by Katharine Doob Sakenfeld. Nashville: Abingdon, 2006–2009
NISB	*The New Interpreter's Study Bible.* Edited by Walter J. Harrelson et al. Nashville: Abingdon, 2003
NIV	New International Version
NRSV	New Revised Standard Version
OBT	Overtures to Biblical Theology
OTL	Old Testament Library
TDOT	*Theological Dictionary of the Old Testament.* 15 vols. Edited by G. Johannes Botterweck and Helmer Ringgren. Translated by David E. Green. Grand Rapids: Eerdmans, 1978–2006
VT	*Vetus Testamentum*

ONE

Ruth

Introduction

THE BOOK OF RUTH tells a marvelous story, complete with surprises, hilarity, and emotion. The characters spring to life because most of us can imagine "walking in their shoes." This tale about Naomi, Ruth, Boaz, and others has been crafted with the playful use of ambiguity, double entendre, sexual innuendo, wordplay, rhyme, repetition, and foreshadowing. Through those strategic methods, the storyteller does not force meaning, so much as hint or even tease about it. Amid all this, the book of Ruth gives testimony to a God of unsurpassed lovingkind-ness, manifested through the least likely individuals and situations.

The tale begins at a rapid pace, covering more than ten years in the first five verses. The narrative then slows dramatically, and the rest of the book follows a real-time rhythm of deep feelings and carefully chosen words and actions. The outline below shows four main sections that correspond to the four chapters of the book.

Date and Purpose

The time of this book's composition has been—and will likely remain—the subject of significant controversy. The book of Ruth contains minimal historical markers. The first instance appears obvious enough to settle the matter. In the very first verse of the book we read that the story takes place during the premonarchic time of the judges (1:1), not long after Israel had settled in the land of Canaan (That would be approxi-

1

mately 1100 BCE). Upon closer inspection, however, the text makes clear that the writing or telling of this story took place some time much later than that. In 4:7, the narrator inserts an aside, explaining a way of doing business "previously" in Israel (NRSV, "in former times"). Such a comment would not make sense if the narrative were circulated in the time of the story's setting. Therefore, the story either must either be an old tale that was revived much later, with the addition of this clarifying comment; or it must be a story developed at that much later time but set "long, long ago" for a particular purpose. Another piece of evidence for dating this book appears in 4:17, which names King David, indicating that we cannot date the book any earlier than his reign, approximately 1000–960 BCE.

Many scholarly and religious commentators over the centuries have agreed that the story itself is not as old as the time of the judges, but that it originated much later. In that case the literary setting served the storyteller's purposes rather than historical ends. At the same time, arguments also exist placing the book in the time of the monarchy— King David's time or shortly thereafter. Such assertions originate with everyone from academics to rabbis. Neither view is completely irrefutable. Though many arguments have been crafted to date the book of Ruth based on linguistic evidence, those endeavors have been similarly inconclusive.[1]

When an ancient text is so difficult to date, one strategy is to hypothesize about when and how it might have fit the purposes of the community. This method proves fruitful for the book of Ruth. I will join other commentators who have helpfully argued that Ruth's story played a role in the dialogue of the postexilic, restoration community of the sixth- to fifth-century Jews.[2]

---

1. Jan De Waard and Eugene A. Nida offer a concise summary of the situation. "The frequent repetition of the term 'Moabitess' in connection with Ruth has led to the suggestion that perhaps this book was written in the time of Ezra and Nehemiah as a protest against the stern measures taken by these leaders against men who had married Moabite wives, but there is really nothing substantive either in the grammatical forms, the choice of vocabulary, or reference to historical events which can tell us precisely when this book was written," *A Translator's Handbook*, 1. Over twenty years later, this statement still accurately reflects what scholars as a whole say about dating the book of Ruth. Katharine Doob Sakenfeld provides a helpful and more current summary of scholarship on this matter, though she ultimately arrives at the same point (*Ruth*, 1–5).

2. A strong proponent of this view among contemporary commentators is André LaCocque, *Ruth*.

To briefly recall the biblical history relevant to this postexilic community: The Babylonian Empire conquered Jerusalem around 597 BCE; in 587 they razed the holy city and carried its religio-political leaders into exile in Babylon (2 Kings 24–25; Jeremiah 32, 40; Ezek 33:21). For fifty years, these followers of YHVH lived away from their home. While that was truly a lamentable time (evidenced by the book called Lamentations), it proved fertile in terms of literature production. During this time many of Israel and Judah's sacred stories were written down, collected, edited, and refined. Those texts became the unifying force for a people who would seemingly have been lost, aimless, and splintered otherwise. Remarkably, that cohesive literature contained many and varied stories, representing the diversity of the people rather than homogenizing them. This feature caused the Scriptures—and the "people of the book" who lived by them—to be "adaptable."[3]

That exilic period ended in 539 BCE when a Persian king named Cyrus conquered Babylon and sent the Israelites home. His appearance on the scene was itself cause for theological innovation. One postexilic prophet called Cyrus "anointed one," or "messiah" (Isa 45:1)—a rather shocking designation for a foreigner. As one might imagine, after fifty years in another land, some of the Israelites had developed close, even familial bonds with some of the people they lived with during that time. Indeed, one of Israel's prophets had encouraged them to do so (Jer 29:6). For over fifty years there were deaths and births and marriages; due to the destruction of the Jerusalem temple and their separation from it, there were new ways of worshipping YHVH; indeed, there were new sacred stories and new ways of telling them.

When the exiled community returned to the homeland, a whole new kind of havoc was created. Not all the people of Jerusalem left for the exile; the land was by no means deserted for those fifty years. Conquerors like Babylon did not exile the peasants of a land, except to take them as slaves. Rather, exile served to destroy the leadership and political cohesiveness of a community so that there would be no more rebellion against the new empire. Many of the poor would have remained in the land, perhaps squatting on property that they had rented before. Furthermore, archaeology tells us that even people of some wealth remained behind in Jerusalem. All those who had stayed in Jerusalem and its surrounding areas became known as "the people of the land"

3. Sanders, "Adaptable for Life," 531–60.

(Ezra 4:4; Jer 52:16; Hag 2:4). They, like the exiles, had gone on with life during those fifty-plus years, being born and dying, planting and harvesting, and even worshiping YHVH in ways that evolved over time. When the exiles began returning, it sparked understandable conflict with "the people of the land."

The postexilic community continued to write texts that eventually became Scripture. One scroll from that time is Ezra-Nehemiah, which appears in English Bibles as two consecutive books. They address similar periods, starting with the return of the exiles and including the rebuilding of the city walls and the temple. The priest Ezra comes off as a legalist. His infamous message to the men returned from exile is, "Separate yourselves from the people of the land, and from your foreign wives!" (Ezra 10:11).

This one-line summation exaggerates an attitude that is easy to criticize as exclusionary. The people of Israel, had they been paying attention to their faith history—and the priests had been doing just that during the exile—learned that anything foreign might lure them away from YHVH (Exod 23:23–33; Josh 23–24; Isa 2:5–10). Furthermore, ancient Israel viewed foreign women as especially risky (1 Kgs 11:1–13). Israel's King Ahab made a Sidonian (Phoenician) woman his queen (1 Kgs 16:29–33). The biblical text identified that woman, Queen Jezebel, as culpable for Ahab's downfall (1 Kgs 21:25–26; 2 Kgs 9:4–10, 22, 30–37). The eventual fall of the northern kingdom of Israel and the destruction and exile of Judah and Jerusalem were attributed to the reins of disobedient kings such as Ahab, and other similar situations (2 Kings 17; 21:1–16; Mic 6:16).

Many careful Bible readers over the centuries have noticed, however, that the rather legalist and exclusionary views of Ezra-Nehemiah were not the only ones of the time. For instance, in the postexilic portions of Isaiah we read some remarkably inclusive statements about foreigners as well as those who the priests would have considered "unclean" (Isa 56:1–8). The book of Jonah presses this point as well, portraying an Israelite prophet who was loath to save his foreign enemies when he received word from YHVH that was his task (Jonah 1:1–2; 3:10—4:3). We should be careful not to exaggerate these two views by placing them at opposite ends of a spectrum. The Isaiah passages, while they present a relatively inclusive view, cannot be described as universalistic, for they require that YHVH's people keep the Sabbath and the covenant

(Isa 56:2–6). Furthermore, the Ezra-Nehemiah passages are not xenophobic; they include provisions for the acceptance of outsiders into the community of faith (Ezra 6:21).

In the end, the restoration period was one in which the community of faith understandably struggled with "who's in" and "who's out." It may well be that the book of Ruth was a voice in that conversation. Because it came in story form—and in a story set "long, long, ago"—it may have been perceived as less threatening to the other party. As we will see, however, this book implies views that would have struck some as scandalous, especially during the restoration period. That very reality suggests the likelihood of the restoration period as the rhetorical context for this story. Thus one good reason to conclude that the book of Ruth was written during the restoration period is the fact that it engages precisely the issues that were hotly debated during that time: What is the definition of a foreigner? Are the "people of the land" of Judah and Israel Jews if they didn't go off to exile? Are the people who came back to Judah from exile Jews if they didn't originally come from Judah? What is the place of foreign wives? How would they carry on kin-based ownership of the land? How would they define ancestral lines? In what ways and through what persons does YHVH act?

Like other attempts to historically locate the book of Ruth, this line of reasoning is similarly inconclusive. Such questions could possibly have been relevant in another time of Israel's history.[4] And the book of Ruth does not give us much else to corroborate the argument that it was a restoration-era story. Nonetheless, this hypothetical rhetorical setting gains much support from the story itself. Furthermore, it is a plausible historical background in light of minimal evidence.

Type of Literature and Authorship

Understanding the book of Ruth relies greatly on what literary label one assigns to it. The post-Enlightenment, modernist culture of the twentieth century lent itself to a reading of the Bible as history. Yet, as we have seen, identifying the historical setting of Ruth is a problematic task, much less reading it as historical. This raises further questions. Could

---

4. Sakenfeld's comment about the date and setting of Ruth is helpful here: "Noting the repeated need to challenge narrow exclusivism in the life of the ancient community should remind readers that the story of Ruth addresses a perennial issue in the human community" (*Ruth*, 5).

the book be nonhistorical? Further, if the book is not history, then what kind of literature is it?

This text follows a story line with a clear beginning and satisfying ending; it carefully develops characters whose names brim with meaning, it layers irony on irony, and teases with suspense. It monopolizes on wordplays, stings with sarcasm, pulls punches that might garner as many gasps as laughs—all the while dealing with subject matter of the utmost seriousness and controversy to its readers or hearers. While the irony, humor, name meanings, and careful wordsmithing in Ruth direct us away from understanding it as history, each reader should take the opportunity to consider whether it falls into the category of short story, parable, didactic fiction, fairy tale, or some other genre.[5]

One possibility is to view Ruth as a play in four acts, corresponding to each of the four chapters. In fact, a helpful exercise for reading Ruth with a group is to copy and paste the text into a word processor and divide the book into parts for each character and the narrator. This works smoothly with minimal editing, only taking out the "he/she/they said" lines. This allows a group to experience the story with cast members assigned to parts in a readers' theater. The story truly comes alive when read that way. In addition, the readers' theatre method clearly illustrates how many lines each character has, and it shows where those lines are concentrated. That is one way to determine how much power each player has in the book as a whole, and in its various parts.

Some have described the book of Ruth as a historical short story,[6] others as a novella. Andre LaCocque states that the "only rule of the novella is verisimilitude; it is a history-like story."[7] Though we can identify any number of features that recommend against understanding the book as history per se, it purports to tell of events that have significance for Israel's history. At the same time, Ruth tells a story with infinitely greater meaning and creativity than a historical account.

We may also read this book as a parable. Many of us have experience with this type of literature from the gospels. There, familiar narra-

5. Helpful discussions about the literary form of Ruth appear in LaCocque, *Ruth*, 9–18; and Nielsen, *Ruth*, 5–8.

6. Campbell, *Ruth*, 3–18.

7. LaCocque, *Ruth*, 9.

8. Kathleen A. Farmer argues for this in *Ruth*, 2:891–946, 895–96; and "Ruth" 383–84.

tives such as the Prodigal Son (Luke 15:11–32) introduce characters who have meaning for our own lives, beyond their explicit role in the story. Parables provide at the least something to think about; at the most they preach a clear message with moral or theological significance. The characters in the book of Ruth embody men and women who could easily be any of us. Therefore every reader or hearer may quickly take to heart the story's morals. The book of Ruth also lends itself to the parable designation because nearly all of the character names have meanings that speak to each character's role in the story. That helps us to see more deeply into the story and to personally identify with it.

Certainly, this feature relates to other types of literature as well, such as fairy tales where the characters' names give away their roles in the story. We may recall, for instance, "Snow White," so named for her purity, "Cinderella," for her chore of cleaning the cinders out of the fireplace, and the ubiquitous "Prince Charming," whose name stands without need for further clarification. Furthermore, as my outline illustrates, the story's opening and closing can easily be aligned with the basic structure familiar from fairy tales: "Once upon a time, in a land far, far away . . ."; ". . . and they lived happily ever after."[9] A related possibility is the fable, in which a fantastical story highlights a particular moral. Another strong prospect is the folk tale, which relies on standardized characters and story line.[10]

Related to the question, What kind of literature is the book of Ruth? is the matter of who wrote the book of Ruth. The book contains no claim to authorship, so we have very little to go on in solving this dilemma. A helpful starting point is to develop a reasonable hypothesis about the date and purpose of the book, and then determine who a likely author would be in that scenario. Based on the discussion above, the writer would be someone in the restoration period arguing for a more welcoming view of foreigners than that presented by Ezra-Nehemiah. Perhaps this author circulated among writers with similar views, for we find similar views in Isa 56:1–8.

Another consideration regarding authorship has to do with the content of the book and the perspectives it represents. In this vein, numerous commentators have discussed the possibility that perhaps the author

9. With Sakenfeld, *Ruth,* 1.

10. For a detailed analysis of this option see Sasson, *Ruth,* 196–221.

was a woman.[11] After all, the story is about women—assertive, expressive women who work to ensure their own survival. Furthermore, the story attends to women's concerns: marriage, widowhood, childlessness, motherhood, and poverty. Throughout the book, but predominantly in chapters 1–3, women support, help, talk to, and plan with other women.[12] While these features of the text point to the possibility of female authorship, they are certainly not proof. Along with uncertainty about the date of the book, we similarly cannot be sure of its authorship.

Throughout this chapter, I will often refer to the book's author as "the storyteller." This expresses several of my views about the book of Ruth. Much of the biblical literature originated in an oral form. A book like Ruth, with its similarities to fairytales and parables, would easily fit the scenario of a storyteller surrounded by a group of listeners. I propose this setting in much the same way as I did the historical context: It is a rhetorical context that makes sense hypothetically, but it cannot be proven. Consistent with that, I will frequently use the term "hearer" to denote the book's audience. "Reader" applies more often in our own time, and was certainly the case in some ancient contexts, so I will refer to the audience that way as well. In fact, to the extent that our own culture is becoming less and less text based, "hearer" may become the more relevant term again in the near future.

Ruth the "Foreigner"

Who is Ruth, and what is her relationship to the other characters in this story? The book includes several strategies to get the audience thinking about this question. From her first introduction in 1:4, Ruth is on the one hand a Moabite; on the other hand she is a family member to Naomi, Mahlon, Chilion, and Orpah. According to the flow of the story,

---

11. Campbell, *Ruth*, 22–23; Sakenfeld, *Ruth*, 5; Meyers "Returning Home," 92–93 (also see below re: 1:8); Bledstein, "Female Companionships"; van Dijk-Hemmes, "Ruth."

12. Ilona Rashkow analyzed the dialogue patterns in the book of Ruth. She found that Naomi had more "lines of direct speech" than Ruth. Interestingly, Ruth has a higher percentage of lines when she is with Boaz. These comparisons indicate relative relational power between the characters in the narrative. Indeed, she asserts that "discourse is often viewed as a form of domination." Rashkow comments further: "Naomi's discourse reveals an emphasis, rare in biblical narrative, on relationships between women, specifically mothers and daughters, rather than the customary emphasis on fathers and sons" ("The Discourse of Power," 28–29).

she becomes a widow and wanderer in fairly short order (1:5, 14–19); when she gets to Bethlehem, she could be identified as a "come-here" (to employ a colloquialism from the rural southeastern United States, referring to someone who lives here but is not from here). Throughout the book, Ruth's homeland is assigned as an identifying characteristic for Ruth to the extent that "Moabite" functions practically as her surname (1:4, 22; 2:2, 6, 21; 4:5, 10).

From the beginning of the story, the narrator emphasizes that Ruth is an outsider. One way that the book of Ruth identifies its namesake as "other" is through a label that the storyteller places on Ruth's own lips.[13] In 2:10, we find the Hebrew word נכריה, *nakriyah*, which the NRSV translates "foreigner." Ruth uses this word to identify herself when she asks Boaz why he would show great kindness to an outsider such as herself.

In the wider context of the Hebrew Bible, we find no small amount of controversy related to the concept of "foreigner" or נכרי *nakri*. This term labels the "others" so that the "insiders" can stay separate from them. In most cases, the category carries a negative connotation. There is a law against having a "foreigner" as king (Deut 17:15), and the laws commanding jubilee and interest-free loans do not apply to "foreigners" (Deut 15:3; 23:20). "Foreigners" were not to partake of the Passover meal; it seems they could not even become eligible through circumcision—that was apparently only an option for the "resident alien," or גר *ger* (Exod 12:43–49). The word *ger* connotes a more positive image of the "other" in the Hebrew Bible. It is often translated "sojourner," or "stranger," and indicates a "resident alien" who could enjoy even the rights (Deut 1:16, 29:10–13) and responsibilities (Lev 17:8; Deut 26:10–11) of Israelites. This word even referred to the Israelites themselves, when they were slaves (Deut 10:17–19).

Foreign gods could incur YHVH's wrath (Josh 24:20, Ps 81:8–15, Jer 5:7–31; 8:19); the Ten Commandments make clear that any gods besides YHVH were forbidden (Exod 20:3–5; Deut 5:7–9). When Job laments his situation, he states that his servants had begun to view him

13. Various cultural analysts use the term "other" to describe persons or groups whom dominant society deems the outsider. The process of "othering" often involves stereotyping, vilifying, ridiculing and ultimately excluding the out-group. Postcolonial critics often scrutinize the phenomenon of "othering." A particularly relevant source for feminist studies is Simone de Beauvoir's *The Second Sex*; applicable to biblical studies is Edward W. Said's *Orientalism*.

as a "foreigner" (19:15). Often "foreigners" were the enemies (Obad 11; Lam 5:2), and "foreigners" who were not rejected were blamed for the waywardness of Israelites (1 Kgs 11:1–13). In a vision of Israel's restoration, "foreigners" were the rebuilders of the land, rather than the oppressors of it (Isa 60:10, 61:5), a scenario that the conquered Israelites would presumably have received with some glee. And in Ezekiel's temple vision, he brings a word from God that "no foreigner, uncircumcised in heart and flesh, of all the foreigners who are among the people of Israel, shall enter my sanctuary" (44:7, 9).

The root of "foreigner" is נכר *nakar*, which means, "to regard, recognize, understand." The word for "foreigner" may or may not be related to the verb *nakar*. While the words share a three-letter root and sounds, they indicate virtually opposite ideas: A foreigner is one who *cannot* be "recognized."[14] In cases both inside and outside the book of Ruth, biblical authors clearly monopolize on the fact that the same-sounding words indicate contrary ideas. For instance, in Neh 13:24, the governor Nehemiah criticizes mixed-background children for not being able to "recognize" (*makkirim*, from the root *nkr*) the language of Judah. Practically in the same breath, Nehemiah argues that the downfall of the returned exiles—like that of King Solomon—would be their "foreign wives" (13:26; *hanakriyot*). The homonym-antonyms build toward Nehemiah's rhetorical aim of condemning the "other" cultures to which he attributes Israel's downfall.

The storyteller of Ruth similarly plays with the root *nkr*. For instance, in 2:10, Ruth asks Boaz why he would "regard" her (*lhakkireni*, from *nkr*), since she is a "foreigner" (*nakriyah*). The use of these two similar-sounding words with opposite meanings in the same sentence challenges not only Boaz but the audience of Ruth to think about whether the "other" warrants recognition or inclusion. An interesting parallel to these opposite meanings of *nkr* is the homophone-antonyms *hostile* and *hostel* in English; one represents rejection, while the other relates to welcoming or hospitality (see the Ruth Conclusion, below, for more on hospitality in Ruth.)[15]

14. Scholars debate whether or not the two words have an etymological relationship. In Arabic, sometimes the same root can represent opposite meanings. If a related principle is at work in Hebrew with *nkr*, then the same word lies behind the opposites *nakri* ("foreigner") and *nakar* ("to regard; recognize; understand"). See Ringgren, "*nkr*," 9:423–32.

15. The conclusion reached by many Hebrew scholars about *nkr* is similar to the decision about the homophones *hostile* and *hostel*—that the words have different et-

In some places within the Hebrew Bible, "foreigner" has sexual connotations, in either a metaphorical or actual sense. For instance, in Deut 31:16, when giving Moses his final instructions, YHVH tells the prophet that after he dies, "this people will begin to prostitute themselves to the foreign [*nkr*] gods in their midst, the gods of the land into which they are going; they will forsake me, breaking my covenant that I have made with them" (NRSV). Furthermore, in the book of Proverbs, *nakriyah* usually refers to the "foreign woman," who stands as a literary foil over against "Woman Wisdom." The NRSV translates this "adulteress" (Prov 2:16; 5:20; 6:24; 7:5; 23:27). Thus, the storyteller of Ruth may be making a considerably negative point about Ruth the Moabite in applying *nakriyah* to her; perhaps more negative than the connotations English readers usually apply to the word "foreigner." In one Bible study I taught on the book of Ruth, I asked my favorite question of the group: "What do *you* think happened on the threshing floor (3:6–15)?" A woman responded, with a tone and look of shock and disbelief: "It sounds to me like she's a *whore!*" One of my undergraduate students remarked with a smirk, "Naomi's a *pimp!*" Based on the use of "foreigner" as applied to a woman in the book of Proverbs, that may be precisely the impression the author intended. On the other hand, "prostitute" may be an overly interpretive rendering of *nakriyah*. In the context of Proverbs, it may rather refer to "the other woman," possibly as in the wife of another man, whether Israelite or foreigner.

In the historical books Ezra and Nehemiah, the community of returned exiles attempted to regroup as a people of faith. A major emphasis in this endeavor was to separate from the "foreigners" in the midst; particularly the foreign wives. The end of Ezra consists of a systematic, communal divorce (10:2–44). The priest Ezra had told the men that they must put away their "foreign" wives, their marriages to whom were considered acts of disobedience to YHVH. The final verse of Ezra concludes a long list of men who had married "foreign" women and states that "they sent them away with their children" (10:44, NRSV). This historical context, which stresses dissociating from both foreign wives and even the children they have borne with Israelite men (Neh 13:27) clearly heightens the irony in the book of Ruth, in which the heroine herself

---

ymologies. See "Hostile" and "Hostel," in Onions et al., *Oxford Dictionary of English Etymology*, 449. Thanks to Dr. Kendall K. McCabe for bringing this correspondence to my attention.

was a foreigner. Perhaps the storyteller expected the audience to have precisely this divorce scene in mind, and used the end of the Ruth story as a critique of the directive, "put away your foreign wives." (See also the discussion below on 4:13–22.)

Here, as in Proverbs, a "foreign woman" appears as a scapegoat of sorts for the waywardness of the Israelite people. Indeed, in Neh 13:27 the governor suggests that the people of Israel, like Solomon, sinned because their "foreign" wives made them do it. In turn, the Israelite men were condemned for marrying foreigners in the first place. Nonetheless, the assertion that the women were blameworthy surely remained in the minds of Ruth's hearers as an overarching irony for a story about a Moabite heroine. Incidentally, Ezra-Nehemiah's lack of interest in foreign husbands reminds us of the biblical world's patriarchal ethos. This similarly highlights Ruth's emphasis on husbands, and in so doing suggests the possibility that our storyteller is female.

While this negative view of foreigners certainly prevails in the Hebrew Bible, there is an opposing view as well. At issue is whether outsiders belong in the community of Israelites, and if so, what qualifies them for acceptance. For instance, in 2 Samuel, when King David and his supporters were fleeing from Absalom, we meet the "foreigner" Ittai the Gittite (15:19–22). In a very Ruth-and-Naomi-like scene, David sends Ittai home with a blessing. All the other foreigners in David's entourage have taken their leave, but Ittai offers a soliloquy of protest and loyalty quite like Ruth's (Ruth 1:16–17). With requisite drama and even an oath, he proclaims to the king in 2 Sam 15:21: "As the Lord lives, and as my lord the king lives, wherever my lord the king may be, whether for death or for life, there also your servant will be." David then concedes that the foreigner may come along with his party. In a more cultic arena, we find that in Solomon's prayer to dedicate the new temple he asks YHVH to hear the prayers even of the "foreigners" who would worship there (1 Kgs 8:41, 43//2 Chr 6:32–33).

The lack of hostility toward foreigners in these passages from Samuel, Kings, and Chronicles makes some sense because they were set in the time of the monarchy, when the kingdom of Israel was powerful, and outsiders were not such a threat. After the united Monarchy had split into the north (Israel) and south (Judah), each of which then fell violently to foreign rule in 722 and 587 BCE respectively, those identified as "other" became a serious problem for Israelites. Ezra and those of his ilk viewed the assimilation of Jews with "foreigners" as a potential identity crisis for this now scattered people struggling to survive.

Circumcision was a mark of inclusion in the Israelite community, and therefore becoming circumcised could even change a "sojourner's" status (Ezekiel 43–44). Ezekiel 44:7 indicates that allowing "foreigners" entrance to the temple required not only their physical circumcision but that of their hearts. The postexilic Isaiah greatly expanded such ideas in some strikingly inclusive passages:

> Do not let the foreigner joined to the LORD say,
>   "The LORD will surely separate me from his people";
> and do not let the eunuch say,
>   "I am just a dry tree."
> For thus says the LORD:
> To the eunuchs who keep my sabbaths,
>   who choose the things that please me
>   and hold fast my covenant,
> I will give, in my house and within my walls,
>   a monument and a name better than sons and daughters;
> I will give them an everlasting name
>   that shall not be cut off.
> And the foreigners who join themselves to the LORD,
>   to minister to him, to love the name of the LORD,
>   and to be his servants,
> all who keep the sabbath, and do not profane it,
>   and hold fast my covenant—
> these I will bring to my holy mountain,
>   and make them joyful in my house of prayer;
> their burnt offerings and their sacrifices
>   will be accepted on my altar;
> for my house shall be called a house of prayer
>   for all peoples.
> Thus says the LORD God,
>   who gathers the outcasts of Israel,
> I will gather others to them
>   besides those already gathered. (Isa 56:3–8, NRSV)

Here the prophet actually chastened Israelites for excluding the "foreigner" (Isa 56:3, 6). They were to include even the eunuch, who would have been due double "other" status for being castrated and a foreigner (Lev 21:20).[16] The key was no longer genealogy or even priestly law, but

---

16. See chapter 2 on Esther, below, for a discussion on the category of eunuch. Also see Spencer, "Eunuch," 2:355–56.

rather love of YHVH, the keeping of Sabbath, and the covenant with a God who appears more than eager to include the "other."

Despite Ezra and Nehemiah's overall hostility to foreigners, those books agree to some extent with the inclusive passages from third Isaiah. In Ezra 6:21 we find that the Passover was eaten not only by the returned exiles, but "also by all who had joined them and separated themselves from the pollutions of the nations of the land to worship the LORD, the God of Israel" (NRSV). These differing overall views on the "foreigner" indicate that there was a debate going on in Israel at this time as to what to do with these outsiders, and how to think about them theologically. The book of Ruth may well belong to this debate, joining in with the postexilic Isaiah and challenging Ezra-Nehemiah. Unfortunately, we cannot be certain that this is the case. While Ruth scholars have long supported this view, they have not done so unanimously.[17] Because the book's purported historical setting is the time of the judges, and there are few other firm historical markers, we simply cannot be sure if the author intended the story about Ruth as a statement about how the "other" can become the hero/ine of Israel when included in the community of believers.

Moab

Moab lay just to the east of the Dead Sea and was bordered on the east by the desert. The Bible's etiological story about Moabites explains that they were the result of the infamous incestuous union between Lot and his daughters following the destruction of Sodom and Gomorrah (Gen 19:30–38). This narrative explanation of the Moabites' origins constituted an Israelite insult hurled at these bitter enemies.

Additional background on Moabites appears in Numbers. During the wilderness wandering, the Israelites conquer two Amorite kings in northern Moab (Num 21:21–35//Deut 2:26—3:17) when they were refused passage through that land (cf. Judg 11:12–28). In the following scene, King Balak of Moab hired Balaam to curse Israel (Numbers 22). During the time of the Judges, which is the literary setting of the book of Ruth (1:1), the Moabite King Eglon is directed by YHVH to oppress the Israelites as punishment for their evil deeds (Judg 3:12). The people

---

17. Ringgren ("nkr," 9:428) rejects the idea that Ruth is about including foreign women, while LaCocque in *Ruth* asserts this is precisely the topic of the book.

were subject to him for eighteen years until the people begged YHVH to help (3:14). YHVH sent the judge Ehud, who led a slaughter of the Moabites (3:15–30).

In the legal code of Deut 23:3–6, we find a Scripture that greatly condemns Moabites:

> No Ammonite or Moabite shall be admitted to the assembly of the LORD. Even to the tenth generation, none of their descendants shall be admitted to the assembly of the LORD, because they did not meet you with food and water on your journey out of Egypt, and because they hired against you Balaam son of Beor, from Pethor of Mesopotamia, to curse you. (Yet the LORD your God refused to heed Balaam; the LORD your God turned the curse into a blessing for you, because the LORD your God loved you.) You shall never promote their welfare or their prosperity as long as you live. (NRSV)

This legal background serves as crucial context for understanding how the original hearers of Ruth would have reacted to a story about a Moabite heroine.

These biblical records may well reflect later Israelite animosity against Moab more than they report actual historical events. Nonetheless, these Hebrew Bible texts effectively express the kinds of assumptions the earliest audiences of Ruth would have had about this story and the homeland of its protagonist. If the pentateuchal stories against Moab reflect later feelings against that territory and its people, perhaps Ruth's story was written specifically to contradict such anti-Moabite sentiment by Israelites who had intermarried or intermingled with Moabites or other foreigners (Ezra 9:1—10:12; see the Ruth Introduction—the section on Date and Purpose, above).

As this suggestion illustrates, the Hebrew Bible does not contain a uniform opinion about Moab. Certainly, negative sentiments about Moab abounded, including its origin in an incestuous relationship (Gen 19:30–38), its inhospitality to the Hebrews (Num 21:21–35//Deut 2:26—3:17), and the temptation to idolatry that it posed because of its worship of the god Chemosh (1 Kgs 11:7). At the same time, the Bible reports Moab as the burial place of Moses (Deut 34:5–6), a sanctuary for King David's parents (1 Sam 22:3–4) and part of King David's ancestry through Ruth (Ruth 4:21–22, see below). At the end of Deuteronomy, despite these legal proscriptions against its inhabitants, we read that

Moab was the location from which Moses viewed the promised land that he would never reach. It was the place where Moses died and was buried (34:1–6), and the place where Joshua was said to have divvied up all the tribal lands (Josh 13:32). Isaiah 15–16 and Jeremiah 48 express Israelite ambiguity—even sympathy—regarding Moab, and may reflect the sentiments of those who circulated the story of Ruth.

The words *Moab/Moabite/Moabitess* occur in some form in Ruth thirteen times in a book with a total of eighty-four verses, emphasizing Ruth as the "other."[18] The frequency with which the storyteller applies this label to Ruth emphasizes to the audience her status as an alien from a despised people. Perhaps the narrator intends a comical effect from this hyperbolic repetition, as if to say, "This is a story about a Moabite named Ruth, who was from Moab—did I mention she was a Moabite?" Given the legal background in Deuteronomy, some may have perceived the book of Ruth as scandalous due to its closing genealogy indicating that King David was the descendant of a Moabite (Ruth 4:17).

The storyteller of Ruth presents an intriguing interplay between "Ruth as a Moabite foreigner" and "Ruth as kin to the Judean Bethlehemites." At the same time, the author identifies Ruth as one of the family, calling Ruth Naomi's "daughter-in-law" seven times, "daughter" eleven times (eight by Naomi and three by Boaz) and using "mother-in-law" ten times to label Naomi's relationship to Ruth. While "daughter" does sometimes refer to one who is technically a "daughter-in-law" (Gen 37:35; Judg 12:9), the repetitive use of "my daughter" in Ruth may act as a catalyst for debate about who really is the "other" in this story, and indeed in the wider community. It may pique the interest (and ire) of an intermarried, postexilic community struggling with the question of whether or not a foreigner may ultimately be considered a Judean's daughter, daughter-in-law, wife, or indeed the ancestor of a king.

The Hebrew word for "daughter-in-law" is the same as that for "bride": כלה, *klh* (see Song of Songs chapter for more on this), which indicates the importance of a woman's relationship to her husband's (or betrothed's) family. Furthermore, the crucial milestone in an ancient Israelite woman's life was the birth of her first son rather than her marriage.[19] With that, her dependence shifts from her husband and his family to her son and his future family. The significant relationship between

18. Ruth 1:1, 4, 6 twice, 22 twice; 2:2, 6 twice, 21; 4:3, 5, 10.

19. Leipzig J. Conrad "כלה," 7:166.

a woman and her husband and her son(s) highlights the widowed and childless Ruth and Orpah's original refusal to return to their homeland and to each of their "mother's houses" (1:8). That in itself would have been an unexpected destination, since most widows would be expected to go back to their *father's* house. (See below for further discussion on this matter.) This also makes Ruth's soliloquy of 1:16–17 toward a foreign, desolate mother-in-law that much more poignant.

Redeemer/Redemption/Redeem גאל *g'l*

The Hebrew root of "redeemer/redemption/redeem" represents another significant theme in Ruth. Various forms of the Hebrew root גאל, *g'l* appear twenty-one times in the book of Ruth (2:20; 3:9, 12, 13 [four times]; 4:1, 3, 4 [five times], 6 [four times], 7, 8, 14). English translations of the root and its permutations include "redeemer," "redeem," "redemption," "kinsman," "kinsman-redeemer," "next-of-kin," or simply "kin." While these sound straightforward in English, they represent a legal concept in Hebrew. A *goel* (pronounced "go-ALE," גֹּאֵל) was an Israelite's closest adult family member, responsible for helping the other out of a problematic situation such as financial or legal trouble. In all cases the biblical text explicitly refers to a male blood relative as the *goel*, though I will explore the possibility that Ruth—a female foreigner with no blood ties—may function that way.

Jeremiah 32:6–8 illustrates the law of "redemption." There, the prophet has the "right of redemption" (גְּאֻלָּה *geullah*), and thus fulfills his role as *goel* by purchasing his cousin Hanamel's property in the doomed city of Jerusalem. That act signified that the people would one day return to their sacred Zion. Leviticus 25:25 provides the legal background for this, explaining that the "near redeemer-kin" (גֹּאֲלוֹ הַקָּרֹב, *goalo haqqarov*) shall "redeem" (גָּאַל, *gaal*) land sold to creditors. Similarly, an Israelite who fell into debt slavery was to be "redeemed" by the nearest relative (Lev 25:47–54).

Leviticus 27 lists prices assigned to various offerings so that one could "redeem" what they had committed to YHVH—whether human, animal or land—rather than sacrificing it. *Goel* means "avenger" in Num 35:19–27 (NRSV, NIV), which describes a relative trying to take revenge following a murder. Such situations require the existence of "cities of refuge," where the innocent could live safely (also see Deut

19:1–13). Furthermore, Job uses *go'el* when stating his laments as though in a courtroom. He calls on his legal counsel or "redeemer" (19:25) to defend him from his suffering. Contrary to popular Christian musical renditions of the verse, whether in hymns or praise songs, the reference was not originally messianic. Possible parallels to the *go'el* in our own time could include an "ICE" (in case of emergency) contact person, or a power of attorney. It would be the person expected to "bail out" some-one—from jail, from debt, from poverty, or from other kinds of trouble.

Levirate Marriage

Orphans received protection from a *go'el* family member (Prov 23:10–11). Widows were often categorized along with orphans in the Hebrew Bible as some of society's most vulnerable (Exod 22:21–22; Deut 24:19–21; Ps 146:9; Isa 1:17; 4:1; Jer 7:6–7; Ezek 22:7; Mal 3:5), but widows were to be specially protected by their kin through a law called "levirate (pronounced LEVV-uh-ritt) marriage." Deuteronomy 25:5–10 describes this code, mandating that the brother of the widow's deceased husband "go into her," consummating a marriage between the two. In so doing, the brother-in-law was expected to impregnate the widow in order for her husband's family line to continue. A man who refused this responsi-bility was to be publicly shamed in a ceremony that included removing his shoe (Deut 25:7–10); we may see something related to this in Ruth 4:7–8. The emphasis here on what to do when a man refuses this respon-sibility betrays yet again the lowly place of women in that society: There is no caveat for a situation in which brothers argue over the widow.

Inequities notwithstanding, this method of protecting widows of-ten strikes contemporary readers as bizarre and even immoral. Indeed, Lev 18:16 and 20:21 prohibit sexual relations between a man and his sister-in-law. However, the cultural context provides crucial background for understanding levirate marriage. Ancient Israelites, like many other ancient peoples, adhered to strict gender roles. When a woman in the ancient world was a widow, especially one left without any sons, she was quite vulnerable. In most cases, an ancient woman could only oc-cupy one of two legitimate roles: a virgin in her father's household or a childbearing wife in her husband's household. (As we will see, Judith is a notable exception to this gender restriction.) Outside of these scenarios, a woman rarely had viable options for her survival. The levirate marriage secured the widow's place in society and prevented her from becoming "desolate." In addition to protecting the widow, levirate marriage cared for the memory of the deceased man. It ensured an heir for his inheritance, and allowed his "name" to continue even in his absence (Deut 25:6).[20]

The story of Tamar and Judah in Genesis 38 tells a story that is the classic Hebrew Bible example of this practice. Tamar was childless when her husband Er died. Er was the eldest son of Judah, and he reportedly suffered this fate as divine punishment for his wickedness (38:7). Er's brother Onan foiled his levirate duty to Tamar by premature withdrawal during intercourse (38:8–9). The text tells us God killed him for that. Judah, the father of these two wayward sons, similarly did not ensure the levirate custom for Tamar's sake. He avoided giving his third son Shelah to her, fearing for his life as well (38:11). Following these foiled attempts at fulfilling the levirate law, Tamar seemingly took matters into her own hands. Though there are ambiguities in the narrative, she apparently tricked her father-in-law into impregnating her (38:15–24). This was ironically the same man who had denied her the protection of levirate marriage. Eventually he admitted his guilt, proclaiming, "She is more in the right than I, since I did not give her to my son Shelah" (Gen 38:26, NRSV).

The story of Tamar and Judah suggests an interpretation of the levirate law that goes beyond the "letter" of Deut 25:5–10: the father-in-law taking on the role of the brother-in-law for the widow, if there are no brothers who can or will accept that responsibility. What we find in Ruth goes beyond the precedent of even Judah and Tamar for levirate marriage. Indeed, as we will see below, scholars debate to what extent this code informs the book.

Because Boaz is not Ruth's brother-in-law, and Boaz and Elimelech did not "dwell together," according to a strict interpretation of Deut 25:5–10 Boaz would not have been legally bound to marry Ruth. Even if we were to assume that Ruth actually stands in for Naomi, no legal obligation would apply to Boaz. Perhaps the storyteller is relying on an otherwise unknown form of levirate marriage, in which even a distant family member may take on the role of redeemer if there is no closer relative available to do so. Our limited understanding about levirate

20. LaCocque in *Ruth* cites Josh 7:9; Isa 14:22; and Zeph 1:4, along with Ruth 4:10, to show the importance of continuing one's "name" (121).

marriage and its various forms prevents us from fully understanding the situation between Ruth, Boaz, Naomi, and the "nearer redeemer-kin." We can rightfully wonder if the storyteller intended the ambiguity we experience from this as twenty-first-century readers. Perhaps it made perfect sense to an ancient audience. Nonetheless, we must admit the limitations this uncertainty puts on us as we try to interpret Ruth's story.

Lovingkindness חֶסֶד hesed

The Hebrew word חֶסֶד hesed appears in the book of Ruth three times: 1:8, 2:20 and 3:10. Throughout the Hebrew Bible, the word refers to acts of kindness or lovingkindness, but it also suggests deeds of loyalty and faithfulness. Both humans and YHVH show hesed, though its frequent use in reference to YHVH lends the term an air of holiness even in passages that deal exclusively with humans.[21] In its "secular" uses hesed involves reciprocity; one who receives hesed from another will return it to that person, or will at least be expected to do so. In some cases, a person offers the wish for YHVH's hesed in return for another person's lovingkindness.[22] Because it involves reciprocity, hesed occurs in the context of relationships.[23]

Twice when hesed appears in Ruth the word refers to YHVH's lovingkindness. In 1:8, Naomi urges her daughters-in-law Ruth and Orpah to return to their mothers' homes; she follows that directive with the blessing that (in a very literal translation) "YHVH do hesed with you like you have done with the dead and with me." Here Naomi attempts to reciprocate the lovinkindness of her daughters-in-law by calling on YHVH's hesed toward them. In 2:20 Naomi again calls on YHVH's חֶסֶד hesed, and makes it a blessing for Boaz. Naomi apparently understands Boaz' hospitality to Ruth as an illustration of YHVH's hesed.[24] That

---

21. According to Zobel's count, which he concedes "must be interpreted with some caution," "roughly 63 of the 245 occurrences belong to the secular sphere." ("חֶסֶד," 5:45). Also see Clark, 267, who writes, "The use of the word in the Hebrew Bible indicates that חֶסֶד is characteristic of God rather than human beings; it is rooted in the divine nature, and it is expressed because of who he is, not because of what humanity is or needs or desires or deserves." Clark cites Morris who says, "in men [sic] it is the ideal; in God it is the actual."

22. Zobel, "חֶסֶד," TDOT 5:47, 50.

23. Sakenfeld summarizes it as "deliverance or protection as a responsible keeping of faith with another with whom one is in a relationship" (The Meaning of Hesed, 233).

24. The Hebrew here is somewhat ambiguous, and could actually be translated to

becomes a turning point for Naomi—who had become "bitter" due to YHVH (2:20–21)—to regain hope in her God.

The final instance of *hesed* in Ruth applies to the namesake of the book. In 3:10, Boaz commends Ruth for her acts of *hesed*, which he says went from good to better (see discussion below). To preface that remarkable compliment, he calls on YHVH to bless her. The connection of these two statements may link Ruth's *hesed* with that of YHVH.

The uses of *hesed* in the book of Ruth raise the question of whose "lovingkindness" is operative in this story. As we have seen, the word *hesed* functions in the Hebrew Bible as a seemingly secular word yet has persistent implications of divine action. Similarly, the word's use in Ruth indicates that the heroic gestures of Naomi, Ruth, Orpah, and Boaz are initiated and reciprocated not only by those characters, but also by God.

Ruth Outline

1) Naomi and Ruth: An Unlikely Pair (1:1–22)

    a) Once upon a time (1:1–5)

    b) From Moab to Bethlehem; from sweet to bitter (1:6–22)
        i) Leaving Moab (1:6–7)
        ii) Naomi sends her daughters/daughters-in-law back (1:8–15)
        iii) Ruth refuses to go; pledges her loyalty (1:16–17)
        iv) Naomi stops speaking to Ruth (1:18)
        v) Arriving in Bethlehem (1:19–21)
            (1) Greeting from the women there (1:19)
            (2) Naomi replies; pledges her bitterness (1:20–21)
        vi) Narrator's summary comment (1:22)

2) In Boaz's Field (2:1–23)

    a) Narrator's description of Boaz (2:1)

    b) Ruth goes out to glean; meets Boaz (2:2–17)
        i) Conversation between Ruth and Naomi; Ruth gleans (2:2–3)
        ii) Conversation between Boaz and the reapers; Ruth gleans (2:4–7)

---

indicate either YHVH's or Boaz's *hesed*. Sakenfeld argues for it as Boaz's (*The Meaning of* Hesed, 105–7); Campbell argues for it as YHVH's (*Ruth*, 106–7).

        iii) Conversation between Boaz and Ruth; Ruth eats and
gleans abundantly (2:8–17)
          (1) Conversation (2:8–13)
          (2) Abundant eating, thanks to Boaz (2:14)
          (3) Abundant gleaning, thanks to Boaz (2:15–17)

    a) Ruth and Naomi discuss the day of gleaning (2:18–22)

    b) Narrator's summary comment (2:23)

3) Ruth and Boaz: A Likely Pair? (3:1–18)

    a) Naomi instructs Ruth in the strategy (3:1–5)

    b) Ruth and Boaz on the threshing floor (3:6–15)

    c) Ruth and Naomi discuss the night on the threshing floor
(3:16–18)

4) And They Lived Happily Ever After (4:1–22)

    a) Boaz and Ruth live happily ever after (4:1–13)
        i) Boaz takes care of business with the nameless closer next-
of-kin (4:1–8)
        ii) Boaz and witnesses (4:9–12)
        iii) Boaz and Ruth marry and have a son (4:13)

    b) Naomi lives happily ever after (4:14–17)
        i) The women bless Naomi (4:14–15)
        ii) Naomi's son Obed (4:16–17)

    c) Genealogy from Perez to David, through Boaz (4:18–22)

Chapter 1: Naomi and Ruth: An Unlikely Pair (1:1–22)

Once upon a Time (1:1–5)

The book of Ruth opens with apparently mundane details that orient
us to the story's setting. The narrator lists facts that include place and
character names as well as the book's purported historical context. These
place and character names carry weighty meanings that offer greater insight to the story's meaning.

    The time is that of the judges (1:1), which explains the placement
of the book in the Christian canon, where it follows Judges. The book of
Judges recounts a repeating cycle of events. First, the people "do what is

right in their own eyes," then they are oppressed by an enemy as punishment until they cry out for God's help. At that time, God sends them a charismatic leader who will help in that particular situation: a judge. The cycle then begins again. (For a sample of this, see the Othniel cycle in Judg 3:7–11, then the Ehud cycle in 3:12—4:1.) This cycle repeats throughout Judges, and the situation of the ancient Israelites continues to disintegrate until the book ends with the statement "there was no king in Israel; all the people did what was right in their own eyes" (Judg 21:25, NRSV). This statement immediately precedes the book of Ruth, implying that there was neither king nor ordered morality at the time of this story. This sequence provides an opportune segue for Ruth's tale about a heroic rescuer, though with many unusual differences from the Israelite leaders and battlefield settings usually found in Judges.

In the Jewish canon, Ruth appears in the final collection of books, called the *Kethuvim* or "Writings." Within this group, Ruth is part of the *Megillot*, or "Five Scrolls." These include Ruth, Song of Songs, Ecclesiastes, Lamentations, and Esther; they follow Proverbs. In Jewish tradition, each of the Five Scrolls relates to a festival day and is read on that occasion. The book of Ruth is read for the Festival of Shavuot (also called Pentecost, or the Feast of Weeks), a celebration of the grain harvest and the Torah. This association makes sense given the book's emphasis on food security, and its field and threshing floor scenes. The context of the Five Scrolls gives readers a particular idea about what kind of literature Ruth is. In contrast to the Christian canon, where the book of Ruth appears among historical books, the Jewish canon places Ruth with wisdom literature (Ecclesiastes), love poetry (Song of Songs), psalms of complaint (Lamentations), and another hopeful Jewish diaspora-era story (Esther). The Five Scrolls most likely represent Israel's later history during and after the exile. This literary context supports the view I articulated above, that Ruth is a *story* (rather than history) of the *restoration era*.[25]

The first location mentioned in the book of Ruth is "Bethlehem in Judah." This city stood out for the original hearers of the story because it was the hometown of King David (1 Sam 16:1–13), who despite his transgressions (2 Samuel 11–12) was exalted by the Deuteronomist as a model king (1 Kgs 14:8). Since the story is set as though it took place prior to the monarchy, but was likely told long after the monarchy (as well

---

25. For a similar view, see Farmer, *Ruth*, 2:894.

as the kingdom of Judah) had been destroyed, this location effectively foreshadows the end of the story, where we find out that Ruth was King David's forebear (Ruth 4:18–22). Furthermore, if the story of Ruth was told for a postexilic community attempting to rebuild in Judah, perhaps this setting served as a hopeful reminder that righteous people coming out of Judah would join with righteous people from foreign lands to produce God's work.

Ruth 1:1 gives the audience two bits of shocking information. The first comes in finding that "there was a famine in the land," when "the land" in question is Bethlehem in Judah. The word *Bethlehem* in Hebrew (pronounced *bait-LECH-em*) literally means "house of bread," so for the narrator to tell us that there was a famine in *that* land effects a palpable irony, and probably even humor. To draw in the audience even further, the narrator adds a second shock: The place to which Elimelech and his family sought relief from the famine was Moab. While Moab was a reasonable enough place to find food, Israel shared a contentious history with this neighboring land. (For more on Moab and its relationship to Israel, see the Ruth Introduction, above.)

In the first four verses of this book, the narrator introduces us to the story's characters one by one. English-speaking audiences miss the meanings of these characters' names, and instead just struggle to pronounce them. First we meet Elimelech (elly-MEL-eck). His name only appears in Ruth; it means "my God is king." This name effects some irony in the Christian canon, where it follows the book of Judges, which closes with the statement "there was no king in Israel" (Judg 21:25a NRSV; see above). In addition, the name indicates the faithfulness of this character and his family—something the narrator might have needed to emphasize, in light of their famine-induced foray into territory where Israel's longstanding enemies worshiped a foreign god. Next the narrator introduces us to Elimelech's wife, Naomi.[26] This main character's name also only appears in the book of Ruth. Her name has a somewhat less certain meaning than Elimelech's, but it likely suggested to the original audience the related Hebrew words for "pleasant," and "delightful." Shortly, Naomi claims a new name, "Mara," which means the opposite, "bitter" (1:20). I like to think of her as "sweetness and light," a fitting English description for her Hebrew name.

26. The pronunciation and accompanying spelling nay-OH-me remains predominant, though according to the rules of Hebrew pronunciation, it should be pronounced NO-me, with an opening short "o" rather than long "a."

The children of this couple were Mahlon (makh-LOAN) and Chilion (chilli-YOAN). Those rhyming names[27] would probably have conjured the meanings of similar-sounding words for "sickness, disease," and "failing, pining, annihilation," respectively. The Moabite wives of these doomed men were Orpah (or-PAH) and Ruth. "Orpah" sounds like the Hebrew word for "neck," or "back of the neck." We will see shortly how these names help illustrate the story line. Finally, we turn to Ruth. The meaning of her name is somewhat disputed. "Ruth" has similarities to the word for "friendship." However, a number of scholars find more convincing its relationship to a word that indicates "to drink one's fill," or "saturated."[28] For a very visual rendering of her name, I will call her "My-cup-runneth-over."[29]

From Moab to Bethlehem: From Sweet to Bitter (1:6–22)

After only six verses, Naomi has few reasons left to feel like "Sweetness and Light." Her blood relatives are all dead, she is in a foreign land, and her only apparent hope is in making the journey home to Bethlehem and prevailing upon the kindnesses of family and friends. For a woman in her time, she had little assurance that she would be anything other than desolate. The prophets were well justified in leveling judgment against those who oppressed widows because of their vulnerability in society (Isa 10:2; Mal 3:5; Zech 7:10). While the "uppity women" in this book (Esther, Judith) and elsewhere in the Bible (for instance Leah and Rachel [Genesis 29], Tamar [Genesis 38], Rizpah [2 Sam 21:8–11], among others) seem to find ways around that vulnerability, many of those same women also illustrate it by going to great lengths to ensure their well being. Ruth and Naomi most certainly belong in that category.

In 1:6 the storyteller moves beyond the background and setting to the plot of the story. There we read that Naomi and her daughters-in-law "started to return" (NRSV), or literally, they "arose to return." In colloquial English we might say she "got up to go back" from Moab for Bethlehem. This marks the beginning of the journey. As we see soon enough, however, the topic of "return" has not yet been settled. The Hebrew word for "return," שׁוּב *shoov* appears repeatedly in this

27. Sasson, *Ruth*, 18.

28. Ibid., 20; Trible, *God and the Rhetoric*, 146; LaCocque, *Ruth*, 40.

29. I owe credit for this name idea to my wordsmith husband Frederick Focke Mischler.

section and indeed becomes a theme for the chapter, and perhaps for the book. This Hebrew root appears fifteen times in Ruth, twelve times in chapter 1.[30]

Elsewhere in the Hebrew Bible *shoov* is most prominent in the prophets, who often use it in a metaphorical sense. For instance, in Jer 31:18–19, a repetition of this root in 31:18a pleads to God "bring me back, let me come back," and in 31:19a the metaphorical, theological use becomes even clearer: "For after I had turned away (*shoov*) I repented" (NRSV). In addition, Hosea repeatedly uses this word to make theological points. The prophet chastises Israel for "turning" from their God, and at the same time admonishes them to "return" to their God. (For example, see Hos 7:16 and 14:1, though this word-theme runs throughout the book.[31])

The storyteller of Ruth similarly plays with the various meanings of this word-concept, especially throughout chapter 1. First, Naomi starts to "return" (*shoov*) to her homeland (1:6). At the same time, she implores her daughters-in-law to "*shoov*" (1:8, 11, 12; NRSV has "go back/turn back," respectively) to their Moabite homes. When Orpah agrees to this, then Naomi focuses her efforts exclusively on Ruth: "Your sister-in-law has returned (*shoov*) . . . return (*shoov*) after your sister-in-law" (1:15). Ruth resists this command to the word in her soliloquy: "Do not ask me to leave you; to return (*shoov*) from following after you" (1:16). Chapter 1 ends with a distinct emphasis on this word, which appears twice in 1:22: "So Naomi returned (*shoov*), and Ruth her Moabite daughter-in-law returned (*shoov*) with her." After all the talk and dispute about turning and returning, in the end the two traveled together to Bethlehem.

Perhaps the storyteller's play with this word involves the irony that while Ruth is turning toward Bethlehem, she is turning away from her Moabite home. Furthermore, Ruth's soliloquy (1:16–17) and the whole chapter's reflection on *shoov* foreshadow a change in identity that we will discover through the remainder of the story; rather than simply being a Moabite foreigner, Ruth has "turned" into someone loyal to Naomi, Bethlehem, and YHVH. Furthermore, might she be trying to "return" to her existence as wife, attempting to deny her situation as a grief-stricken widow? We will see that while Naomi first "turns" from "sweet" to "bitter" (1:13, 20–21), in the end she will "turn" yet again, this time into some-

30. 1:6, 7, 8, 10, 11, 12, 15 (twice), 16, 21, 22 (twice); 2:6; 4:3, 15.

31. See Fabry, "שׁוּב," in *TDOT* 14:487–89.

one surprised by the lovingkindness (*hesed*; see the Ruth Introduction, above) of YHVH as expressed through a Moabite woman.[32]

For all the death that has already taken place in this story without any reported emotion, it seems notable that beginning in 1:9 the storyteller finally reports weeping. The tears shed are not over the parting of blood-relatives, but of in-law foreigners. The blood-relatives who held these women together as family had died back in 1:3 and 1:5. The weeping continues through 1:14. In 1:9 and 14, the narrator tells of Ruth and Orpah's emotion at the prospect of leaving their mother-in-law. We could rightly wonder if the storyteller intends humor or irony that these two weep while Naomi apparently does not. We could furthermore wonder if this should be read as some kind of "bitterly" sarcastic foreshadowing that Ruth would shed tears for a woman who will rename herself "Bitter" (1:20), and show more silence than interest in Ruth's companionship (1:18; see comments below).

In 1:8 Naomi specifies the location to which Ruth should return: "her mother's house." This comment has stood out to many a commentator, since it almost sounds as though the kinship system were matriarchal, and usually a woman would return to her "father's house."[33] Scholars have proposed various explanations for the use of "mother's house," including the possibility that it was simply a mistake.[34] However, Carol Meyers argues persuasively that this reference marks the book of Ruth with "the language of female experience," and "constitutes powerful evidence for the presence of a female text."[35] We could even view this remark as support for the argument that the author of Ruth was a woman.

Following the instruction that her daughters-in-law return home, Naomi asks for YHVH's blessing of *hesed* on them in return for Ruth and Orpah's lovingkindness to her family (1:8b–9a). Her request is quite specific in 1:9a, where she pleads for YHVH to "grant that [the young women] may find security" (NRSV) or "rest" (NIV) in the house of a

32. See Sasson, *Ruth*, 37, re: *shoov*.

33. Carol Meyers cites other references to "mother's house," including Gen 24:28 ("Returning Home," 99–102); and Song 3:4; 8:2 (103–6). She also argues that the term is "represented" in Proverbs.

34. In fact, some of the ancient texts read "father's house" instead of "mother's house" in 1:8. See Campbell, *Ruth*, 60.

35. Meyers, "Returning Home," 114.

husband (see also 3:1, below). When Ruth and Orpah respond emotion-
ally and refuse (1:9b–10), Naomi asks some rhetorical questions that
contemporary readers may find odd. In 1:11–13 Naomi indicates that
she can neither remarry nor bear more sons, nor would these young
women wait for those sons to grow up to remarry themselves. These
strange comments may be the storyteller's effort at foreshadowing by
alluding to the concept of levirate marriage (see Introduction, above), in
which these young widows would bear children with a brother of their
deceased husbands in order to continue his name. The storyteller will
get back to this idea in 3:9, though the matter remains unclear throughout the book.

In 1:13, Naomi begins to announce her new identity. As we saw
above, both her disposition and her name change from "Sweetness and
Light" to "Bitter." The Hebrew word for "bitter" is מָרָא *mara'*, a name
that Naomi claims specifically in her 1:20 soliloquy. Also significant in
both 1:13 and 1:20 is the fact that Naomi attributes her changed identity
to her God, identified as YHVH and *Shaddai*, respectively. This accusation opens the book with a theological tension: is God culpable for
Naomi's worsened situation and attitude? If so, what will God do to re-
dress this woman's woes? The storyteller hooks the audience with those
loaded questions, and challenges them to consider them throughout the
tale. We will revisit these questions and their various implications as we
work our way to the end of this story: Can God turn around (*shoov*)
Naomi's situation and attitude? If so, how? Will Naomi's bitterness allow
for such a change?

In 1:14–15, the two daughters-in-law live up to their names. Orpah
shows the "back of her neck," "returning" to her people. Ruth, "saturated" with lovingkindness, "clung" to Naomi. The Hebrew for "clung"
is דָּבַק *dabaq*; it marks closeness, commitment, and desire for another
throughout the Hebrew Bible, including between Adam and Eve (Gen
2:24[36]), between Shechem and Dinah (Gen 34:3), with foreign spouses
(Josh 23:12; 1 Kgs 11:2), the king (2 Sam 20:2), and God (Deut 11:22;
Josh 22:5; Ps 63:8 [Heb: 63:9]).

---

36. I cannot conclude with Mieke Bal that the use of this word here is a "slip"
suggesting an analogy between Adam and Eve in the Garden of Eden and Ruth and
Naomi on their way to Bethlehem, despite the differing gender pairing. While this
creative suggestion intrigues me, and could possibly be the storyteller's playful intent,
the wide semantic range for this verb throughout the Hebrew Bible leads me to find her
proposal solely speculative. See "Heroism and Proper Names," 42–69.

Following Naomi's theological challenge and Orpah's departure, we find Ruth's famous soliloquy. Her moving speech in 1:16–17 notably includes the theme-word *shoov*, right near the beginning. Ruth does not want Naomi to force her to *shoov* ("turn back," NRSV) from her journey to Bethlehem with her mother-in-law. In making her case against such coercion, she dramatically pledges her loyalty to Naomi. From land to kin to divinity to burial ground, in 1:16–17 Ruth puts words to the action we saw in 1:14, where Ruth "clung" to Naomi. Ruth punctuates her pledge of loyalty with an oath—imagine a dramatic hand motion suggesting choking to death, slitting the throat, or falling to the ground—as she says "thus may YHVH do to me, and thus; even more if death makes a division between me and you" (1:17b).

One of the Bible's best examples of understatement follows this poignant scene. After Naomi has heard Ruth's moving refusal to return to her homeland rather than stay with Naomi, the mother-in-law offers a chilling response (1:18b). It's as though Naomi never even heard Ruth; the Hebrew reads, "she ceased to speak to her." English translations vary widely in their rendering of this phrase. NRSV gives "she said no more to her," while the NIV reads "she stopped urging her." Eugene Peterson's *The Message* offers the greatly interpretive "she gave in." Here we see that different renditions of the terse Hebrew suggest vastly different characterizations of Naomi. The translations that indicate Naomi had simply become convinced of Ruth's rightness may well be missing the point, just like Naomi herself. Instead, the narrator has created a stark contrast between Ruth's melodramatic proclamation of love and Naomi's response, and punctuated it with what could be characterized as the silent treatment.

This effect increases in Naomi's speech to the women of Bethlehem in 1:19–21. Naomi responds to their simple question "Is this Naomi?" (1:19) with her own soliloquy. Rather than articulating her gratitude for Ruth—or even introducing her exceedingly loyal daughter-in-law—she proclaims her new name: *Mara*, which means "bitter." She contrasts not only her old name with her new, but also her former state of being "full" with her current state, which she labels "empty" (1:21a). Furthermore, Naomi blames her situation on YHVH, the same God to whom the Moabite Ruth had just proclaimed her devotion, as opposed to the hated Moabite god Chemosh (1 Kgs 11:31–33). Elsewhere Naomi calls YHVH Shaddai (שַׁדַּי, 1:20, 21), a name that ironically seems to indicate God's nourishment and care.[37] Though the etymology is ultimately uncertain, the name may somehow relate to the word for "breasts" (שָׁדַיִם *shaday-im*) or "fields" (שָׂדֶה *sadeh*), both of which have to do with sustenance through food.[38] The theological contrast between her use of this divine name and her blame of God contribute to a conflicted and even humor-ously dejected characterization of Naomi.

In the storyteller's elegantly crafted narrative of 1:6–21, each of Naomi and Ruth's words—and silences—brilliantly illustrates their situ-ation and their feelings about it. Just to recap the contrasts in this chap-ter: The woman whose name means "Sweetness and Light," Naomi, has become "Bitter" (Mara, 1:13, 20). The Chemosh-worshiping Moabite Ruth has sworn fealty to the God YHVH (1:16) while the Bethlehemite widow of "My-God-Is-King" (Elimelech) holds YHVH accountable for her sorry state of affairs (1:13, 20, 21). Ruth, who has no reason to be devoted to Naomi, powerfully and poetically proclaims her loyalty to her widowed and menopausal mother-in-law (1:16–17), while Naomi, who has no reason to reject Ruth, apparently ignores her (1:18–22). Naomi calls herself "empty" (1:21) while the one who can and will make her "full"—Ruth, or "My-cup-runneth-over" has just followed her all the way home to Bethlehem (1:22). Naomi's selfish blindness to Ruth's devotion comes off as rather comical. If Naomi had a New York City "girlfriend" (*a la* HBO's *Sex and the City* comedy about four women friends), this friend might respond, "Naomi, *honey*, get on some meds!"

The chapter ends with comparatively unemotional comments in v. 22, which simply states that Naomi and Ruth went back to Bethlehem at harvest time. The narrator reminds us both of Ruth's relationship to Naomi ("her daughter-in-law") and of Ruth's otherness ("Ruth the Moabite"). On a final note, we learn that their return coincided with the start of the barley harvest, a detail that will become crucial for the next two chapters.

For another recap of chapter 1, I offer below a retelling of it, with names and locations translated, and possible storyteller "asides" insert-ed. It is not itself a translation or even a paraphrase, but it does follow the text fairly closely. The intent is an English rendering that would illustrate the story's effect on its earliest audience.

37. See Rose, "Names of God," in *ABD* 4:1005; Seow, "God, Names of," in *NIDB* 2:593; H. Niehr, G. Steins, "שַׁדַּי," in *TDOT* 14:424–46.

38. See Lutzky, "Shadday," 15–36.

Once upon a time in House-of-bread-land, there was a famine!
(You can almost hear the drum cue for laughter: "*buh-dum-DUM!*") At a time when "there was no king in Israel and all
the people did what was right in their own eyes" (Judg 21:25,
NRSV), there was a man named My-God-is-King. (Again, the
drums: "*buh-dum-DUM!*") He left House-of-bread-land for the
Land-of-the-despised-enemy with his wife and two sons. (And
wouldn't he need to be such a pious man to endure faithfully in
that place?) His wife's name was Sweetness-and-light; his sons'
names were Sickness-and-disease and Annihilation. Then, My-
God-is-king died, leaving Sweetness-and-light with these two
sons. The sons married women from the Land-of-the-despised-
enemy, one of whom was named Back-of-the-neck. The other
was named My-cup-runneth-over—who knew one could find
a woman of such overflowing friendship in the Land-of-the-
despised-enemy? After about ten years, the two sons died (what
could one expect, with names like that?), leaving Sweetness-and-
light with neither husband nor sons; she only had two foreign,
widowed daughters-in-law.

At that time, Sweetness-and-light decided to leave Land-of-
the-despised-enemy, having heard that House-of-bread-land was
again abundant. Back-of-the-neck and My-cup-runneth-over
started back with her as well. But she instructed her daughters-in-law to return to their mother's houses in Land-of-the-
despised-enemy. She blessed them and sent them on their way.
She kissed them, but these foreign daughters-in-law cried and
protested that they would go with her to the people of House-of-
bread-land. Sweetness-and-light then chastised them, telling her
foreign daughters-in-law that she could provide no more sons for
them, and that even if they were willing to wait, it would take too
long. (Surely she must have been joking that these women from
the Land-of-the-despised-enemy would have waited for *that!*)
Sweetness-and-light said that life had been most bitter for her;
Sweetness-and-light said that her bitterness had come from her
God's abandonment of her. The daughters-in-law from the Land-
of-the-despised-enemy cried again, and Back-of-the-neck finally
showed the back of her neck, and returned home.

But My-cup-runneth-over stayed by Sweetness-and-light.
My-cup-runneth-over gave a moving soliloquy of her loyalty to
Sweetness-and-light, and to her land, and to her people, and to
her God throughout her life. She ended the soliloquy with an
oath, for good dramatic measure. It was a most poignant scene of
devotion, after which Sweetness-and-light . . . *ceased to speak* to

My-cup-runneth-over. (And when the silence begins to sink in, the audience breaks out in scandalized laughs at the irony! *This* is how you respond to such a profession of loyalty and love?) Thus, they returned to House-of-bread-land in silence.

Upon their arrival at House-of-bread-land, the women there began chattering about these two women, wondering if the one was their old neighbor Sweetness-and-light. But Sweetness-and-light then took her own turn for a soliloquy. She said, "I'm not Sweetness-and-light anymore. I'm now Bitter, for the God of Sustenance has been bitter to me. I went to Land-of-the-despised-enemy full; God has brought me back empty." (The audience is incredulous: she came back with *My-cup-runneth-over*, when she had left with *Sickness-and-disease* and *Annihilation*! How is it that she was full then, and bitter now? She really picked the right new name, that Bitter!)

And that is the story of how Sweetness-and-light and My-cup-runneth-over came to leave Land-of-the-despised-enemy and arrive at House-of-bread-land together.

This interpretation of Ruth chapter 1 may give a sense of the assumptions of and interactions between the original storyteller and audience.[39] For instance, as mentioned in the Ruth Introduction, this may more easily help us classify the book of Ruth as a folktale or even parable, rather than as history. Furthermore, this speaks to the possible purpose of the book as sarcastically addressing those Israelites who would put out the foreigners in their midst.

Chapter 2: In Boaz's Field (2:1–23)

Narrator's Description of Boaz (2:1)

As chapter 2 opens, the storyteller introduces us to a new character: Boaz. His name does not have as certain a meaning as many of the other characters' names in this story, but it may have suggested strength or sturdiness to the audience. The name could be a combination of the preposition "in" בּ *b* and the adjective עַז *'az*, which means "mighty," or "strong." Second Chronicles 3:17 reports that the word "Boaz" was inscribed on a pillar of Solomon's temple; it is unclear whether it indicates

---

39. The above section is greatly inspired by Kathleen A. Farmer's analysis of Ruth as parable in "Ruth," in *NISB* 383–90; and *NIB* 2:889–946.

a donor's name, describes the building itself, or refers to something else entirely.

Even before we learn his name, though, we get a description of this new character in 2:1. The narrator assesses him as an אִישׁ גִּבּוֹר חַיִל *'ish gibbor hayil*, which literally means a "great and worthy man." The NRSV translates it as "prominent rich man," and the NIV reads, "a man of standing." The Hebrew phrase *'ish gibbor hayil* and its closely related forms appear rather frequently in the Old Testament. The NRSV translates it in varying ways according to the context, including as "mighty warrior" for Jephthah in Judg 11:1, as "man of valor" for David in 1 Sam 16:18, and as "man of wealth" for Saul's father, Kish, in 1 Sam 9:1. The plural of the phrase similarly indicates "soldiers" (Josh 6:2), "warriors"—both "mighty" and "valiant" (Josh 1:14; 10:7 and Neh 11:14, respectively), and the "wealthy" (2 Kgs 15:20), also in the NRSV. These examples illustrate the wide range of meaning of this Hebrew phrase. Despite the ambiguities, the expression places Boaz in a category with ancient Israel's heroes. Furthermore, it may indicate his standing in the community as based on his physical, moral, or economic prowess.

In addition to describing Boaz's character, the storyteller explains his kinship role in this story. He is somehow related to the widow Naomi's deceased husband, Elimelech. The fact that we do not know the exact nature of Boaz and Elimelech's kinship leaves us with a narrative gap—a hole in the story line or a lingering question that the text simply does not answer. In this case, because we cannot know what relation Boaz is to Elimelech, we are unsure if he is bound by the law of levirate marriage; if he is a redeemer-kin or *go'el* (see the Ruth Introduction, above, for explanation of these concepts). Later in the story, Boaz tells us that while he is indeed a redeemer-kin or *go'el*, Elimelech has a "*go'el* nearer than me" (3:12). Therefore, we can assume Boaz is not Elimelech's brother and they clearly were not living in the same household, which, according to Lev 25:25 are the criteria for the code of the *levir*. Throughout this chapter, we will return to the matter of levirate marriage and the implications of that for understanding the book of Ruth.

Ruth Goes out to Glean; Meets Boaz (2:2–17)

Following the information-loaded opening verse, we finally return to the action. Ruth, who is again referred to as "the Moabite," just so we don't forget, announces her plan for putting food on the table (2:2). Apparently

Naomi is speaking to her again, for she sends the Moabite on her way to glean. Gleaning provided for the needy by allowing them to harvest the leftovers at the edges of the fields. In fact, biblical law mandated the ancient Israelites to leave the "gleanings" לקט *leqet* of their crops for just that purpose (Lev 19:9; 23:22). Not surprisingly, we learn that Ruth ends up gleaning in the field of the story's newest character, Boaz (2:3).[40] Having exchanged greetings with his workers, Boaz inquires about Ruth to his foreman (2:4–5). The head reaper first emphasizes Ruth's status as a foreigner by twice mentioning her Moabite origin (2:6), he then communicates Ruth's request to glean there (2:7).

Unfortunately, the details of Ruth's words and actions as described by the foreman in 2:7 are unclear. The Hebrew text has numerous problems here; both the Latin Vulgate and the Greek Septuagint conflict with it. To summarize part of the difficulty: It may be that having been given permission to glean by the foreman, Ruth put in a long, hard day's work in the field, with a short break (as in the NIV) or no break (suggested by the NRSV, though it allows for some ambiguity). Or, perhaps Ruth's seemingly special request to "gather among the sheaves" (as opposed to gleaning on the edges of the field, and where the grain had already been harvested) was a privilege only the field's owner could grant, so she stood waiting all day for Boaz to come consider this possibility. Furthermore, Kathleen A. Farmer suggests that Ruth may have needed special permission to glean at all, due to her status as a foreigner.[41]

If indeed Ruth waited to request permission from the field's owner himself, it would notably provide a way for Ruth to meet Boaz in person. That could appear as another coincidence, or it could have been intentional on Ruth's part. It is impossible to say whether Ruth would have known the significance of meeting Boaz, since we do not know if she was privy to the narrator's background information from 2:1, that he was a relative of Naomi.

---

40. Commenting on the coincidence in 4:1 where the nearer redeemer-kin shows up at just the right moment, LaCocque also notes 2:20 and 3:2 as coincidences. He goes on to say that "a story such as Esther will proceed from one coincidence to another. This is a distinctive sign of a late narrative and particularly of the novella. The miracle in the ancient stories has now been replaced by opportune events" (127).

41. Farmer cites Lev 19:9–10; 23:22 and Deut 24:19 to show that a "sojourner" or "resident alien" (*ger*) would have had these rights, but that a "foreigner" (*nakriyah*) would not (*Ruth*, 2:916).

Finally, Ruth and Boaz speak to each other (2:8). He offers her hospitality and protection in the forms of water and assurance of a safe place to glean (2:8–9). Ruth's gratitude is both physical and verbal. In 2:10 she bows to him, and her words articulate the irony that Boaz would "recognize" (לְהַכִּירֵנִי *lhakkireni,* from the root *nkr;* NRSV "take notice of") her when she is one beyond recognition (נָכְרִיָּה, *nakriyah,* also from the root *nkr,* NRSV "a foreigner"). (See the Ruth Introduction, above, for more on the concept of "foreigner" in Ruth.) Boaz's response indicates that he recognizes Ruth for being more than a foreigner. He has heard about Ruth's selflessness in leaving Moab for Bethlehem (2:11)—a striking contrast to Naomi's silence on the issue (1:18–22). His answer highlights that Ruth herself came voluntarily to a land where she did not know anyone (2:11b), and suggests that her graciousness to Naomi has earned her Boaz's graciousness in return. In 2:12 Boaz waxes theological, wishing Ruth *shalom* (יְשַׁלֵּם, *yeshallem*) from the God of Israel, to whom she had professed loyalty back in 1:16. Furthermore, this blessing suggests that not only Boaz but also YHVH would want to reciprocate Ruth's behavior. Boaz prays further that Ruth will find the protection of YHVH's "wings" (כָּנָף, *kanaph*). This description of divine care also appears in Ps 91:4. As we will see, this illustration of shelter and redemption reappears later in the story (3:9). Boaz's sentiments do not go unnoticed by Ruth, who thanks him for his compassion and anticipates his continued hospitality to her (2:13).

When it is time to eat, Boaz offers Ruth even more hospitality, this time in the form of food to eat until she was full (2:14). (The sour wine was probably a dipping sauce for bread, comparable to what we would use for salad dressing.) Boaz's hospitality to Ruth continues after their meal, when he allows her to harvest from the main crop, not just from the gleanings on the edges of the field (2:15)—the same thing she requested in 2:7.

He goes beyond even that, instructing his workers to give her some of what they picked as well (2:16). In the end, Ruth's harvest amounted to an *ephah* (2:17). It is impossible to say exactly how much this would be in current measuring systems, but scholars have commonly estimated it at 10–20 liters. It would probably have been enough to feed Ruth and Naomi for about a week. Despite all the translation difficulties in 2:2–17, the passage highlights one message: The woman named "My-cup-runneth-over" has found a place and a person of abundance for herself and her mother-in-law, "Bitter."

Ruth and Naomi Discuss the Day of Gleaning (2:18–23)

When Ruth leaves the field, she returns to her mother-in-law with the fruits of her day's hard work (2:18). Here we finally meet a Naomi whose bitterness appears to have been overcome with gratitude. She is quick to bless the owner of the field where Ruth gleaned, even before she learns his identity (2:19). When she does learn his identity, it is a transformative moment for the one who had changed her name to "Bitter." Her hope in YHVH seems to return with the statement "blessed be he by YHVH, who does not withhold his lovingkindness [*hesed*] from the living or the dead" (2:20). Here, she introduces the theme of *hesed*—it is YHVH's *hesed*, and Naomi has renewed hope in it. (See section on *hesed* in the Ruth Introduction, above.) Perhaps we could editorialize on Naomi's blessing in 2:20, and add to "blessed be he by YHVH, who does not withhold his lovingkindness [*hesed*] from the living or the dead"— or the bitter!

Naomi's postscript to this blessing is to identify Boaz as a closely-related redeemer-kinsman, or *go'el* (2:20b). Here is the first suggestion that he might fill the role of redeemer-kin for the women. For now, however, the suggestion acts as little more than foreshadowing; no details are provided. (See section on *go'el* in the Ruth Introduction, above.)

At the end of the chapter, Ruth again notes Boaz's hospitality (2:21), and Naomi instructs Ruth to continue working with Boaz's women workers, warning her that circumstances might not be so pleasant elsewhere (2:22). Naomi's comment here may sound ominous, but the text does not give us anything more than implication about what she thinks might happen in another field. In any case, Ruth does not seem difficult to convince; the narrator tells us that Ruth followed Naomi's instructions all through the harvests of both barley and wheat (2:23).

Chapter 3: Ruth and Boaz: A Likely Pair? (3:1–3:18)

Naomi Instructs Ruth in the Strategy (3:1–5)

At the beginning of chapter 3, Naomi continues to give direction to her daughter-in-law. Naomi wants to ensure some "security" (NRSV) for

Ruth; the NIV reads "should I not try to find a home for you . . . ?" In a very literal translation, the Hebrew reads "shall I not find rest for you, that it will be well with you?" In this context, what Naomi apparently has in mind is a state of rest for Ruth, which would connote security and perhaps even a home; it is the very thing (and the same Hebrew word) that Naomi prayed for Ruth and Orpah in 1:9a.

With this brief statement of intent, Naomi lays out her plan. As the audience might have guessed from 2:20, it has to do with Boaz, who Naomi here calls "relative" (not *goʾel*). Naomi knows that Boaz will be at the threshing floor that evening, separating the grain from the chaff after the harvest (3:2). Now that the person and place are established, Naomi goes on to instruct Ruth. She tells the young woman to "get all dolled up" (as my grandmother would have said)—to get herself looking and smelling good for this occasion (3:3). Then Ruth is supposed to secretly watch Boaz until, having been contentedly filled with food and drink, he lies down to sleep. At that point, Naomi instructs her to "uncover his feet, and lie down, and he will tell you what you should do" (3:4). Their conversation ends with Ruth agreeing to follow Naomi's guidance (3:5).

This interchange may sound odd to the English-language reader. Ruth is to get washed and dressed and smelling sweet, only to go hide at the outdoor location where Boaz was processing the grain. Once he is asleep, having topped off his day's work with a little partying, Ruth is supposed to uncover his feet, lie down, and wait for further instructions. What kind of a plan *is* this? Naomi's instructions may strike a twenty-first-century audience as bizarre, but also as rather innocuous. In fact, through implication and double entendre, the storyteller has Naomi suggesting a rather bawdy plan.

The threshing floor was, on the one hand, the flat area where one would go to separate grain from chaff. Thus Naomi's direction to Ruth could sound fairly innocent, since Boaz would have been at the threshing floor to process his crop. On the other hand, the threshing floor could be described as the ancient world's "red light district." Hosea 9:1 illustrates that the threshing floor was known as a place for prostitution. By the end of Naomi's instructions, the audience would likely have thought about that "other" use of threshing floors.

Naomi directs Ruth to literally "know the place" where Boaz lies (3:4, NRSV translates "observe the place"). Since a string of double entendres is yet to come, perhaps "know" here initiates those other wordplays by connoting the "biblical sense" of the word that many are familiar with in Gen 4:1. Next Naomi gives Ruth the apparently odd instruction to "uncover his feet." What many readers of English do not know is that "feet" in Hebrew is a common euphemism for "genitals." In other parts of the Hebrew Bible, translators sometimes interpret this euphemism for us. For instance, in Judg 3:24 Eglon's servants did not disturb him in his chambers because they assumed he must be "covering his feet," in a literal rendering of the Hebrew. The NRSV and NIV, however, translate this as "relieving himself." In 2 Kgs 18:27 a people under threat of siege are warned they may have to literally "drink the water of their feet." The NRSV and NIV both render this "urine." Furthermore, Deut 28:57 and Ezek 16:25 use "feet" as a euphemism for female genitals.

The origin of this euphemism may relate to the practice of using one's robes as a tent around the lower body while urinating or defecating.[42] Since in this scenario one would risk urinating on the feet, that could explain the euphemism "foot water" for urine. Thus the phrase "covering the feet" (as in Judg 3:24) was a way to avoid mentioning unmentionable body parts and acts by instead naming only a most innocuous body part.

Knowing all this, we can see that the storyteller may well have had something more than a foot massage in mind by using the phrase "uncover his feet" in 3:4. Further accentuating the storyteller's playfulness with this scene, the Hebrew for this phrase rhymes: Both the verb for "uncover" and the noun for "feet" contain a g-l-(t) sound: מַרְגְּלֹתָיו וְגִלִּית *vegillet margelotayv*; "and uncover his feet" in 3:4 and מַרְגְּלֹתָיו וַתְּגַל *vatgal margelotayv*; "and she uncovered his feet" in 3:7.

After her instruction to "uncover his feet," in 3:4 Naomi tells Ruth to "lie [down]" (שָׁכַב *shakav*). To "lie" (used three times in 3:4) has similar connotations in both English and Hebrew. Numerous passages clearly illustrate the sexual meaning of this Hebrew word. Not only is it used in Ruth 3:4, 7, 8, and 13 with possible sexual implications, but that meaning of the word is much more explicit in Gen 19:33, 35; 30:15–16; 39:7, 12, 14; Exod 22:16; Deut 22:22–23, 2 Sam 11:4; 12:24; 13:14; and Ezek 23:8. Like in the case of "foot," translators sometimes omit euphemisms for the sake of English-language readers. For instance, the first part of Lev 19:20 reads in Hebrew "a man who lies with a woman," yet the NRSV makes the scene explicit: "a man has sexual relations with a

42. Pope, "Bible, Euphemism," 1:723.

woman." Because the Hebrew itself contains ambiguity, it is not entirely fair to criticize the translators for their renderings. For instance, sometimes a foot is just a foot (*a la* Freud's "sometimes a cigar is just a cigar")! The text does not explicitly say that Ruth was to lie *with* Boaz (as do most passages with clear sexual connotations) but simply reports that she should "lie down" after she had "uncover[ed] his feet." That word choice and narrative context allow the storyteller to retain a delightful— or irritating—level of ambiguity about what exactly was to happen on the threshing floor.

Ruth and Boaz on the Threshing Floor (3:6–15)

As chapter 3 continues, both Ruth (3:5) and the narrator (3:6) emphasize the main character's detailed obedience to her mother-in-law's instructions. This highlights the fact that in 3:9 Ruth will depart from those instructions in a slight but significant way. In 3:7 the scene unfolds just as Naomi had directed. When Ruth makes her move, the text says that she does so "stealthily" (NRSV). The Hebrew here is לַט *lat*, which means "secrecy," or "mystery." Interestingly, this word also appears in Judg 4:21, in which Jael approaches the sleeping Sisera with tent peg, mallet, and murderous intent. There, the word describes that foreign woman's sneaky movement in a scene with Israel's enemy. Other citations of *lat*, such as 1 Sam 18:22 and 24:5 indicate that Ruth was trying to be both "hidden" and "quiet" (NIV translates "quietly" in Ruth 3:7). We could say she was "sneaking up" on the sleeping Boaz. When she neared him, she did just what her mother-in-law had instructed her in 3:4: she uncovered his feet, and lay down.

In 3:8 we get a bit of insight as to Boaz's perspective. First of all, he wakes up "in the half of the night," which could mean "midnight" (so NRSV) or just "the middle of the night" (NIV). Second, as one would expect, the man was "startled" (NRSV, NIV) to find "a woman lying at his feet." The word for "startled" (חָרַד, *harad*) usually connotes "terror" or "trembling." His reaction could be explained by the potential implications of "lying" and "feet," or just by the fact of being unexpectedly awakened in the night by a woman he does not recognize.

Naomi had told Ruth that Boaz would tell her what to do next, but the scene takes a slight turn at this point. He understandably asks who it is lying at his feet (3:9). After Ruth identifies herself, she does not wait for Boaz to tell her what to do. Rather, she tells Boaz what to do. She says to him, "Extend your cloak over your servant, for you are *go'el*" (redeemer-kin; see the Ruth Introduction, above). Here she utters yet another double entendre. Her instructions connote more than her need for covers on a cool night sleeping outdoors. Adding to our list of euphemisms, a man who "extends his cloak (כָּנָף, *kanaph*, as in Ruth 3:9)" over a woman is likely having intercourse with her.[43] Ezekiel 16:8 makes this clear. Deuteronomy 22:30 contains a related use of *kanaph*. The NRSV translates: "A man shall not marry his father's wife, thereby violating his father's rights." A literal rendering of the Hebrew reads: "A man shall not take the wife of his father, and shall not uncover the *kanaph* of his father." Clearly, the prohibition was against a man having intercourse with his father's wife; the second part of the verse makes that explicit despite the euphemism, and suggests that the transgression has to do with shaming the father as much as adultery.

In an additional—and bizarre—connection, the Hebrew word for "cloak" is the same as that which is translated "wing" in 2:12 (כָּנָף, *kanaph*). In this way, the storyteller may be suggesting a connection between divine protection (YHVH's "wings" in 2:12) and this human relationship. Indeed, 2:12–13 predict that connection, since Boaz's remark about YHVH's care for Ruth is followed by Ruth's plea for Boaz's continued compassion toward her. If this parallel directs us to conclude that YHVH's care came to these women through some manner of prostitution, it raises some disturbing theological questions for us.

In any case, Ruth justifies her arguably forward request in 3:9 by telling Boaz he is *go'el*, or "redeemer-kin." This, foreshadowed by Naomi's initial identification of him as *go'el* in 2:20 (as well as her comments about being unable to provide more children for Ruth and Orpah in 1:11–13) suggests a connection between the laws of *go'el* (redeemer-kin) and those of levirate marriage (see Introduction section for further explanations of both concepts). Here, and in the narrative following, the storyteller suggests Boaz and Ruth's night on the threshing floor may have had legal—specifically marital—implications.

Boaz responds to Ruth's suggestion by blessing her (3:10). In addition to the connection between *kanaph* for "wings" and "cloak" in 2:12 and 3:9, respectively, this blessing in 3:10 recalls that previous conversation between the two, where he also conferred on her a blessing (2:12). Boaz opens this blessing by calling Ruth "my daughter" for the

43. Pope, "Bible, Euphemism," in *ABD* 1:723.

second time (2:8). This designation may sound inappropriate given the
sexual connotations of the story, but the word also referred to any young
woman, (Ps 45:10; Prov 31:29, NRSV; and the NIV's "women" is from
Heb "daughters"; Song 2:2, NRSV; and NIV's "maidens" is from Heb
"daughters"). Boaz's use of this term may also indicate his acceptance of
his role as redeemer-kin; it connects him to Naomi, who calls Ruth "my
daughter" throughout the book (1:11, 12, 13, 2:2, 22, 3:1, 16, 18). "My
daughter" also undermines Ruth's status as "other" and instead indicates
Boaz's hospitality toward her.

Also in 3:10, Boaz commends Ruth for her two acts of "lovingkindness" or "loyalty" (NRSV; from *hesed*, see the Ruth Introduction, above).
While Boaz does not name these explicitly, we can presume that the first
was Ruth's commitment to Naomi, for which Boaz praised her in 2:12.
Assuming that the second act refers somehow to the events and discussion that night on the threshing floor, this again challenges readers to
consider what exactly took place or was agreed upon there. This is one
line that makes the most sense when the book of Ruth is read as a play.
At one church Bible study on Ruth, when the utterly deadpan Boaz in
our readers' theatre gave the line "this last instance of your loyalty is
better than the first," the whole group appropriately burst into laughter.
The storyteller may well have been most interested in the hilarious implications of Boaz's comment. Yet as we will see in chapter 4, redemption
of land or some form of levirate marriage may have also been at stake.

Regardless of its exact meaning, 3:10 highlights not only Boaz's
hospitality toward Ruth, but also Ruth's hospitality toward Naomi *and*
toward Boaz himself. Boaz compliments—or thanks—Ruth for not
pursuing "young men," indicating that perhaps he is not such a "good
catch," and furthermore suggesting that he is pleased by her choice of
him. Consequently, Mieke Bal has understood this to mean that an
older, unmarried, childless Boaz received lovingkindness (*hesed*) from
Ruth, whose proposition on the threshing floor offered him a life he may
have thought no longer possible. Indeed, perhaps Ruth's lovingkindness
(*hesed*) exceeded that of Boaz, even though he has often been portrayed
as a hero in the story.[44]

Boaz continues in 3:11, calling Ruth "my daughter" again, and as-
suring her that he will follow through with her identification of him as
go'el in 3:9. Indeed, he goes on to say that "his people" consider her a

44. Bal, "Heroism and Proper Names," 22–69.

"worthy woman." This statement first reminds us that Ruth is a foreigner. Second, Boaz's identification of Ruth as a "worthy woman" (אֵשֶׁת חַיִל *'eshet hayil*) directly links her to the storyteller's assessment of Boaz as a "great and worthy man" (אִישׁ גִּבּוֹר חַיִל *'ish gibbor hayil*) in 2:1 (see section on Ruth chapter 2, above). The designation "worthy woman" also appears in Prov 12:4 and 31:10, which the NRSV translates "good wife" and "capable wife," respectively, based on the contexts. The modifier "worthy" has multivalent meanings, including upstanding, efficient, effective (Exod 18:21), praiseworthy, notable (1 Kgs 1:42), and outstanding (Prov 31:29). Kathleen Farmer has remarked that the storyteller, in linguistically linking Ruth and Boaz this way, indicates that they are a well-matched couple.[45]

In 3:12–13, Boaz acknowledges his status as redeemer-kin, or *go'el*. He goes on to say, however, that there exists one "nearer" than he. Boaz will allow that other man the opportunity to be *go'el* for Ruth. If the other man declines, Boaz swears "by the living YHVH" ("as the LORD lives," NRSV, NIV 3:13) that he will take on this responsibility. Unfortunately, we still do not know precisely what that responsibility will be!

Ruth takes her leave of the threshing floor in the veil of dawn's dim light, which Boaz apparently thinks is most prudent (3:14). He does not send her away empty handed, but in yet another act of hospitality, fills her cape with barley (3:15). The amount is ambiguous; the meaning of the gift is what matters here.

So, what did happen on the threshing floor? While the ambiguities tease with a cast of innocence, four possible double entendres suggest that this was an episode involving some level of sex or romance. Were the text to only mention one of the four—"threshing floor" (3:2, 6), "lie [down]" (3:4, 7), "feet" (3:4, 7, 8), or "cloak" (3:9)—we may have good reason to wonder what was going on here. But, with four instances of sexual innuendo as well as Naomi's instructions that Ruth get herself all dressed up for the occasion (3:3), the ambiguity fades. Either something sexual happened on the threshing floor—at the very least, a proposition—or Ruth went to the "red light district" looking and smelling her best, uncovered Boaz from the ankles down, lay beside him asking him to share his covers and take on the responsibility of redeemer-kin, and left with a cloak full of some fresh barley. That absurd picture would

---

45. Farmer, *Ruth*, 2:929–30.

seem to recommend that we read with the double entendres, and assume a sex scene.

Considering the stereotypes of foreign women (see the Ruth Introduction, above, on *nakriyah*), as well as the double entendres and sexual innuendo, ancient audiences may have found this a decidedly bawdy scene. On the other hand, in light of Boaz's comment in 3:10 and the events of the rest of the story, perhaps this scene is about a romantic marriage ceremony between an unlikely pair, sealed with a barley bride price.[46] Perhaps the events of the threshing floor have less to do with sex than with two people who are expressing lovingkindness (*hesed*) to one another. Furthermore, considering the rather crass reality that in Ancient Israel "if you have sex with her you married her,"[47] it may indeed have been a marriage (or at least engagement) ceremony taking place that night on the threshing floor.[48] One church study group gave the sequence of events from 2:14—3:15 a rhyming title: "They sealed the deal after the meal."[49] Because of the time separating us from this text, and because of the story's inherent ambiguity, we cannot be sure which of these options—or some other—best explains the scene.

Kathleen A. Farmer has proposed that Ruth makes two separate requests on the threshing floor: one for redemption of the land, and one for marriage. She supports this by noting that Boaz offers two separate replies to Ruth in 3:11 and 12: the first regarding marriage, and the second for redeeming the land. According to 3:10 Ruth could have chosen someone else for marriage, if her concern were only for herself. The fact that she chose Boaz, however, indicates her concern (*hesed*) not only for herself, but also for Naomi, and indeed for carrying on the name of her deceased husband and father-in-law.[50] This textual analysis provides a rational explanation for an unclear passage.

---

46. See Farmer for this and other possible meanings suggested by the gift of barley (2:930–31).

47. This is illustrated in the legal code (Deut 22:28–29), and in the cases of Dinah (Genesis 34) and Leah (Gen 29:23–25).

48. For further support and articulation of this idea, see Sasson, *Ruth*, 82–99.

49. Christ Episcopal Church, Dayton, Ohio.

50. Farmer, "Ruth," 2:929.

Ruth and Naomi Discuss the Night on the Threshing Floor (3:16–18)

Chapter 3 closes with Ruth returning to her mother-in-law, with plenty of food in hand and quite a story to tell (3:16–17). In 3:16 the Hebrew literally gives Naomi's question as, "who are you, my daughter?" This apparently nonsensical question is actually an infrequent way of inquiring about someone's status (see also Amos 7:2, 5). Having heard the story and received the barley, Naomi assures Ruth—and the audience—that the outcome of this story will not be long in coming (3:18).

Chapter 4: And They Lived Happily Ever After (4:1–22)

Boaz and Ruth Lived Happily Ever After (4:1–13)

Numerous commentators have noticed that Naomi and Ruth's direct dialogue ends in chapter 3. While these two women and the women of Bethlehem especially have significant roles in the end of the story (4:14–17), our female protagonists now largely become subjects in the wheeling and dealing of men. The dialogue about Ruth in 4:1–12 categorizes her as more possession than person. Indeed, the verb in 4:5 that the NRSV and the NIV translate "acquire" can mean "purchase," or "buy" (see below).

This abrupt shift in speech pattern would seem to make a point on the part of the storyteller, but that point remains elusive. Could it be that a female storyteller gets replaced here by a male storyteller? Could this indicate that women's power and autonomy could only go so far before succumbing to the rules of patriarchal culture? Throughout the story Naomi and Ruth appear to have been working carefully within patriarchal culture. Perhaps this shift simply indicates what our characters may have taken for granted all along: given cultural realities, the women's efforts at providing for themselves would eventually have to be formalized by men.[51]

Whether given in female voices or not, chapter 4 wraps up this story in fairly short order, even providing a "happily ever after" ending for all. First, Boaz takes care of business with the "nearer redeemer-kin." The

---

51. For disparate views on this, see Trible, *God and the Rhetoric*, 194–96; and LaCocque, *Ruth*, 125–26.

narrator noted in 3:15b that Boaz returned to the city after his night with Ruth on the threshing floor. Once there, the nearer redeemer-kin Boaz had mentioned to Ruth conveniently appears, and Boaz arranges him and ten of the city's elders for what looks to be a formal, legal gathering. Ten elders would make what amounts to a quorum, and the location of the city gate in ancient times served as the courtroom (4:1–2).

Boaz then explains the situation, though we contemporary readers remain perplexed about the details. He tells the nearer redeemer-kin that Naomi is selling her deceased husband's land (4:3)—completely new information to readers. In 4:4 Boaz formally explains that the nearer redeemer-kin could redeem that land, in a situation apparently similar to that of Jeremiah and Hanamel in Jer 32:6–8.

It may be that selling Elimelech's land was Naomi's way of providing some income for herself and Ruth. The role of the *go'el* in such a scenario would be to buy the land so as to keep it in the tribe or kinship network, and to keep the vulnerable relative out of poverty. Presumably the land belonged to Naomi; perhaps Elimelech originally owned it, and it passed to his widow upon his death. It may be that Ruth, as the widow of one of Elimelech's sons, would also have been a partial owner. However, the storyteller explains none of this explicitly to the readers or hearers. In any case, as 4:4 continues, Boaz states that he is next on the *go'el* list, should the nearer redeemer-kin decline. The final statement of 4:4 is the nearer redeemer-kin's conclusion: "I will *ge'al* it" (אָנֹכִי אֶגְאָל *'anoki 'eg'al*; the NRSV and NIV translate "I will redeem it").

Following this affirmation, Boaz continues with what sounds like a "hitch," or a "string attached" (4:5). Unfortunately, this crucial verse contains significant textual difficulties, creating uncertainty in what the words themselves say, not to mention complicating our already muddled understanding of the legal-cultural implications here. The first textual ambiguity in this verse is whether the redeemer-kin would be acquiring land from *both Naomi and Ruth*, or *just from Naomi*. The NIV translation reflects the former and the NRSV translation indicates the latter, though it includes a text-critical note to show the alternate reading.

The next textual problem relates to whether the nearer redeemer-kin would be acquiring the *land only*, or *both the land and Ruth* (in marriage). The Hebrew text records Boaz's line in 4:5 this way: "on the day *you* acquire the field from the hand of Naomi, *I* will acquire Ruth the Moabite, the wife of the deceased man." In that scenario, the nearer redeemer-kin redeems the field, but Boaz claims Ruth. This differs from the NRSV and NIV translations, in which Boaz says the nearer redeemer-kin would acquire both the land and Ruth: "On the day you buy the land from Naomi and from Ruth the Moabitess, you acquire the dead man's widow" (NIV); "The day you acquire the field from the hand of Naomi, you are also acquiring Ruth the Moabite, the widow of the dead man" (NRSV). Those translations follow the rabbinic tradition about how to read the text, and many commentators over the centuries have concurred.[52]

According to the Hebrew text in which Boaz says "*I* will acquire Ruth the Moabite . . . ," he could here be publicly declaring the private "marriage vows" he made with Ruth on the threshing floor.[53] In that case, Boaz would apparently be taking on the role of the levir "voluntarily."[54] By announcing this to the nearer redeemer-kin, Boaz complicates the situation of the property by showing that one day through him there could be another rightful heir to that land. In other words, that one who redeemed it may not keep it for long but would have to give it to Elimelech's heir through Boaz.

In contrast, following the traditional rabbinic reading "*you* will acquire Ruth," the nearer redeemer-kin would redeem both the land and, apparently, Ruth. In those circumstances, some kind of levirate marriage would be implied, though it would have presumably evolved from the specific forms we know of in the biblical text (Deut 25:5–10). We do not know of another situation that combines redemption of land and levirate marriage in this way. Boaz' comments in 3:12–13 and Ruth's in 3:9 seem to support this scenario, if they are understood as discussion about levirate marriage in general rather than as levirate marriage vows made specifically between Boaz and Ruth. Notably, one implication of this traditional reading is that it could rule out the possibility that anything unseemly happened on the threshing floor.

No matter the exact meaning or implications of 4:5, the nearer redeemer-kin declines his role as *go'el* in 4:6, and turns it over to Boaz. If Boaz were legally proclaiming that he would be Ruth's husband (levir) and produce a child with her, who could claim Elimelech's land again, then the nearer redeemer-kin would have realized that he would redeem

---

52. Campbell, *Ruth*, 146.

53. This proposal is in line with Sasson, *Ruth*.

54. Farmer, "Ruth," 2:937.

Naomi's land only to have to return it again to Ruth and Boaz's child, who would ultimately have been Elimelech's heir. That understanding follows the original Hebrew text rather than NRSV or NIV. If Boaz were suggesting that the nearer redeemer-kin would acquire both the land and Ruth in a "package deal" (with the rabbinic reading), then the nearest redeemer-kin may have been saying that he could not take on another wife.

In 4:7 we find a fascinating narrator aside, and the closest thing to a historical marker that the book offers, aside from the dubious 1:1a. The verse explains the odd manner in which the nearer redeemer-kin declines to redeem, and passes it on to Boaz: the tradition of shoe exchange. By noting that this took place "previously" ("in former times," NRSV; "in earlier times," NIV), the narrator has abruptly betrayed the fact that the story was being told (or at least written down) at a time somewhat removed from "the days when the judges judged" (1:1a). It seems the time must have been at enough of a later date that such an apparently significant gesture could have gone out of use.

Contemporary readers need more than the narrator's explanation, however. The Hebrew of 4:7 provides only a rough description of this sign. Some translations attempt to clarify, such as the NIV's "for the redemption and transfer *of property* to become final . . . this was the method of legalizing transactions in Israel." However, the Hebrew simply says, "regarding redemption and exchange, to confirm every matter . . . this was testimony in Israel." A specification that this had only to do with land is an interpretive addition, though it does have contextual support (4:3). On the other hand, 4:10 suggests that the exchange involved Ruth as well. Ultimately, this verse is ambiguous, and an understanding of whether Ruth and the land were a "package deal" has to do with a wider view of the section and whether or not it involved some form of levirate marriage.

The shoe ceremony in fact may contribute to the idea that a levirate marriage of sorts was being rejected by the nearer redeemer-kin. What we read in Ruth 4:7–8 departs in specifics from Deuteronomy's description of how to reject the levirate responsibility, yet the similarities make comparison of the two irresistible. In Deuteronomy's description of levirate marriage, a shoe signifies a man's rejection of his levirate responsibility; in that case, the widow is the one who is to publicly remove the man's shoe and also spit in his face to declare his unwillingness to "build the house of his brother" (Deut 25:9). Yet the explanation given in Deut 25:7, "to raise up (לְהָקִים *lahaqim*) the brother's name (שֵׁם *shem*)" closely parallels what we find in Ruth 4:5 and 10: of "to raise up (לְהָקִים *lahaqim*) the name (שֵׁם *shem*) of the deceased." The legal text also notes that this ceremony should take place at the city gate (Deut 25:7; Ruth 4:1, 10), with elders as witnesses (Deut 25:7–8; Ruth 4:2).

Despite the similarities, the guidelines of levirate marriage as we know them have not been followed. Boaz and this nearer redeemer-kin were not brothers of Elimelech living in the same household (Deut 25:5). Also, Ruth *chose* Boaz (3:10), while the levir was to be an automatic placeholder for the deceased husband, only to be dramatically rejected by the widow if he refused. Since the scene in Ruth does not stick to all the details of the levirate legal code, it may be that the shoe exchange only represents the property deal. Whatever its specific meaning, the shoe ceremony in Ruth 4:8 apparently symbolizes Boaz's words of confirmation in 4:9, and possibly in 4:10 as well.

It may be that an unusual connection between levirate marriage and redemption by a *go'el* both in the threshing floor scene and in chapter 4 relate to the story's broader aim of challenging legalism in the restoration community. André LaCocque points out that by that time in history the levirate marriage was no longer employed, as it smacked of incest.[55] Furthermore, a strict interpretation of the levirate marriage would not have applied here because Ruth was a foreigner. In light of that, LaCocque argues that the greater law of *hesed* instigated—and allowed for the interrelation of—these previously unrelated laws in a situation where they would never have applied before.[56]

This scene wraps up the book's highly concentrated use of the Hebrew word *go'el* ("redeemer-kin") and its related forms from the root גאל *g'l*. The word first appeared in 2:20, when Naomi told Ruth that Boaz was a redeemer-kin to her through Elimelech. (For further explanation of *go'el*, see the Ruth Introduction, above.) Then, Ruth and Boaz used the word six times on the threshing floor (3:9, 12, 13 four times). At the city gate, Boaz and the nearer redeemer-kin exchanged the word ten times (4:1, 3, 4 five times, 6 four times[57]), followed by two times by the

---

55. LaCocque, *Ruth*, 131.

56. See ibid., 109.

57. The NRSV does not make every use of the Hebrew *g'l* in 4:4 and 6 explicit.

narrator (4:7, 8). The storyteller could not be more persistent in raising the issue of who in this cast of characters will be the redeemer-kin.

Perhaps in focusing so intently on *go'el* in this section, the storyteller intends to challenge the audience with the question, who exactly is our kin? This story's probable historical setting was the restoration period, when Israelites who had recently returned from exile in Babylon were in conflict with "foreign wives" in their midst, as well as with Judeans who had never left. (See the Ruth Introduction, above, for more on this history.) Given this context, it could be that the emphasis here on the redeemer-kin and on who should, will, and could take on that responsibility was a way for the restoration community to reflect on who should or could be part of *their* kin. The community's response to this scene arrives in the form of a unison blessing (4:11–12), which has the feel of a standard choral offering for momentous occasions. Notably, even though Ruth has been physically absent from this whole scene, the words of the people are for her, not Boaz.

Near the end of 4:11, we again find the word חַיִל *hayil*, familiar to us from Boaz's identification of Ruth as a "worthy woman" (*eshet hayil*) in 3:11, and the narrator's assessment of Boaz as a "great and worthy man" (*ish gibbor hayil*) in 2:1. Here in 4:11, the word is paired with the verb for "be," or "do." The phrase is translated variously: "may you *produce children* in Ephrathah" (NRSV), and "may you *have standing* in Ephrathah" (NIV). In any case, the word sounds a familiar note of praise for our heroine; once again, but not for the last time, the storyteller's language pays tribute to Ruth.

As the community continues, they bless Boaz with the helpful request that his "house," or offspring be like that of Perez, the son of Tamar and Judah. The mention of these three Bible characters raises the issue of levirate marriage yet again. Tamar memorably tricked her father-in-law Judah into impregnating her after his first son, and her husband, died; Judah had failed to ensure that one of his younger sons took on the levirate responsibility for the widow (see Genesis 38 and discussion above). In addition, Perez was the youngest son, whose tribe (Num 26:20) had the more prominent position in the kingdom, due to the fact that King David came from its ranks. This serves as a possible connection to our story about another "underdog" who comes out on top. Also, in the postexilic time of the restoration—the time in which the story of Ruth was likely composed and told—Perez's descendents were known as "worthy men" (אַנְשֵׁי חָיִל *'anshe hayil*, Neh 11:6), a designation that clearly runs in the family based on Ruth 2:1, 3:11, and 4:11.

Finally, the optimistic comparison of Boaz to Perez serves as foreshadowing for the end of the story; the original audience may have immediately recognized the connection between Perez and King David, but because the story is set in a time well before the monarchy, the narrator provides that genealogy as a postscript in 4:18–21.

No matter our speculations about what precisely happened on the threshing-floor or at the city gate, 4:13 states that Boaz and Ruth at some time consummated their union, evidenced by the birth of a son. Surely the audience would have been waiting for this very resolution. In fact, it would seem that the story could have ended with this "happily ever after" for Ruth, Boaz, and son, but instead it continues with a "happily ever after" for Naomi, betraying the storyteller's interest in this formerly "bitter" character.

Naomi Lived Happily Ever After (4:14–17)

We hear another group blessing in 4:14, but now it is from only the women rather than the whole group gathered at the gate (4:11). These women hold the status of characters in the story, having first appeared in 1:19. Their concern then and now is with Naomi. Now they bless the same YHVH who, when she last spoke with these women, Naomi had nearly cursed (1:20–21). Specifically, they give thanks that YHVH provided for Naomi's "redeemer-kin," or *go'el*, and in turn they praise the *go'el* himself.

Ruth 4:15 would seem to spell out, finally, the identity of the "redeemer-kin": Ruth and Boaz's son. Yet, playful as usual, the storyteller includes in 4:15 a huge amount of praise for Ruth as well. The women deftly exceed their own praise for the child with rhyming superlative praise for his mother, Ruth. They give thanks in 4:15a that this son will be Naomi's "returner (לְמֵשִׁיב *lemeshiv*)[58] of life and sustainer (וּלְכַלְכֵּל *ulkalkel*) in your old age" (שֵׂיבָתֵךְ *sevatek*); in 4:14b they surpass what they said about the child, and remind Naomi that "your daughter-in-law (כַּלָּתֵךְ *kallatek*) who loves you gave birth to him." The women go on to tell Naomi that this daughter-in-law is better to her "than seven (מִשִּׁבְעָה *mishiv'ah*) sons." In sum, the "*sv*" sound in "returner (*lemeshiv*) rhymes

---

58. See the Ruth Introduction, above, on *shoov* as a theme in Ruth.

with "your old age" (*sevatek*) and seven (*mishiv'ah*); "sustainer" (*ulkalkel*) has similar *kl* sounds as "your daughter-in-law" (*kallatek*). Furthermore, all the "*sv/shv*" sounds in this verse may have appropriately reminded the audience of the root for "abundance," (שׂבע *sb'*), which appeared in Ruth 2:14 and 18 where the two women ate Boaz's grain until they were "satisfied" (NRSV, from *sb'*), and which could be viewed as a theme in the book.

The remarkable verses of 4:14 and 15 start out sounding like a predictable patriarchal happy ending with the birth of the awaited son. Yet 4:15 ends with what could be viewed as a feminist critique, by superseding the birth of the son with words of exceeding honor for his mother, a foreigner. The women's exclamation that Ruth is "better than seven sons" not only rhymes with "returner" and "old age" (see above), it also invokes a number symbolizing completeness (Gen 2:2–4; Exod 20:11). There could hardly be a higher compliment for Ruth. Since within five verses of the story's beginning Naomi loses her husband and sons, and Ruth loses her father-in-law, husband, and brother-in-law, we can see the significance of the end of the story in which Ruth bears a son. That son, Obed, serves as the kinship tie both women needed.

Naomi becomes the boy's "foster parent" (NRSV: "nurse," 4:16). The women call him Naomi's child, but they name him Obed, which means "servant." *A son + a son used interchangeably. — Does Ruth mother ? her son ?*

Genealogy from Perez to David, through Boaz (4:18–22)

The storyteller goes on to give an abbreviated genealogy that cuts to the chase; this child of a Moabite was King David's grandfather. Ruth 4:18–22 fleshes out that genealogy, connecting the dots through Israel's history between Perez—the offspring of an Israelite man who did not require his sons to fulfill the law of the levirate, and his Canaanite daughter-in-law who tricked him into fulfilling it himself (Genesis 38, and see above)—and the flawed yet revered superhero of the Israelite monarchy, King David himself.

Conclusion

Whether the book of Ruth is a novella, fairytale, fable, or folktale, thoughtful readers can hardly help considering its deeper meanings. In that, our egos may tempt us to identify only with the book's heroine,

Ruth. But perhaps the story has much more to teach if we consider how we are like the other figures in the story. Indeed, as evidenced by the number of lines each character has, it may well be that the story is more about Naomi than about Ruth.[59]

And who cannot see the temptation of Naomi? Can we not relate to experiences of bitterness that are palpable? Naomi actually changes her name to "Bitter"; now and then most of us have changed our attitudes or at the very least our facial expressions to bitter. Bitter may feel like the lingering agony and loneliness of loss, like what Naomi experienced. The idea to rename ourselves "Bitter" may come with death or divorce, with illness or chronic pain. It is frighteningly easy to relate to—or become—Naomi. And the effects of a life as "Bitter" linger like a bad taste in the mouth, perhaps even prompting us to blame God for that state, as Naomi did in 1:13, 20–21.

I have a good friend and colleague who teases himself and others about being disgruntled, angry, lonesome, and tired of eating alone by exclaiming—with hand raised as though to gain the attention of a maitre 'd, a sing-songy—"Bitter, party of one!" Certainly, if Naomi had won that early argument with Ruth, she would have gotten just that; she could have sauntered right into Bethlehem to desperately, angrily shriek to her friends, "Bitter, party of one!" In fact, the way she apparently ignores Ruth all the way home, she did practically that.

Fortunately, Naomi's story attests and many of us still today attest to a God who is faithful, who will not let bitterness prevail without persistent, poetic professions of love from a Ruth, or a dozen Ruths. Yet Ruth never looks like we expect. To Naomi, she was her deceased son's widow from a foreign and despised land, willing and able to care for her, though she surely had expected something at least slightly more traditional—like a husband or her own son, rather than the adopted child of her Moabite-foreigner daughter-in-law.

Ruth may be a group of challengingly diverse persons struggling to love one another and love God, all the while calling themselves "church." Ruth may be a small child whose unconditional love has the power to melt away our icebergs of hurt. Ruth may be the job we didn't want, which turns out to be a true joy. She may be the divorce that was heartbreaking yet provided freedom and happiness that never before seemed imaginable. Since Ruth does not look like we would expect (a foreign,

59. See Rashkow, "Ruth," 29.

powerless, destitute widow who should have gone home to her mother), we may ignore her presence, like Naomi did.

Once we begin to recognize her, we all have various names for Ruth. Jesus talked about Ruth in parables: mustard seed, yeast, buried treasure, and valuable pearl (Matt 13:31–33, 45–46). These things are not what we were looking for, but they embody the kin-dom[60] of heaven nonetheless. There she is: Ruth, standing right in front of our faces, and we still have the most difficult time realizing it, much less appreciating her. And then, before we know it, we find ourselves utterly filled with joy, like Naomi holding her newborn baby.

Even when we acknowledge Ruths all around, it can be quite difficult to let go of the desire for what we expected. It may still be what we want. We still long for, fantasize about, and even grieve what was lost, like Naomi must have—her husband, her very own sons, and a family that never suffered famine and was comfortably composed of other Bethlehemites. I imagine that Naomi, even after she finally appreciated Ruth, even as she held the new baby Obed in her arms, still felt some of her bitterness. And who can blame her—or us? We can have a little of the bitter, can't we? Perhaps the trick is to not let that lingering bitter prevent us from seeing the God-given Ruths all around; to allow ourselves the turning point that Naomi had in 2:20, where Boaz's appearance on the scene allowed her to see that YHVH had not abandoned her after all.

By identifying with Naomi rather than Ruth, perhaps we can discover the principle of "undercover hospitality."[61] Could it be that throughout Ruth, in sarcastic, stealthy, and otherwise unexpected ways, the various characters extend hospitality to one another—but especially to Naomi? Contemporary faith communities spend a good deal of time talking about hospitality. While we are caught up with figuring out how we can offer hospitality and to whom, maybe we would do well to remember Ruth's story. Someone who *we* might be very reluctant to welcome into our own lives or congregations could be the very one who will offer hospitality to *us*. In fact, perhaps that person who we might just

60. I owe thanks to my teacher Dr. Carolyn Stahl Bohler for teaching me to use this inclusive and contemporarily relevant alternative to *kingdom*. In addition, it is particularly fitting for the book of Ruth, and its conception of what constitutes community and family.

61. I am grateful to my colleague and good friend the Reverend Alecia Schroedel for this delightful euphemism and double entendre (well in the spirit of the Ruth story itself) as a description of what goes on in this book, especially in chapter 3.

as soon exclude even as a recipient of our hospitality is precisely God's way of offering hospitality to us. Could it be that all kinds of hospitality goes around in all kinds of directions, without us even noticing, because it is happening in such "undercover" kinds of ways? The book of Ruth may serve as a reminder for us to pay attention and look around to see if God's hospitality is moving among us in surprising ways, like it was moving among Naomi, Ruth, and Boaz.

It can also be fruitful to consider in what ways or situations we are most like Orpah. She exits the story early on, so we do not know much about her. We do know that—at least initially—she had the same impulse to loyalty as her sister-in-law Ruth (1:10). But, after Naomi's repeated urgings (scoldings? chastisements?) not to carry through on that loyalty (1:11–13), Orpah tearfully returned home (1:14). What do we learn from Orpah? Rather than eliciting our judgment, perhaps her decision can inspire us to reflect on our own choices to tearfully turn away from a cause or a person. We do not know why Orpah left and Ruth stayed, but we do know that there are times when we do not have it in us to be Ruth; times when we must return to what we know, and who we are, and times when we simply must rest. For infinite practical, personal, spiritual and emotional reasons, we cannot irrationally stick with every needy situation or individual that we encounter. We cannot—and probably should not—always sacrifice ourselves for the sake of someone or something even as important as a widowed mother-in-law. Our God-given lovingkindness inspires us to weep at that, in turning away from a homeless family, or from volunteering to teach Sunday school. We cannot always do what needs doing, and that is indeed cause for grief.

Finally, let us consider identifying with the namesake of this biblical book. Too often that is all we do, yet Ruth should perhaps be the least likely character to garner our aspirations. It may be that when we become Ruth, it happens both unexpectedly and unwittingly. In my experience, it has only been considerably after the fact that it occurred to me I have been Ruth to someone. In most cases, I was not *trying* to be Ruth, but rather I did so in such an unlikely way that I later determined it could only have been God working through me. I recall a friend who quite belatedly thanked me for speaking wisdom and compassion to her when she was struggling immensely. Looking back, I realized at the time I was in no position to be offering wisdom or compassion, because I too was struggling immensely. Perhaps if I were being Ruth in that situation, it was God—not me—who inspired that. Maybe the best we can do to be Ruth to someone is to not suppress the urge to utter a God-inspired soliloquy of unlikely love and loyalty—and then to wholeheartedly act on it. And when a Naomi looks up with thankful tears in her eyes, holding her newborn, perhaps we simply need to share in her joy and gratitude to God.

We also need to regard Ruth as more than an admirable heroine. While it may seem straightforward to aspire to be like biblical heroines (and heroes), the scriptural stories are usually go deeper than that. In regard to the threshing floor scene in chapter 3, we would do well to ask ourselves, for instance, whether Ruth was hilariously sneaking her way to survival, or sadly sleeping her way to survival? Either explanation casts a seriousness on the scene that we might not automatically assume: Ruth and Naomi faced utter poverty and starvation, and needed to find a way to eat. The latter question points out that Ruth took dire risks in approaching Boaz as she did. What was their plan if he refused? What if he took offense at her behavior and made her an outcast in the community? What if he had sex with Ruth and *then* made her an outcast in the community? What would these widows' options have been then? The story calls us not to judge Ruth's actions in this situation, but it certainly challenges us to consider Ruth as something other than a typical heroine.

Returning to the restoration-era hypothesis for which I argued in the Ruth Introduction, we can recall that the family of faith was at that time trying to define itself. It was struggling with "who's in," and "who's out"; it was determining "what is the in-group," and "what is the out-group." The Ruth story likely contributed to that discussion by offering a despised, foreign, idol-worshiping heroine who converts to follow YHVH, and who arguably does so in a more faithful way than many actual Judeans. Naomi's character could have challenged the restoration community to grapple with their post-exilic bitterness and blindness to a divine vision that might have been larger than theirs. Isak Dinesen, the great author who wrote *Out of Africa*, has said, "All sorrows can be borne if we put them in a story or tell a story about them."[62] It is not so difficult to imagine that Ruth's story served that purpose for certain persons within the community of restoration Jews. Indeed, this story continues

---

62. Quoted by Kidd, "A Penguin Readers Guide," 8.

to bear the sorrows of its readers, as evidenced by contemporary devotional readings of the book.[63]

Surely these matters do have present-day relevance, as most Christian and Jewish denominations debate about whether or not to include gays and lesbians in the ranks of their congregations and clergy. Indeed, some continue to struggle about the extent to which they should include women. Are we muffling God's voice through a Ruth who would be ordained to speak that word, while we work to bar her from the pulpit?

At the time of this writing, a pressing controversy within the United States of America has to do with whether and under what circumstances immigrants should be included as citizens. In this country of immigrants, we are hotly debating who is "illegal," and who is not; we are placing National Guard troops at the Mexico border, and building a "super fence" to keep out the "other." Can Naomi, Ruth, and Boaz speak to that situation? Are we fencing out Ruth—herself a sort of "illegal?"

In addition, the book of Ruth may highlight for us the issues of poverty and hunger that plague women around the globe. This is particularly the case in cultures like that of ancient Israel, which required women to be especially reliant on men. Perhaps this should remind us to identify with Boaz. While he had a legal obligation to allow for gleaning, he apparently went well beyond that, to provide food for Ruth and Naomi; perhaps he surpassed that obligation in allowing a foreigner to glean at all,[64] to say nothing of his actions in chapter 4. In what ways do we—as individuals, faith communities, civil society—care for our poor, and how do those compare with what we have learned from Boaz' generosity?

Returning to the subtitle I introduced in the Preface, we could also consider whether Ruth and Naomi fit the description of "uppity" women. Some commentators have marveled at the amount of dialogue these women have and the power they amass in the midst of a remarkably hopeless situation. Depending on one's interpretation, Naomi's directions to Ruth and Ruth's initiative with Boaz on the threshing floor in chapter 3 would most certainly count as "uppity," if not scandalous! However, other interpreters over the centuries and even today would count Ruth's story as an example of women manipulatively eking out a tiny bit of power in the midst of an intractable patriarchy. In that view,

63. For instance, Kates, *Ruth*; Chittester, *The Story*; James, *The Gospel*.

64. Farmer, *Ruth*, 2:916.

Naomi and Ruth diligently obey gender norms, live lives of few options, and have little control over their own destinies. The paradox and brilliance of this story is that its ambiguity allows for both interpretations.

Some interpretations of this story have become dangerously prescriptive. Rather than being an opportunity for all people to reflect on their status as "bitter," "worthy," or graced with a "cup-that-runneth-over," on their acts of "turning/returning," "lovingkindness," or of "showing the back of one's neck," some readers or hearers have tried to freeze the story into one particular message. Of course, applying Scripture to contemporary life as though it is a literal match happens frequently. However, this study on the book of Ruth—as well as the other books discussed in this volume—may serve as a helpful example that the biblical text allows for too many possible interpretations for it to have such particular moralistic meaning. The text is living; it should not (and I would argue cannot) be frozen.

Some Asian women have reported that the story of Ruth has been assigned such certain significance in their culture. In those settings, it has been enlisted among some Christians as biblical support of a cultural requirement that daughters-in-law obey their mothers-in-law. In some cases, those kinship ties have been expressions of oppression rather than of lovingkindness. Anna May Say Pa quotes Wenh-In Ng's comment: "To have 'Wither thou goest, I will go' held up as one's model from the pulpit when one's culture already demands that you do, is far from liberating."[65] Of course, such an interpretation neglects the fact that Naomi pleads for her daughters-in-law to return home (1:11–13), and the fact that the narrator makes no judgment on that. No morals of the story are spelled out for the reader/hearer; there is no one cut-and-dried message to the story. Nonetheless, the story is problematic for women whose culture has demanded loyalty to the mother-in-law. It may be that when a biblical text becomes so overwhelmed by cultural baggage, its good news may need to be carefully reclaimed. Indeed, it may need to be set aside for some time before its story may be properly heard.

I will close with one final question, an opportunity to play with the ambiguities of the story. For each of the book's themes: redeemer-kin/ *go'el*, foreigner, return/*shoov*, lovingkindness/*hesed* and others, we can rightly ask ourselves—and the story—to whom does that theme apply? Whose lovingkindness comes into play—Ruth's, Boaz's, YHVH's? Who

65. Pa, "Reading Ruth 3:1–5 from an Asian Woman's Perspective," 58.

"returns," to where, and in what way? Who is the redeemer-kin—Boaz, Ruth, both of them? Whose "otherness" is at stake here—Ruth's, Naomi's, our own? The book of Ruth offers us ample opportunity to reflect on these questions as they apply to our own lives and spiritual journeys, perhaps even considering different answers every time we "return" to the story.

TWO

Esther

Introduction

FROM A RAGS-TO-RICHES HEROINE to the triumphant vindication of an underdog people, the book of Esther contains all the elements we desire in a good story. At times, the book keeps us on the edge of our seats wondering what will happen next; at other times it paints hilariously absurd scenes and characters that leave us no choice but to laugh. Though it is not an historical account, the book of Esther highlights numerous verifiable details about the Persian Empire, from royal intrigue to harem life. More importantly, it presents utterly true realities for the scattered Jewish people.

Esther so captured the imaginations of ancient Jews that we now have it in three versions: a Hebrew version canonical to Jews and Protestants (Masoretic Text; MT); a Greek version canonical to Catholic and Orthodox Christians (Septuagint or Apocrypha; LXX); and another non-canonical Greek Text (Alpha Text; AT).[1] One of the rare biblical books that in the MT never mention God, Israel's history, nor any overtly religious acts, Esther nonetheless proudly holds its place in the biblical canon, begging its readers to consider why it belongs there.

The book of Esther unfolds with one delicious scene after another, many of which include banquets. The outline below attempts to delineate those scenes so as to illustrate the overall structure of the book in MT, with bracketed portions to include the LXX Additions (Add Esth).

---

1. In the commentary below, I will be referring to MT unless I specify otherwise.

Date and Purpose

Because the book of Esther does not contain obvious information about the date of its composition, scholars have varying views about its origin. The only points of agreement are that it must be later than the time of the historical King Xerxes I (486–465 BCE) since he is the apparent basis of the story's king (Add Esth 1:1), and earlier than 48 BCE, the latest possible date associated with the appearance of the book in Egypt as noted in Add Est 11:1. This fifth-through-first-century span leaves daunting room for speculation about the book's origins.

The tale presents itself as set in the Persian period, which began in 539 BCE when King Cyrus of Persia conquered ancient Babylon. At that time, many of the people of Israel were in exile in Babylon, with their Jerusalem home having been decimated by the Babylonians in 587 BCE. The Babylonian Exile began what we now refer to as the Jewish Diaspora, in which the ancient Israelites were forcibly scattered from their "promised land," never to fully return. It seems perfectly reasonable to expect that the Babylonian exile would have destroyed the ancient Israelites forever. Yet their persistent faith, guided by the priestly leaders and solidified by their religious practices and oral and written sacred stories, sustained them during this uncertain time.

In 539 BCE, Cyrus the Great of Persia offered them a new life in their homeland when he sent them back to Jerusalem with cash and temple furnishings looted by the Babylonians to rebuild their holy city and temple (Ezra 1:1–8; 5:13–17; 6:3–14; Isa 44:28–45:7; 1 Esd 2:1–14). Therefore many scholars refer to the early Persian Period as the Reconstruction period. The Persian period lasted until Alexander the Great conquered the area in 332 BCE, marking the beginning of the Hellenistic, or Greek Period. Compared to earlier periods of biblical history, we know quite a bit about the Persian Period from extrabiblical sources, including Persian records themselves and secondary commentators such as Herodotus and Ctesias. We have good information about who the Persian kings were, when they ruled, and even what they accomplished.[2]

In the case of this time period, we are fortunate to have a significant extrabiblical resource in *The Histories* of Herodotus. Herodotus is our ancient Greek historian par excellence. Born sometime between 490 and

---

2. Moore, *Esther*, 116–17; *Ctesias' History of Persia*; Herodotus, *Hist.*; and Kuhrt, *The Persian Empire*, xxxvii.

480 BCE, Herodotus traveled around the ancient world to Africa, Persia, Russia, Italy, Mesopotamia, Egypt, Palestine, and many other places in between. He recorded what he saw and read and heard, in some cases including conflicting versions. His reports about the Persian period illuminate the study of Esther, corroborating some of what the book reports about the workings of that empire. For instance, he tells of royal women being called upon to join the men's banquet, and praises the speedy and effective Persian courier system—both details that have relevance to the book of Esther (Herodotus, *Hist.* 5.18; 8.98).

Because our knowledge about the Persian period is relatively complete, we can be quite sure that the book of Esther does not report factual events. For instance, no extrabiblical sources can corroborate a key feature of the story: that once a Persian law was established it could not be rescinded (1:19). There are no Persian queens named Vashti known in other sources (Xerxes' queen was named Amestris [Herodotus, *Hist.* 9.109]), and no reports of a deposed Persian queen. In addition, no evidence exists for a Jewish Persian queen, which is not surprising since Persian policies did not allow for a Jewish woman to be the queen. In fact, a Persian king was required to choose from one of seven royal families for his queen.[3] The king in Esther is the only character with a clear historical corollary. Ahasuerus may well be a fictionalized version of Xerxes I (486–465 BCE). Herodotus tells about the extravagance of Xerxes I; thus the king in Esther may have been meant in part as a spoof of this historical figure.[4]

Another factor that betrays the fictional nature of this book is its violence. There was no massacre known in the Persian period such as is described in Esth 9:5–16. And, from what we know about Persian rule, there would be no need for such a bloody defense on the part of the Jews. Though the Jews were scattered from their home, and their minority status itself threatened their existence, the Persians were generally known for their tolerance of other religions, not for their persecution of them. Nonetheless, that was neither an ideological view nor a policy; it was simply the usual practice. Xerxes I may well have been responsible

3. Herodotus, *Hist.* 3.84.

4. On Xerxes' extravagant military procession, see Herodotus, *Hist.* 7.41; Xerxes insisted on a lavish meal for himself and his men (7:118–20); Xerxes foolishly acted on others' advice (7:213–15, 234–38).

for destroying cult sites of various peoples when they rebelled against his rule.[5]

However, Herodotus tells a story with remarkable parallels to Esther, in which a woman in the Persian king's harem takes the opportunity to help her father find out that the throne has been usurped so that he and other loyalists could win it back. That tale also ends with a massacre of the rebels, which is in turn marked by a festival (Herodotus, *Hist.* 3.68–79). Indeed, the book contains a good deal of historically believable information relevant to the Persian Empire. For instance, ancient Persian documents contain references to eunuchs' assassination attempts of the king, making plausible the plot along those lines that the book of Esther includes (2:21–23).[6] We also have records that Persian kings did send out communiqués in a variety of languages to their diverse subjects.[7]

Thus we see features in the book of Esther that both reflect and challenge extrabiblical information about the Persian era. As Kuhrt has pointed out, the stereotype of the Persians as exhibiting remarkable "religious tolerance" appears to be overstated and unsubstantiated.[8] Reports in the books of Ezra (Ezra 1:1–8; 5:13–17; 6:3–14) and Isaiah (Isa 44:28—45:7), which have largely led to this view, cannot be corroborated in the extrabiblical materials. Kuhrt concludes from her research that "there was no empire-wide law code. The Persian authorities seem to have implemented and observed local norms." In that sense, we cannot make accurate generalizations about Persian policy in terms of the ruling of faraway subjects. Thus we cannot know for sure why Ezra and Isaiah reported Persian generosity, such as financial and material help with rebuilding the Temple. In contrast, not every instance of Persian rule bore out such treatment.[9] Perhaps in the Jews' case, King Cyrus

5. Kuhrt, *The Persian Empire*, 242.

6. The eunuch Bagoas killed King Ochus and the son who succeeded him, King Arses, and attempted to kill the next king, Darius (Diodorus Siculus XVII, 5.3–6, in Kuhrt, *The Persian Empire*, 424). Also see Kuhrt's discussion of eunuchs, 577, and further explanation below in the commentary on Hegai in Esth 2:3.

7. Kuhrt, *The Persian Empire*, 827–28.

8. Ibid., 828.

9. The Persians' response to the desecration of the Jewish sanctuary in Elephantine by Khnum worshippers around 407 BCE was considerably tempered and more mediatory than what biblical writers report about Persian governance. In that case, according to Egyptian law, the local Persian authority allowed for further dismantling

saw the stability of Jerusalem and the happiness of its people—provided largely by the restabilization of their cultic lives—as geographically strategic to his reign.

Esther's background information on Mordecai also betrays the nonhistorical character of the story. According to one reading of 2:6, Mordecai was taken into exile in Babylon along with King Jeconiah (Jehoiachin; Esth 2:6; 2 Kgs 24:12). If that were the case, it would not make sense for him to still be alive during the Persian period, well over fifty years later. Also attesting to the nonhistoricity of the book is Haman's plot (and the king's agreement to it) to execute Mordecai on the basis of one crime. Herodotus praises the Persians for their policy not to put someone to death except in the case of multiple offenses.[10] Finally, the genre of Esther does not in the least suggest a historical retelling. We will see below that commentators have proposed a variety of genres, but they all assume that Esther is fiction of one sort or another. Though the story was not historically factual, Esther was an utterly truthful tale about the struggles of a people living in diaspora. What some storytellers have been known to say could be said of the book of Esther: "I don't know if it really happened this way, but it sure is true."

If we know that Esther is not a historical tale, then can we at least determine when it was told and written? Other than between the span of Xerxes I's reign beginning in 486 BCE and the appearance of the book in Egypt as late as 73 BCE, the most honest answer to this is that we don't know. The book simply does not give us enough information to definitively settle this matter. Different scholars use historical and linguistic evidence to argue for dates across this time span.

A number of current scholars place the book in the range of the fourth to third centuries BCE.[11] This locates the book roughly in the late Persian period or the early Hellenistic period, though at some distance from the time of Xerxes I himself. The first verse includes an explanation of who this king was, a clarification that would only be necessary some time after his rule.[12] Since the book includes a fair amount of insider

---

of the sanctuary, as the Jews could not prove they owned the land on which it was built. The case was not settled to allow the Jews to rebuild until a few years later. Furthermore, the Egyptian Jews appealed not only to Persian leadership but also to authorities in Jerusalem and Samaria (ibid., 828–30; 854–59).

10. Herodotus, *Hist* 1.137, in Kuhrt, *The Persian Empire,* 424

11. Berlin, *Esther,* xli; Levenson, *Esther,* 26; Crawford, *Esther,* 3:856.

12. Levenson, *Esther,* 26.

information about the Persian court, particularly the harem, that could be evidence that it was not written very long after the time of Xerxes I, perhaps still within the Persian period. If the book were intended to make fun of a Persian reign, it would primarily have had a comic effect during that general time period.[13] Additionally, the king in Esther may be a "doofus" (see below), but he is not malicious. This fits with what we know about the Persian period, in which the kings were benevolent or at least benign to the Jews in diaspora. It does not fit so well with the later Hellenistic period, in which we do find more fearsome rulers.

Another possibility is to place the book in the late Hellenistic period, in the late third through second centuries BCE. Jewish novels similar to what we find in Esther arose in that era, often starring women with newfound prominence.[14] Furthermore, with that amount of distance from the events that inspired it, it would have been possible for the book to have been intended to sound historical at the time of its writing. In that case, what we now read as the book's historical inaccuracies could have been overlooked by original audiences through forgetfulness or ignorance of the earlier time.[15] After a couple hundred years, perhaps some of those details were simply irrelevant. The book of Esther does have some similarities to other literature of the diaspora from the late Hellenistic period; similarities include themes such as Jewish heroism in the face of persecution, the realities of isolation, and the fear of assimilation.

The time in which these issues were most intense was during the reign of the Hellenistic Selucid ruler Antiochus IV Epiphanes (175–164 BCE). Antiochus IV Epiphanes' rule was marked by his persecution of Jews for their religious practices (see 1 Macc 1:10–64; 2 Macc 6–7). While earlier literature such as Ezra-Nehemiah and Ruth address early restoration-period apprehensions about the place of foreigners in the community, Esther's concerns about the annihilation of the Jewish people could fit into the late Hellenistic period, along with Judith and Daniel, which are similar hero stories possibly told to help the community endure Antiochus' persecutions.[16] Finally, it is also feasible that Esther's concluding revenge against the Jews' enemies (Esth 8:11–12;

---

13. Berlin, *Esther*, xlii.

14. Wills, *The Jewish Novel*, 1–39; 130.

15. Fox, *Character and Ideology*, 139.

16. Wijk-Bos, *Ezra, Nehemiah, and Esther*, 103.

9:5–16) places it in the time of the Jewish backlash against Antioches Epiphanes: the Maccabean Rebellion (167–164 BCE).[17]

Of course, none of these arguments is airtight. Someone distanced from the Persian court and harem could nonetheless write credible material about it, just as books today can reconstruct the past with some accuracy. The absence of Greek loanwords in Esther could indicate that it was pre-Hellenistic, or the lack of loanwords could in fact be due to a Hellenistic period Jewish author avoiding any Hellenizing tendencies out of disdain for Greek rule.[18] If the book of Esther were from the later Hellenistic Period, some argue, there would be clearer references to Antiochus Epiphanes' persecutions and the revolt of the Hasmoneans.[19] For instance, the king would be portrayed as a more despicable character. On the other hand, while the book of Esther does not characterize King Ahasuerus as a tyrant, surely no ruler would want to be painted as the buffoon we meet in Esther. Perhaps a text from the time of Antiochus Epiphanes would be clear that Haman's malice was due to religious persecution, or maybe a book meant to lampoon his rule would intentionally be more opaque in order to avoid political repercussions. We have little Jewish literature from the fourth or third centuries, so we can gain little evidence by comparing the book of Esther to similar material from that time.[20] Although diaspora Jews suffered gravely under Antiochus Epiphanes, they undoubtedly faced continuous threats beginning at the time of the exile.[21]

In the first half of Daniel, we read stories purportedly from the Babylonian period but belonging to the diaspora era. These Hellenistic and Maccabean-era tales portray great Jewish heroes who show unwavering loyalty to God's laws despite oppression and torment. Because of their obedience, and only with the help of God, they surmount life-and community-threatening events like ancient superheroes. The second half of Daniel is likewise set in the Babylonian period, yet it was most likely written in the Hellenistic period as a critique of the vicious persecutor of Jews, Antiochus Epiphanes IV. By placing it in the Babylonian period, the writers of Daniel were able to disparage this tyrant without risking

17. 2 Macc 8; 10:14—12:28

18. Wills, *The Jewish Novel*, 98, 100.

19. Moore, *Esther*, lix–lx; Berlin, *Esther*, xlii; Fox, *Character and Ideology*, 140.

20. Levenson, *Esther*, 26.

21. Van Wijk-Bos, *Ezra, Nehemiah, and Esther*, 103.

their lives. Such themes in books like Daniel and Judith accommodated the needs of diaspora Jews who were trying to retain their identity and religion while living as minorities who were often persecuted. It is certainly possible to view Esther as a similar type of story, sustaining diaspora Jews in a time when their survival as a distinctive people was particularly threatened.

Ultimately, we still cannot be sure of how to date the book. As we have seen, logical arguments exist for placing Esther's origins in the fifth through the second centuries; sometimes the same evidence bolsters very different arguments. Another wrinkle in this debate is the likelihood that the book contains a number of different sources, which themselves belong to different time periods. (See Text Criticism section below.) Perhaps each layer of the book served a unique historical purpose in its own time. For instance, court tales about Mordecai and Haman, and then about Esther, could logically belong to the time of Persian rule in the fourth century. Later editing and sources may have supplied the portions about the aggressively averted pogrom and Purim. These may have been more important at a later date to bolster the courage of a minority people in the Hellenistic period and to justify the celebration of a non-Mosaic festival. Still later portions, the "additions," which now reside in the Apocrypha, provided overtly religious interpretations of the events in Esther. As with much of the Bible, mystery prevails as the final answer to these questions about date and text history. Nonetheless, we will learn much from examining the evidence and understanding the arguments. We shall simply have to be humble about drawing conclusions.

Type of Literature and Authorship

The genre of Esther has been identified in numerous ways. The first relates to the above section, and the probability that it is not a historical narrative. The broad genre designation is fiction or story, with lengthy discussion available on Esther as Jewish novel.[22] Beyond that, we can identify it as a Persian court tale.[23] Adele Berlin has categorized it as comedy, farce, and even burlesque. As it is utterly tied up with the cel-

---

22. Wills, *The Jewish Novel*, 96; Linda M. Day helpfully reviews the genre possibilities (*Esther*, 11–12).

23. Sasson, "Esther," in *The Literary Guide to the Bible*, 335–42.

ebration of Purim, it is a story of a carnival for a carnival celebration.[24] Berlin explores connections between it and Greek comedy, while Kevin McGeough compares it to the Wisdom literature.[25] All those designations primarily apply to Hebrew Esther; Greek Esther is more a tale of piety and even romance, with a praying and swooning Esther gracing its pages. In the end, all these various genre options for Esther provide some helpful illumination for the text.

For a nontechnical genre description, I like to think of Esther as a historicized tale, as if told by filmmaker Tim Burton, where everything is exaggerated (see section on excesses, below). In Burton's film *Edward Scissorhands*, an adolescent is not just awkward, he has scissors for hands; a suburb is not merely a façade of happiness but contains rows of identical homes painted in shockingly cheery colors. The ending is bittersweet, with the whole town chasing down its gentle but outcast and misunderstood hero at the end. Similarly in Esther we find a palace not just fancy but gaudy; a tale inhabited not by characters but by caricatures; the audience cheers not for outcomes of simple justice but for complete reversals of fortune fully foreshadowed on one end and dramatically drawn out on the other. The bawdily comedic Esther may not initially appear quite as bittersweet as Burton's *Scissorhands*, yet it certainly is not all a happy story either. It does after all include the planned annihilation of Mordecai and all his people (3:6, 9, 13; 5:14), and then the carried-out execution of Haman and the bloody self-defense killings of the enemies of the Jews (9:5, 16).

As for authorship of Esther, we are similarly uncertain about it as we are about its historical setting. As I discussed above, the book as we have it in Hebrew and both Greek texts (AT and LXX) indicates editing so that ultimately we must ask about the multiple authors of Esther. As with many folktales, it would be difficult to pin down a particular author as opposed to a community of authorship. Whoever did write the book of Esther was familiar with the setting of the Persian court and harem. Stories of such could have been fairly widespread, depending on the time period, as evidenced by the writings of Ctesias, Herodotus, and others. Because the book exhibits familiarity with the harem and boasts a female protagonist, some have suggested that at least part of Esther

24. Berlin, *Esther*, xvi–xix; xxi–xxii.
25. Ibid., xxi; McGeough, "Esther the Hero," 44–65.

might have been written by a woman.[26] Certainly it was not only women who knew about harem life (for instance, some eunuchs did), nor would women be the only ones to make a woman the champion of a story. Nonetheless, of all the writings in the Hebrew Bible, Esther is certainly a likely candidate for having female authorship, especially the early Esther Source (see below).

Text Criticism

The Greek version of Esther (Add Esther, LXX) contains six "additions" to what we find in the Hebrew. Roman Catholic and Eastern Orthodox Bibles include these portions along with the rest of the book, translated from the Greek. Lettered from A through F, the additions also appear in the Apocrypha sections of Protestant Bibles. The additions appear as a unified collection now, but they did not originally. They vary in date, authorship, and even original language (between Greek, Hebrew, or Aramaic).[27] These six Septuagint additions of Esther significantly change the complexion of the MT story by including overt religiosity and even apocalyptic features, so that it lines up more closely with other biblical books such as Daniel.

Some versions of the Apocrypha contain only the additions, out of context from the rest of the book, numbered as though they were tacked on to the end of the "core" Hebrew text (the MT). The text-critical discussion below points out that this way of presenting the Additions to Esther relied on erroneous assumptions about how the Hebrew and Greek developed and relate to one another. More helpful are the recent translations that integrate the additions into the rest of the Greek text, as they would have occurred originally (for instance, the NRSV). Unfortunately, the verse numbering for Esther was already set based on the additions as a sort of appendix to the rest of the book. This creates a strange situation in which the Greek translation begins with 11:2. This numbering does, however, provide us with an easy way to identify material from the additions: It consists of any chapter and verse number above 10:3.

The commentary below will primarily treat the Hebrew text (MT), which is primarily used in Jewish and Protestant traditions. In the case

26. For instance, DeTroyer, "An Oriental Beauty Parlor."

27. Crawford, *Esther*, 3:945; Fox, *Character and Ideology*, 265–66.

of the additions, I have included them in the book's outline in square brackets, and will address them briefly as they appear throughout the book. I will likewise discuss the Greek Esther Additions (Add Esth or LXX), and elsewhere when they contain different story-lines and possible clarification for the Hebrew. When the text version is not otherwise specified, it is safe to assume that my comments relate to MT, which is my primary focus here.

Except in rare instances, this commentary will not deal with material in the Greek Alpha Text (AT), which is another slightly different version of the Esther story that does not have canonical status in any tradition.[28] These tenth- through thirteenth-century Greek manuscripts include versions of the additions, so AT looks like the Septuagint version. Yet text-critical work in recent decades has shown that the Alpha Text was most likely a Greek translation of a Hebrew version separate from the precursor of the MT, though it was similar to it in content.[29] The additions in the LXX were probably also added to the AT. In all likelihood, the LXX represents the same Hebrew version as MT, which is different from AT. Both the LXX and the AT adopted the additions. Furthermore, it may have been that separate stories about Esther and Mordecai/Haman preceded either of the Hebrew originals. To summarize, here is a hypothetical, approximated reconstruction of the texts:

---

28. Crawford and Fox's commentaries more thoroughly integrate material from AT. Also see Wills, *The Jew in the Court*, 153–192, and Clines, *The Esther Scroll*.

29. Fox, *Character and Ideology*, 255–59; Clines, *The Esther Scroll*, 139–73 and 215–47, for the Greek AT and Clines' English translation of it.

Figure 1

1. Mordecai/Haman Source (not extant; likely originally circulated in oral tradition)

2. Esther Source (not extant; likely also oral, perhaps added to the Mordecai/ Haman source)

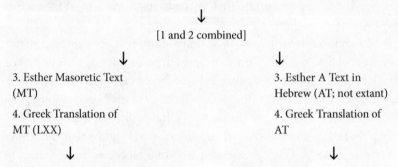

[1 and 2 combined]

3. Esther Masoretic Text (MT)

3. Esther A Text in Hebrew (AT; not extant)

4. Greek Translation of MT (LXX)

4. Greek Translation of AT

5. Greek, Hebrew and Aramaic Additions adopted by LXX; then AT[30]

The existence of two Hebrew versions of the book of Esther points to the importance of the story in the world of early Judaism. Wills asserts that the latest version, the LXX with additions, has much in common with the Greek novels of the period.[31] Throughout the book, we will notice some inconsistencies, rough spots, and repetitions in the text. Some scholars view these as evidence of more than one ancient story preserved by editors in what we now know as the book of Esther.[32] In fact, there appear to be fairly consistent linguistic and grammatical markers to show which parts of the book belonged to the earlier layers of the book (such as the Esther source), and others that mark the hand of the later editors.[33]

Banquets

More than one scholar has noticed that the number of banquets or feasts in the book of Esther comes to the nice round number ten. Some schol-

30. Also see Clines, *The Esther Scroll,* 140; Fox, *Character and Ideology,* 255; Crawford, *Esther,* 3:860–62.

31. Wills, *The Jewish Novel,* 130.

32. Wills, *The Jew in the Court,* 159–91; Bickerman, *Four Strange Books,* 171–240.

33. For instance, Wills notes that 1:1 and 1:2 begin with "and it happened in the days of . . ." and "in those days" respectively. This redundant chronological note "indicates that a seam has resulted from the insertion of the intervening digression about Ahasuerus [1:2–3]" (*The Jew in the Court,* 159).

ars have even used those banquets as a way to structure the book, noting symmetrical similarities and subgroupings of the banquets.[34] Even without counting the banquets or focusing on them as organizing devices, noting their presence and importance in Esther is unavoidable. Virtually every scene in the book either arises from or culminates in a feast. The first banquet occurs in 1:3; it is the king's banquet for his higher-ups. Not wasting any time at all, the king follows that with a banquet for everyone in Susa (1:5). Then we meet Queen Vashti, who is throwing a banquet of her own for the women of the kingdom (1:9). After Vashti is deposed and Esther is chosen as the new queen, the king throws her a wedding banquet (2:18). Later, when Haman has devised his plan to destroy all the Jews, and the king has issued the decree saying so, the two of them have a little drinking party (3:15). All the remaining banquets are thrown by Jews. The next two banquets are given by Esther for the king and Haman (5:4; 7:1–8) in her efforts to win the king's favor for the Jews and to undo Haman's planned massacre. Fully illustrative of the book's reversals, the last three banquets have no Persian involvement at all, but arise as Jewish celebrations. First there is a banquet in honor of Mordecai's decree undoing Haman's decree (8:17). Then the Jews celebrate both on the fourteenth and fifteenth of Adar (9:17 and 9:18, respectively).

Thus, the Persians (King Ahasuerus or Queen Vashti) give the first five banquets, the Jewish Queen Esther gives the next two, and the Jewish people are responsible for the final three. The numbered list of banquets below illustrates this:

(1) King Ahasuerus' banquet for higher-ups (1:3)

(2) King Ahasuerus' banquet for all in Susa (1:5)

(3) Queen Vashti's banquet for the women (1:9)

(4) Queen Esther's wedding banquet (2:18)

(5) King Ahasuerus and Haman's postdecree drinking party (3:15)

(6) Esther's first banquet (5:4)

(7) Esther's second banquet (7:1–8)

(8) Celebration of Mordecai's Decree (8:17)

(9) Celebration on fourteenth of Adar (9:17)

(10) Celebration on fifteenth of Adar (9:18)

34. Berg, "The Book of Esther," 31–57; Crawford, *Esther*, 3:857; Fox, *Character and Ideology*, 156–58.

Each banquet on this list except for one uses the Hebrew word מִשְׁתֶּה *mishteh*. The middle party on the list, 3:15 uses the related word שָׁתָה *shatah*. A *mishteh* was indeed a celebratory meal (Gen 21:8; Judg 14:10) and something provided for the sake of hospitality (Gen 19:3; 26:30); but being rooted in the word for "drink" (שָׁתָה *shatah*), it often emphasized drinking (1 Sam 25:36; Isa 5:12; 25:6; Jer 51:39; Dan 1:5, 8, 10, 16). It was also not unheard of for a banquet to last quite a while (Judg 14:12, 17), though the king's opening banquet in Esther tops them all.

There are ample material remains and even commentary from ancient historians of the Persian era documenting the prevalence of banquets in that setting.[35] Lavish banquets abound in the writings about and by ancient Persians, and ornate goblets have been found to attest to those festivities.[36] While references to ancient Persian banquets do not agree in all the details with what we see in Esther, this extrabiblical information shows that the banquets throughout the book of Esther refer—even if in caricature—to a significant feature of ancient Persian culture. Notably, Esther herself does not avoid the banqueting of her Persian setting. Indeed, she uses it fully to her advantage (5:4; 7:1–8). Yet in stark contrast to the ubiquitous banquets is the fast that Esther calls in 4:16. In fact, the banqueting context makes Esther's fast seem all the more somber and significant.

Decrees

The book of Esther contains at least four instances of official decrees being issued, either from the king or from Esther and Mordecai. Not all of these use the same vocabulary, but in each case some kind of command is written and distributed to the people. The first example occurs in 1:19–22, where the king "sent letters . . . that every man should become ruler in his own house." The next decree is Haman's command to kill all the Jews (3:12–13). The third essentially undoes Haman's previous edict, being Mordecai's command to kill all the enemies of the Jews (8:9–12). The final official letter—or set of letters—is issued repetitively by Esther and/or Mordecai to establish and legitimate Purim in 9:20–32. This jumbled passage makes it a bit difficult to sort out who is sending

---

35. Kuhrt, *The Persian Empire*, 610–13.

36. For illustrations of these goblets see ibid., 613 and Moore illustration, *Esther*, fig. 6 (after p. 22); online: http://www.britishmuseum.org/, search on "fluted silver drinking horn"; www.louvre.fr, search on "Achaemenid rhyton."

out how many letters about Purim. The verses may well be the result of editing.[37] These four decrees effectively track the major plotlines of the book, and clearly illustrate the reversals it will enact. At the same time, these written orders reflect the Persian penchant for letter writing and distribution through their reportedly efficient courier system.[38]

Reversals

The story of Esther, like much of the rest of the Bible, thrives on reversals. A central articulation of this in particularly theological terms occurs at the beginning of 1 Samuel as we read in Hannah's song:

> The bows of the mighty are broken,
>   but the feeble gird on strength.
> Those who were full have hired themselves out for bread,
>   but those who were hungry are fat with spoil.
> The barren has borne seven,
>   but she who has many children is forlorn.
> The LORD kills and brings to life;
>   he brings down to Sheol and raises up.
> The LORD makes poor and makes rich;
>   he brings low, he also exalts.
> He raises up the poor from the dust;
>   he lifts the needy from the ash heap,
> to make them sit with princes
>   and inherit a seat of honor.
> For the pillars of the earth are the LORD's,
>   and on them he has set the world.
> He will guard the feet of his faithful ones, but the wicked shall
> be cut off in darkness; for not by might does one prevail.
> (1 Sam 2:4–9, NRSV)

These words foreshadow what will happen to Israel, its leaders, its people, and even its enemies as its history continues. That motif is so crucial to the wider biblical narrative that it is not at all surprising that the gospel writers report Mary reprising Hannah's song (Luke 1:46–55), and Jesus repeating it in his own way, "But many who are first will be last, and the last will be first" (Mark 10:31, NRSV).

This theme—and audiences' interest in it—was certainly not lost on the author(s) of Esther. Reversals are so common and so poetically por-

---

37. See discussion below on 9:20–32 and Fox, *Character and Ideology*, 123–27.

38. Kuhrt, *The Persian Empire*, 827–28; Herodotus, *Hist.* 8.98.

trayed in the book of Esther that it makes for an enjoyable Bible study exercise to look for them. I encourage readers to reflect not only on my list of reversals, which follows, but to look for additional ones as well as nuances within the ones I name here.

Not only do Vashti and Esther each experience reversals, but they reverse roles with each other. Vashti goes from being queen to being deposed (1:13–22), while Esther goes from being the unknown Jewish orphan (2:7) to being the new queen of Persia (2:17). Sidnie White Crawford points out the irony that while Vashti gets into trouble by not appearing when summoned by the king (1:12), Esther risks getting killed by approaching the king when she has not been summoned to do so (4:10–11; 5:1–8).[39] Vashti is asked to wear a crown but refuses; Esther uses the crown for her purposes when necessary. Vashti is deposed so that men in the kingdom will be masters of their own homes (1:16–22); while it may be debatable whether Esther becomes master in the palace, she surely gains a huge amount of power there (5:1–8; 7:2–3; 8:1–8; 9:12–13). We could even consider, in light of 1:21–22, whether the book reflects a reversal of gender roles in terms of power. Women were supposed to be put in their places of minimal power; in the book of Esther, however, one woman in particular gains the utmost power in the kingdom.

Mordecai begins as a man who apparently has some small role in the royal court (2:5, 19); he later becomes the king's right-hand man (8:1–2, 9–10, 15; 9:4; 10:2–3). In fact, he switches places with the king's right-hand man, Haman, the man who hates him so much. The text foreshadows this in 6:1–12 when Haman devises what he thinks will be a tribute to himself, and the honors instead go to his enemy Mordecai. By the end of the book, Mordecai and Esther reverse places with Haman down to the detail: Haman is killed in the very way he had devised just for Mordecai (7:10); the people Haman had targeted for genocide defend themselves and destroy their enemies on the very day they were to have died (9:1–2); the king gives his signet ring, which Haman had worn and used for his purposes, to Mordecai and Esther, who then use it for the opposite purposes (8:7–8). Furthermore, Mordecai and Esther receive Haman's house and possessions (8:2b). As the citations attest, we see much of this reversal in the decrees, which in some cases indicate

---

39. Crawford, "Esther," *NIB* 3:904.

that the reversals constitute poetic justice through some word-for-word repetition among them (3:11–15//8:8–14).

In a bigger-picture reversal, the book exchanges the positions of Persians and Jews. While in the beginning the Jews in Esther feel it necessary to hide their identities (2:20), by the end the turnabout is so effective that it is good to be a Jew; the Persian non-Jews claim to be Jews (8:17). The Persians are originally in power (1:1–4); while that never completely changes, by the end, the advisors who drive the king's decisions are Jews (10:3). In reference to the previous theme of banquets, we see that the early banquets, given by and for Persian interests (1:3, 5, 9; 2:18; 3:15), shift to Jewish banquets given by and for Jewish interests (5:4; 7:1–8; 8:17; 9:17, 18). In addition, during a crisis point in the story Esther's fast poses a major reversal of this banqueting theme, effectively highlighting the severity of the circumstances (4:15–16). The finale of these reversals seems to be the celebration of Purim, which itself co-opts what was to be a day of death (3:7, 13//9:1–2) into an official celebration (9:26–28). The text articulates this explicitly: "the month was turned for them from sorrow to joy, and from mourning to a festival day" (9:22).

Excess

The final theme I will identify in Esther is that of excess. The book overflows with details that go way beyond even a good fictional reality. In most cases the excess pushes into the realm of ludicrous to the extent that it gives the story a comic edge. The character of the king is a good first example. He is just *too much*, from his partying to his reactions in any given situation. Thus, one of the nicknames I endow him with is "King Over-the-top." He is the masthead for this book full of excess. His first banquet lasts six months (1:4), and the second a full seven (1:5); this is beside the fact that he even has a second banquet after having a six-month-long one! Another of the king's excesses is his overreaction to his queen's act of disobedience: he deposes her (Esth 1:19). This decision not only has to do with Queen Vashti but is enacted in order to teach a lesson to all the kingdom's women and in order to establish the men of the kingdom as masters in their own homes—an excessive response indeed (1:16–20). When the story turns to the choice of the next queen, the preparations involve lengthy cosmetic treatments applied to the harem, which included all of the kingdom's young girls (2:1–4, 12).

Haman's response to Mordecai when he will not pay him homage is as excessive as the king's response to Queen Vashti when she refuses to appear at his banquet. Haman not only wants to punish Mordecai; he plans to kill him on a ludicrously tall post (5:14). As if that weren't enough, Haman's disproportionate final solution is to kill all the Jews in order to appease his anger toward the one Jew Mordecai—a plan for which he offers the king an unbelievably large sum of money (3:9). When Haman thinks he has the opportunity to devise his own ceremony of honor, he proposes a multifaceted event with numerous allusions to his designs on the throne (6:1–9).

One of the final excesses arises in chapter 9, where the amount of killing necessary to circumvent Haman's pogrom rises into the tens of thousands of people. Here the excesses are not so funny, not only because the scene is a bloodbath, but because this extremity reflects the dire circumstances of those telling the story.

Esther Outline

[ADDITION A: 11:2—12:6
Mordecai's dream foretells the story (11:2–12)
Mordecai angers Haman by foiling an assassination plot (12:1–6)]

1. King Doofus and His Dilemma (1:1—2:1)
    a) Setting up the story (1:1–9)
        i) Introduction: Geographical and chronological markers (1:1)
        ii) A banquet given by King A. (1:2–4)
        iii) A second banquet given by King A. (1:5–8)
        iv) Queen Vashti ("Queen V.") Introduced: She gave a banquet for the women (1:9)
    b) The story begins: King A. and his queen (1:10—2:1)
        i) Calls for his seven eunuchs to bring her: How and why (1:10–11)
        ii) Vashti becomes the antagonist (1:12)
        iii) King A. makes his case against Queen V. (1:13—2:1)

2. Queen ? To the Heroine, Queen Esther (2:2–23)
    a) King A.'s servants: Find a new queen (2:2–4)

    b) New characters (2:5–11)
       i) Mordecai (2:5–6)
       ii) Hadassah a.k.a. Esther (2:7)
       iii) Why these characters matter to the story (2:8–11)
          (1) Esther was taken to the palace with the other young women (2:8–10)
          (2) Mordecai hung around to keep an eye on Esther (2:11)

    c) "Extreme Makeover: Persian edition"; Contestants and rules (2:12–14)

    d) Esther becomes the queen (2:15–18)

    e) [Side-Story: Mordecai foils an assassination plot (2:19–23)]

3. The Villain Haman: His Rise; His Demise (3:1—9:17)

    a) Haman's rise; Haman's scheme (3:1–15)
       i) Haman's grandiose demands; Mordecai's refusal (3:1–4)
       ii) Haman's anger and plan (3:5–9)
       iii) The king approves and decrees (3:10–13)

[ADDITION B: The King's Decree against "a Certain Hostile People" (13:1–7)]
       iv) Copies of the decree available; delivery in Susa (3:14–15a)
       v) The king and Haman have a drink while disorder ensues (3:15b)

[ADDITION C: 13:8—14:19
    Mordecai's prayer for his people (13:8–18)
    Esther's prayer for her people (14:1–19)]

[ADDITION D: Esther's successful request of the king (15:1–16)]

    b) Mordecai and Esther respond to Haman's plan (4:1–17)
       i) Mordecai's anguish reflected all Jews' anguish (4:1–3)
       ii) Esther's anguish and investigation (4:4–5)
       iii) Mordecai and Esther communicate via Hathach (4:6–17)

    c) Esther's successful request of the king (5:1–8)

    d) Haman responds to Mordecai: he and Zeresh plot against Mordecai (5:9–14)

TURNING POINT: BEGINNING OF HAMAN'S DOWNFALL

    e) King A. wants to honor Mordecai (6:1–13)

  i)   Discovers Mordecai's loyalty and wants to honor him
       (6:1–3)

  ii) Enter Haman, with his would-be self-serving but backfir-
       ing plan (6:4–13)

  f)   Esther's Second Banquet; Haman's Bitter End (6:14—7:10)

  g)   Esther and Mordecai get Haman's place and power (8:1—9:17)

  iii) House and ring (8:1–2)

  iv) At Esther's request, the plot is reversed (8:3–14)

[ADDITION E at 8:12: King's Decree: Reviews situation; condemns
Haman's decree; gives freedom to Jews (16:1–24)]

  v)   Situation of the Jews reversed: now it's good to be a Jew!
       Celebrate and feast! (8:15–17)

  vi) Mordecai's plan is carried out, with the help of King A.
       (9:1–15)

  vii) Chronological note and Sabbath celebration (9:16–17)

  viii)Additional celebrations (9:18–19)

4.   THE POINT OF THE STORY: Purim (9:20—10:3)

  a)   The new official Mordecai makes the feast official (9:20–23)

  b)   The origins of the festival (9:24–28)

  c)   The festival confirmed: Purim (9:29–32)

  d)   Summary, epilogue, and corroboration (10:1–3)

[ADDITION F: 10:4—11:1
   Mordecai's Dream: Remembered, completed, exposed (10:4–13)
   Colophon: Authentication of the Letter (11:1)]

Scene 1: King Doofus and His Dilemma (1:1—2:1)

This book begins with a daunting name to pronounce: Ahasuerus.
According to the Hebrew spelling, it contains four syllables: ah-chash-
VAY-roash. The Greek version of the king's name is only slightly easier
on the tongue: Artaxerxes (arta-ZERK-zeez). Ahasuerus is the Hebrew
version of a Persian name. Because Ahasuerus tongue-ties so many of
us, I have proposed a few nicknames for the first character we meet in
Esther: Above I suggested "King Over-the-top." "King A" lacks creativity
but is fast and easy and sticks to the text. My preferred moniker for him

is "King Doofus"; the word *doofus* describes his character as presented in Esther, which I will elaborate further below.

While the opening words in the Hebrew purportedly present King Ahasuerus' reign as a way to date the book, as we have seen above, "the days of King Ahasuerus" (1:1) does not in fact provide a reliable historical marker. In contrast, the geographical range of his rule does relate to what we know of the ancient Persian Empire. It covered a massive domain—what the original audience may well have perceived as the known world. Esther 1:1 paints a sweeping landscape "from India to Cush, one hundred and twenty-seven provinces"—Cush being the area of southernmost Egypt, or Ethiopia. The "one hundred twenty-seven provinces," however, is a greatly exaggerated number in light of what we know about ancient Persia. It could be yet another way to express this king's extravagance, or it could be a symbolic number composed of twelve times ten plus seven—significant because twelve was the number of Israel's tribes (Gen 49:28), ten indicated "completeness" (Exod 27:12, 34:28), and seven was an important number for the composition of the Persian court (1:10, 14) as well as a highly symbolic number throughout the Hebrew Bible (Gen 2:2–3; 7:2–4; 8:10, 12; 18:32; Exod 12:15; 25:37; 29:37; Lev 8:11, 33, 35; 23:34).[40]

These geographical markers in the opening verses of Esther seem to place this story at the height of the Persian Empire. Biblical historians usually view that time as a good one for the ancient Jews rather than one of persecution like Esther describes. Susa was the capital of Persia during the sixth through fourth centuries BCE; it was a city centrally located in this widespread empire. It correlates to the contemporary Iranian city of Shush in the province of Khuzestan, southwest of Tehran. The "citadel" of vv. 2 and 5 refers to the western part of the city, fortified against military attack, and primarily housing the royalty.[41]

The book of Esther opens with the first of ten banquets in the story, and it sets the standard for the king's opulence. The first banquet is said to have lasted six months (1:4) and includes officials from every corner of his massive kingdom. This leads to yet another banquet (1:5), this time for the sake of entertaining not only dignitaries from throughout his realm, but also all the residents of the citadel at home. So far what we

40. Levenson, *Esther*, 43.
41. Miroschedji, "Susa," 6:244.

know about this king is that he can be defined by excesses: the size of his kingdom, the extent of his parties, his drinking, his décor, his guest list.

Thus far, the text effectively characterizes Ahasuerus as "King Over-the-Top." The only way in which the nickname "Doofus" applies in the first five verses is that the king spends six months partying rather than ruling. With even his governors joining him, the whole domain is left utterly neglected for half a year, requiring the king's subjects to fend for themselves. Indeed, in such a scenario the royal court would have relied on its subjects to provide for their wasteful extravagance, entailing a gross mismanagement of funds. This description offers an early, uncomplimentary portrait of the king and his cronies.

Though Ahasuerus is surely fictionalized, it may well be that some aspects of his character as well as his kingdom would have rung true to hearers of the book of Esther, who might have known of the Persian Empire and its King Xerxes. As we saw above, Herodotus described the historical figure Xerxes I as extravagant and foolish.[42] He was also such an idiotic tyrant that he ordered physical punishments of a body of water that had the audacity to foil his plans to cross it; on the second try at traversing he enacted an offering of apology to the river.[43] Ancient inscriptions tell that Xerxes believed himself divinely chosen for the monarchy, a case he may have needed to make since he was not his father's eldest son.[44]

The luxurious furnishings and decoration of Ahasuerus' palace in Esth 1:6 correlate to ancient texts describing a royal residence, as well as some excavated remains from Susa.[45] Interestingly, these palace descriptions use language that recalls the priestly temple specifications and vestments.[46] It is odd to see this vocabulary and descriptive style in a biblical passage that does not elucidate holy scenery. This king's palace is certainly as fancy a place as the most elegant scene described in ancient

42. On Xerxes' extravagant military procession see Herodotus, *Hist.* 7.41; Xerxes insisted on a lavish meal for himself and his men (7:118–120); Xerxes foolishly acted on others' advice (7:213–15, 234–38).

43. Herodotus, *Hist.* 7.34–35, 54.

44. Smith-Christopher, "Xerxes," 1401.

45. Herodotus, *Hist.* 9.82 describes an equally lavish palace.

46. NRSV "blue" וּתְכֵלֶת, Exod 25:4; 26:1; NRSV "purple" וְאַרְגָּמָן, Exod 27:16; 35:25; NRSV "fine linen" שֵׁשׁ, Exod 28:5; 35:25; 39:29) and Ezekiel's temple vision (NRSV "pavement" רִצְפָה, 40:17, 18; 42:3).

Israel's writings. Whether it is a place that welcomes the divine presence remains to be seen.

Esther 1:7 and 8 describe the drinking at the king's banquet. The Hebrew of v. 8 has most often been translated to say that "the drinking was according to the law, without constraint," where "law" is based on the noun דת *dat* and has to do with a regulation about drinking.[47] Another translation option, which we find in the NRSV, reads this Hebrew noun and its prepositional prefix (כדת *kadat*) according to an Aramaic cognate for a large drinking goblet, or "flagon:" "Drinking was by flagons, without restraint" (Esth 1:8, NRSV).[48] The Greek contains an apparently opposite statement in order to make a similar point: "And this banquet was not according to the appointed law" (Add Esth 1:8, LXX). That the drinking was not according to the law here meant that the partygoers could have as much as they wanted. All the translations emphasize the bounty of beverage contributing to gluttony and drunkenness. Furthermore, if we understand *dat* here as "law," or "decree," it provides the first of many instances in which King Ahasuerus blithely uses his legislative power.

In v. 9 our narrator introduces the third banquet, with details likely to spark the audience's interest. It was a women's banquet, with the queen herself as its hostess. Here we meet Queen Vashti—her name means "best" in Persian—, who has a brief but crucial part in this drama. The conflict of this story arises on the final day of the king's second banquet, when he determines to show off his queen to his party guests, who are now presumably a drunken and overfed horde made up of the kingdom's elite men. So, on this final, seventh day of the second banquet (1:5, 10), the king calls for his seven eunuchs to go fetch his queen wearing her crown (1:11). Interestingly, in the Greek version of Esther, the list of eunuchs includes Haman (Add Esth 1:10), who was even introduced once before in Addition A (12:6; see below); in the Hebrew we have to wait until 3:1 to meet this villain.[49] Such eunuchs as these seven who had

47. This word appears numerous times throughout Esther, often referring to various decrees of the king: 1:8, 13, 15, 19; 2:8, 12; 3:8 [twice], 14, 15; 4:3, 8, 11, 16; 8:13, 14, 17; 9:1, 13, 14.

48. See John Gray's proposal "that *kdt* is a cognate of the Aram. *kaddā*, a large vessel' or 'flagon'; thus [the Hebrew phrase] could be translated 'the drinking was by flagons without restraint'" (Moore, *Esther*, 8). Also see the section above on banquets, and the note about goblets.

49. Moore counts this as "an obvious error" because of Haman's family status (*Esther*, 2, n. i).

responsibilities within the harem were very likely castrates, so that they could not sexually threaten the king or vie for the throne through one of the king's women. The eunuchs' plot against the king later in the book (2:21) is an example of how these higher-up officials could be a threat.[50]

In the king's summons to his queen, the narrator enlists marvelous ambiguity, which the best bards would have undoubtedly called on for effect. The eunuch had been ordered "to bring Queen Vashti before the king, wearing the royal crown" (Esth 1:11, NRSV). Imagine a storyteller's pregnant pause right before "the royal crown" (v. 11), suggesting that perhaps Queen Vashti was called on to wear *nothing* but her crown.[51] Such a scenario would more readily explain her refusal to parade before the partygoers. Or, maybe the queen was to show herself in all her finery, but was simply more interested in entertaining her own banquet guests than being the after-dinner show for a bunch of drunken men. Apparently the Persian convention was that wives dined with kings until the drinking began, at which time "music-girls and concubines" entertained them.[52] Any of these explanations for Vashti's refusal of the king's summons are plausible. Probably the most important way to interpret the king's command, however, is in terms of good storytelling. First and foremost, the ambiguity in this terse line suggests an author who makes good use of the audience's imagination. Indeed, many of the strange and ridiculous goings-on in Esther make the most sense in terms of telling a good story.

In v. 12, the narrator flatly lays out the initial conflict of the story. For whatever reason, Queen Vashti defies the king's command to appear at his banquet. Enraged, the king turns to his oft-used leadership strategy: he asks his advisors what to do. The long list of their names in 1:14 provides the kind of detail that could make the story sound historical, if it weren't for the similarity to the list in 1:10.[53] These advisors look

---

50. For more on eunuchs, see discussion below on Hegai in the commentary on 2:3.

51. Crawford cites *Meg., Tg. Esth I, Tg. Esth II* to show that this interpretation accords with Jewish tradition (*Esther*, 3:882).

52. "When the Persian kings have their dinner, their lawful wives sit beside them during the dinner and eat with them. But when the kings want to divert themselves and indulge in drinking, they send them away and have music-girls and concubines come. And they are quite right to do so, as, in this way, they do not involve their wedded wives in their debaucheries and drunkenness," Plutarch, *Moralia* 140b (cited in Kuhrt, *The Persian Empire*, 593).

53. On the one hand, seven was a typical number of courtiers in Persia (Moore, *Esther*, 10). Yet Adele Berlin suggests that the reverse repetition between this verse and

into the "law" for the king. The word for "law" here is not *torah*, which we find throughout the Pentateuch. Rather, it is the same as in 1:8, the Persian word *dat*. Because this word appears so frequently, it highlights the ironic theme that royal decrees would presumably provide structure and order but instead they reveal a kingdom of impulsiveness and near-chaos.

The officials respond with a paranoia that punctuates various parts of the book. The king's advisors overreact by assuming that this one decision of one royal woman will set a far-reaching precedent for all women in the kingdom, whom they feared would "look with contempt on their husbands" (1:17, NRSV). The Greek goes so far as to say that they would "insult their husbands" (Add Esth 1:18, NRSV). In 1:16–20 their obsessed justifications go on ad nauseum. It was apparently not enough to just explain the rationale for this decree (1:16). The officials go on to quote the imagined words of the women whom they worry will be influenced by Vashti's behavior (1:17), and they detail their fabricated nightmare scenario of female rebellion throughout the realm (1:18). They therefore plan to make an example of Vashti in order to prevent the female revolution they fear she has begun. This overreaction sets the tone of the book, contributes to the characterization of the king as a "Doofus," and additionally depicts his officials as highly insecure. Furthermore, it sets up a central irony of the story: The king and his men depose Queen Vashti so that all Persian men will be masters of their own homes (especially the king), while in the end the Jewish interloper Queen Esther becomes the master of the king's home. The courtiers' repeated explanations in 1:16–20 increase the comic effect of this passage. Not only do they overreact, but they spend too much time explaining their overreaction. Both features portray them as foolishly anxious. It seems that such a stunt would not have been beyond the historical King Xerxes. As Herodotus tells it, Xerxes procured for himself a mistress to take the place of a woman he could not attain. When his wife, Amestris, discovered this, she turned the tables on him and arranged for the gruesome abuse and disfigurement of the woman who was the object of the king's lust (Herodotus, *Hist.* 9.108–12). This history is nearly as dramatic as what we read in Esther about King Ahasuerus.

1:10 make it sound "playful," comparing it to the seven dwarves (*Esther*, 16). In Add Esth 1:14, there are only six "friends," and their names are different from those in MT; three of them are noted as governors and close to the king.

Esther 1:19 explains that Persian laws are irrevocable. This imprac-
tical statute has no extra-biblical corroboration, though the book of
Daniel does mention it (Dan 6:8–15). In any case, it plays an important
part in the story of Esther, setting up a legal dilemma that can only be
resolved by implementing a new law to counteract the first rather than
the apparently obvious solution of revoking the unjust law. This will become a key point in the narrative in chapter 8 (8:8). Besides the fact that
the decree cannot be revoked, the narrative in 1:19–22 contains some
confusion as to what exactly the king's law says. In 1:19 it seems a clear
enough irony. Vashti shall no longer be allowed to appear before the
king, because she would not appear before the king. Thus, there shall be
a new queen. The absurdity of this decree mocks the officials. The point
of this decree was to convey the import of wifely obedience (1:20).

In v. 22 however, we apparently get an additional decree, that "every man should be master in his own house" (NRSV). Is the law about
Vashti's demotion or about the marital relations of everyone in the
kingdom? Surely the latter was not even subject to legislation, though
some husbands may have welcomed such a royal ruling as a providential
resolution to their marital conflicts! Adele Berlin shows that the grammar and structure of the verse points to v. 22 as the justification for the
pronouncement in v. 19, rather than articulating a new decree entirely.[54]
In any case, the narrative makes the crucial points for the sake of the
story: Vashti is out; a new queen will be found; men are to rule their
wives.

This passage contains the intriguing implication that Vashti's refusal undermines the king's power, thus suggesting that Vashti herself
has a great deal of power. Might we view Vashti as a hero because she
refuses to be pushed around by the king, and in so doing betrays the
amount of power women held? These questions will be important to
reconsider in light of Esther's character. The brief but significant appearance of Queen Vashti stands over against Esther throughout the rest of
the book, intensifying the new queen's actions by virtue of comparison.
How might the original hearers of this story have responded to these
issues, and would that have depended on whether they were male or
female? We cannot know the answers to those questions for sure, but
they invite us to consider the effect of the story on various audiences.

54. Berlin, *Esther*, 20.

A transitional verse, 2:1, closes this section and opens the next. Once he's no longer so angry, "King Doofus" looks back on this episode, propelling him to commence—in the words of one of my Bible study participants—"Extreme Makeover: Persian Edition." Perhaps he can move on to the next woman once he has finished fuming about the last.

Before moving on to this would-be Miss Persia contest, let us backtrack to discuss Addition A (Add Esth 11:2—12:6) which opens the Greek version of Esther. These seventeen verses effectively lead into the events of Esther's story. They open with a different king, Artaxerxes the Great (465–424 BCE), who as a historical figure was the son of and successor to Xerxes I.[55] However, it seems that the LXX actually means to refer to Xerxes I here, in which case the LXX Additions and MT connect with a logical chronology: 11:2 occurs in the second year of the king's reign (484 BCE); 1:3 in the third (483 BCE).[56] Addition A includes some of the necessary details about Mordecai, including his genealogy (11:2), which repeats in 2:5. This introduction of Greek Esther also includes a comment about Mordecai's place in Israel's history (11:4), which we will see again in 2:6. Fully in the spirit of other biblical heroes such as Joseph and Daniel (Gen 37:5–10; Dan 7:1–28), Mordecai has an apocalyptic dream foretelling the divine plan for coming events. In it, he sees two warring dragons, marking a global threat against a "righteous nation" that sought divine help (11:7–10). As Addition F will make clear, the figures in this dream at least loosely relate to the characters in the upcoming story, with Esther as the little stream (11:10; 10:6), and Haman and Mordecai as the warring dragons (11:6; 10:7). The people cry for help with the same language that they use in Judges when they need a deliverer (11:8b, Gk//11:10a, NRSV; Judg 6:6; 10:10, ἐβόησαν *eboēsan*). Mordecai dreams that God's intervention in this combat will follow much the same pattern as it does elsewhere in the Hebrew Bible, with the exaltation of the lowly and the demise of the powerful (11:11; cf. 1 Sam 2:1–10).

Addition A goes on to give an abbreviated version of a scene that the Hebrew text will narrate later, in which Mordecai foils a plot against the king. Thus this portion of Addition A makes no chronological sense in the context of the larger book.[57] Here, the potential assassins are iden-

---

55. Klein, "Artaxerxes," 1:275.

56. Levenson, *Esther*, 38; Fox, *Character and Ideology*, 14 n. 2.

57. Crawford points out that since 11:12–17 does not appear in Old Latin or Josephus,

tified as "Gabatha and Tharra" (12:1), in contrast to the Hebrew where they are called "Bigthan and Teresh" (2:21). Furthermore, Haman has some connection to this episode, though the text does not explain why exactly he would be angry with Mordecai's seemingly heroic intervention (12:6). This may have been intended to implicate him in the plot, which would make him a villain not only to the Jews, as is the case in the Hebrew version, but also to the Persians. While the Hebrew version suggests Haman's interest in the throne, it is fairly implicit. This last verse of Addition A more clearly paints him as a usurper. Finally, 12:6 (and 3:1) identify Haman as a "Bougean," which may have been a later way of identifying an enemy of the Jews, without such specific historical relevance as the Hebrew's "Agagite" (3:1, 10; 8:3, 5; 9:24).[58]

Scene 2: Queen "?" to the Heroine, Queen Esther (2:2–23)

Chapter 2 opens with what sounds like a beauty contest, with the winner being crowned the new queen of Persia. It would be easy to read into it all the trappings of a Disney movie, with all the kingdom's "beautiful young virgins" (NRSV 2:2; cf. "beautiful and virtuous girls" in Add Esth 2:2) enjoying months of spa treatments, ending in a fairy-tale wedding for the contest's winner, complete with frilly dresses and bridesmaids in pink. This, however, would be a misleading parallel to say the least. In describing the scenario, we read that the royal soldiers were to "collect" (קבץ *qvts* in 2:3 and 8) and "take" (לקח *lqh* in 2:8) the young women into the harem for the sake of the king. Though it is possible, we cannot necessarily assume that anyone signed up for this like an eager young would-be Miss Persia. Instead, it may have looked more like kidnapping and sexual slavery (though in a posh setting), with the woman who most "pleases the king" (2:4a) being named queen. What would have "pleased" Ahasuerus in a young woman's night with him was probably nothing like the talent portion of the nationally televised Miss America Pageant. Though the text is not explicit about it, this was most likely about the king's sexual pleasure.[59] Notably, the Hebrew text makes no

---

it was probably added after the other additions (*Esther*, 3:950).

58. Duran, "Bougaean," 1:494. Also see Schmidt, "Bougaean," 1:773–74. He cites *Iliad* 13:824 and *Odyssey* 18:79 for using "Macedonian" to express disdain.

59. See Day, *Esther*, 51–52 for a helpful discussion about the ambiguity about what

mention of Esther avoiding unclean foods while in this foreign court (over against Add Esth 14:17 and Dan 1:8–16), nor does it in any way skirt the fact of her sexual encounter with the king (in contrast to Add Esth 14:15).

On the other hand, we also cannot necessarily assume that the young women felt they were dragged away to live like captives. While the women may not have volunteered for this contest, it may have been viewed as an opportunity for ordinary—even poor, foreign, orphaned—young women to live a life of luxury. The fact that the passage ignores the women's own desires for their lives probably betrays something about gender roles at the time. Most women did not get to make such decisions about their own lives, so this chance for an increased standard of living may have seemed like a pretty good scenario.

In the end, we must remember that this scene is the narrator's fabrication, and not history. The ancient historian Herodotus tells us that no Persian king would have been allowed to choose his queen this way, but had to select her from one of seven royal families.[60] Esther and many of the other contestants apparently brought no family connections and no political alliances—apparently all the king cared about was his new queen's sexual prowess. This may have (and still would) raise eyebrows, but it contributes to the characterization of the king as "Doofus." Here, perhaps he is a doofus with the mindset and decision-making criterion of a hormone-driven adolescent. Indeed, the outcome of the story of Esther attests to precisely why no Persian king would have been permitted to choose just anyone for his queen—she might manipulate him for the sake of her own people! Finally, this beauty contest including every young woman in the kingdom serves as yet another example of the king's excesses.

In the midst of this story about the search for a new queen, we get a fairly lengthy narrator's sidebar (2:5–11) for the purpose of introducing the book's namesake, Esther. She is introduced by way of her cousin and adoptive parent Mordecai. The text identifies him as a "Jew" who lives "in the citadel of Susa" (2:5). Not just any old commoner would live in the citadel, so this is an indication that Mordecai may have had an official role in the royal court. Mordecai's name may be related to the name of the Babylonian god Marduk, or it could mean something like "the

"pleased" meant in this passage.

60. Herodotus, *Hist.* 3.84.

man par excellence."[61] If it seems odd for a faithful Jewish man to have such a foreign name, note that one of the returning exiles in Ezra 2:2 and Neh 7:7 also had this name. Furthermore, Esther is a Persian name—the narrator gives her Hebrew name as Hadassah in 2:7.

As any good biblical introduction would, this passage reaches back into the ancestry of the character at hand, first announcing Mordecai and tracing his genealogy back to a man named Kish (2:5). In contrast, the Greek version has already given this information about Mordecai in Addition A, 11:2–4. The Kish we know in the Hebrew Bible is the Benjaminite father of Saul (1 Sam 9:1–2). Shimei is another one of Kish's sons who is memorable in the biblical narrative for having angrily cursed David for destroying the house of his brother Saul, and in turn having supported Absalom's rebellion against David (2 Sam 16:5–13). Shimei recants those words and pleads for his life when Absalom's try for the throne failed, at which time David did spare him (2 Sam 19:16–23).

We cannot know for sure if the Kish and Shimei named in Esth 2:5 are intended to refer to these biblical figures from approximately five hundred years earlier. Alternatively, the Kish and Shimei mentioned here could be meant to name Mordecai's father and grandfather, who in that case just not so coincidentally have names that handily invoke the stories associated with these biblical figures. In either case, the text calls to mind the Kish and Shimei of 2 Samuel. By placing Mordecai in the house of Saul, the text sets the stage for us to meet the villain of the story, Haman. Haman was descended from Agag (Esth 3:1), who was Saul's enemy and downfall (1 Sam 15). Agag arose from the line of Amelek, whose people had been at odds with the Israelites since the time of the wilderness wandering (Exod 17:8–16; Num 24:20; Deut 25:17–19).

Unfortunately, the purported historical note 2:6 is ambiguous as to who was supposed to have been carried off to Babylon in the exile of 587 BCE. Thus it does not clear up the problem of who this Kish and Shimei were. Neither the A Text nor the LXX clarify this either (Add Esth 11:4 and 2:6). The NRSV translator's footnote after "Kish" in v. 6 betrays the ambiguity: The Hebrew there reads "who." The question is, did Kish go into exile, or does the text here refer to Mordecai? The NRSV translation makes it seem clear that Kish was the one. If so, who exactly was this Kish? It is chronologically possible for a grandfather or great-grandfather of Mordecai to have been exiled in Babylon. On the

61. Clines, "Mordecai," 902, citing R. Lemosín (4:902–4).

other hand, if the referent was supposed to have been the Kish the Bible knows as Saul's father, it would not make literal sense, because he lived hundreds of years before the exile.

In contrast to the NRSV's clarification that Kish went into exile, it seems most likely that Mordecai was the one who supposedly went into exile, with Kish being Saul's father, named in Mordecai's genealogy for the sake of his ancestral opposition to Haman's lineage. Yet had Mordecai gone into exile, he would have been over a hundred years old by the time of Xerxes I, who reigned from 486 to 465 BCE. It may well be that this chronological and linguistic tangle is yet another indication of Esther as a nonhistorical story. It could have been a narrator's wink to tell the audience that the book was fiction, or it could be evidence that the story was told long after anyone would have kept track of those dating details. Next we finally meet the namesake of the book (2:7). She has both Persian and Hebrew names: "Esther," which means "star" in Persian, and "Hadassah," which means "myrtle" in Hebrew. The latter name does not appear in the Greek version of Esther. The narrator explains her relationship to Mordecai. She was his cousin, but when orphaned she became his foster daughter. The Greek adds that she was his cousin through "his father's brother, Aminadab" (NRSV Add Esth 2:7). We also learn that Esther was beautiful, like most heroines. That detail also presumably plays a part in Esther's upcoming rise to royalty. Finally, we learn that as a resident of the citadel of Susa, Esther was "gathered" for the king's new harem along with the other young women who lived there (2:8).

We met the king's eunuch Hegai (called Gai in Add Esth 2:8ff.) back in 2:3. He is assigned as guardian over the newly arrived young women (2:8, 15). Scholars of the ancient world have debated whether all eunuchs would have been castrates, or sterile for some other reason; it may have been that some with the Hebrew title סָרִים *saris* would have been royal officials who were not sterile.[62] In the case of a harem supervisor or any official with responsibilities to the queen, we can assume that the individual would have been a castrate in order to ensure the sexual fidelity of the king's wives and to prevent harem servants from usurping the

---

62. Not every "eunuch" (Heb. סָרִים *saris*) in the Hebrew Bible was necessarily a castrate. The term was also a title for a royal official, such as in the case of Potiphar, who had a wife (Gen 39:1, 7). Also see סָרִים in *TDOT* 344–50.

throne via these women.[63] Hegai's narrative role seems to be as a stand-in for Mordecai as Esther's new father figure. Our heroine "pleased him" (2:9) and gained his compassion, or *hesed* (חֶסֶד). We do not know the details of Esther and Hegai's positive relationship, but it was certainly beneficial to Esther, who gained a high level of status even before she has her night with the king. Indeed, we will see that Hegai apparently helps Esther gain this favor. Even though the narrative setting has moved into the harem, under the charge of Hegai, Mordecai does not lose his important role. Esther's foster father remains present through his admonition that she should not disclose her Jewish identity (2:10). Furthermore, he keeps a close eye on her even from outside the harem walls (2:11).

In 2:12 the story of the search for the new queen resumes, following the aside to introduce these characters. Each woman will have a "turn to go into the king" (2:12). Elsewhere "go into" is a thinly-veiled euphemism for intercourse, though for obvious reasons a man usually is said to "go into" a woman (בּוֹא Gen 6:4; 16:2; 38:8, 9, 16; Deut 25:5; Judg 15:1; 2 Sam 12:24; Ezek 23:44; instances in which the woman is the subject include Gen 19:34 and 2 Sam 11:4). These successive nightly visits only occur after a whole year of beauty treatments, making this sound like an ancient version of *My Fair Lady*. The extended makeover has similarities with the other over-the-top features of the book, such as the six-month-long banquet. More practical explanations for the yearlong cosmetic session include the possibilities that the twelve month period would soften and lighten the most calloused and sun-darkened skin of field hands, and that it would be enough time to ensure that none of the young women were pregnant.

When summoned to the king's chambers, each woman would be given, literally, "whatever she said" to take with her to the king (2:13). This maddeningly vague reference has prompted all kinds of speculation. Perhaps the ancient readers of this story would have known exactly what kind of thing that might have been, but we can only make educated guesses. To be sure, it was not a Star of David necklace, as anachronisti-

---

63. Xenophon reports that Cyrus viewed eunuchs as the utmost in loyalty and protection for the king (*Cyropaedia* VII, 5.59–65 in Kuhrt *The Persian Empire*, 589). In some cases eunuchs helped to raise the royal children (Plato, *Alcibiades* 121d in Kuhrt *The Persian Empire*, 591). Yet they seem to have largely occupied a lowly position, such as being the prize in a game of dice (Plutarch, *Artoxerxes* 17.5–6; in Kuhrt *The Persian Empire*, 590), or in the case of "beautiful" boys, being kidnapped and castrated and sold (Herodotus *Hist.* 8.105).

cally portrayed in the film *One Night with the King*. The Star of David was not adopted as an exclusively Jewish symbol until the nineteenth century.[64] Greek Esther says nothing about the young women bringing anything with them; it only states that Esther perfectly followed Gai's (rather than Hegai's) instructions (Add Esth 2:15), a comment close to that in the Hebrew Esth 2:15. After each woman's turn, her status changed. The women went to the king's chambers with Hegai, and returned with Shaashgaz (this is still Gai in Add Esth 2:14) to the "second harem," the group of women considered the king's wives or concubines. She would only return to the king if he called for her, based on whether he "took pleasure in her" (2:14). The verb for "pleasure" or "delight" is *hafets* חֶפֶץ. It may well be a sexual euphemism indicating what the king was looking for in a new queen, like we see in Deut 21:14.

The narrator next focuses in on Esther's turn, but first inserts her immediate genealogy. Her father was the otherwise unknown man, Abihail; Mordecai was Abihail's nephew, making him Esther's cousin (2:15). However brief and obscure, the mention of her ancestry does increase her prominence, as it does with any biblical character given a genealogy.[65] Besides being beautiful (2:7), the rest of 2:15 builds up Esther's character as one who would fit well into most female fairy tale roles: She did what she was told, and everyone liked her. In the end, everything about Esther pays off. The king found Esther more than sexually pleasing; in fact he "loved" (אָהַב *'ahav*) her, and she gains his "favor" (חֵן *hen*, which may also be euphemistic in Deut 24:1) and "lovingkindness" (חֶסֶד *hesed*, 2:17)—the same feeling she garnered from Hegai back in 2:9. Ahasuerus thus selects her as his queen, notably in the "seventh year of his reign" (2:17), four years after the story began and he ousted Vashti (1:3).[66] To signify her new position, the king crowns her, recalling the incident in which Vashti would not don the crown. Indeed, the narrator takes care to note that the king chose Esther "instead of Vashti" (2:17). All this reminds the audience of the king's whims, highlights Esther's potential risk in her new role, and paints Esther as a foil to Vashti. In fact, 2:17 may prompt us to wonder what the king had originally thought of or felt for Vashti. Of course, to celebrate this new royal

---

64. Scholem, "Magen David," in *Encyclopedia Judaica* 13:336–39.

65. Crawford, *Esther*, 3:889.

66. In the Hebrew this is "the tenth month . . . Tebeth"; the Greek has "the twelfth month . . . Adar" (2:16 in both versions).

bride, the king throws a banquet, granting gifts as well as holiday time or amnesty to his subjects.[67]

In 2:19–23 we read a brief, intriguing, and apparently irrelevant episode in which Mordecai foils an assassination plot against the king. As the story progresses, we will find that this sets up the background for a later plot development. This episode reportedly takes place "when the young women were being gathered together a second time" (2:19a). The Greek here excludes this chronological reference entirely, while NRSV omits the caveat "a second time." Both emendations attempt to do away with the logical problem that 2:19 creates for the narrative. Why would the young women be gathered together again if the court and kingdom have just celebrated Esther's selection as queen? Ultimately, we cannot be sure what this means—surely there was not a second group of women and a second contest after the selection of Esther. Commentators have suggested various ways to understand it—one of the more logical ones being that the reference is to the second harem mentioned in 2:14. Another likely possibility is that 2:19a accidentally repeats 2:8 as the result of an editing error.[68]

Following that obscure reference, we read that at the time of the upcoming episode, Mordecai was at the king's gate (2:19b). This comment probably reveals more than his location. The king's gate would have been a central place for the leaders and the leading citizens of Susa, suggesting that Mordecai had a role of some importance. Very often in the ancient world the city gate was the setting of legal proceedings (for instance Deut 22:15, 24, 25:7; Josh 20:4; Ruth 4:11; Isa 29:21; Amos 5:10, 12, 15). The Bible also names the city gate as a good place to pick up gossip, as it was here (Ps 69:12; Pr 24:7).

At the beginning of this digression appears another apparently out-of-place comment about Esther, who had not divulged her ethnic-religious status as a Jew (2:20). The Hebrew reads that "she had not revealed her kindred or her people"; the Greek states that "she had not disclosed her country" and goes on to clarify that she continued "to fear God and keep his laws" (Add Esth 2:20, NRSV). Even if this is part of the editing

---

67. MT הֲנָחָה is a *hapax* (*BDB* 629B, "a giving of rest, i.e. perh. holiday-making"); LXX has "remission of taxes" (2:18).

68. Fox, *Character and Ideology*, 38, includes discussion of other options as does Moore, *Esther*, 30. See the Text Criticism section above for discussion on the possible editing of Esther.

error mentioned in regard to 2:19a, this repetition of 2:10 will become important to the plot later in the book.

As though to bring the reader back on track following this aside, the narrator repeats Mordecai's location: at the king's gate (2:21a). There, he caught wind of a plot to assassinate the king (2:21b–22a). Greek Esther has already told this story in Addition A (12:1–4), where it served to explain Mordecai's place of prominence in the court as well as Haman's disdain for Mordecai (12:5–6). Whether out of loyalty to King Ahasuerus or fear for his cousin the queen in the wake of a coup, he used his inside connection to Esther to tip off the king about this conspiracy (2:22). This embedded side-story ends quickly, with the culprits' execution, and, importantly, documentation of the incident (2:23b). Though the NRSV and other translations explain that the conspirators "were hanged on the gallows," the Hebrew in 2:23 literally reads, "and the two were hung upon a tree." It is unlikely that was a gallows; in the ancient world, what JPS translation has, "impaled on stakes," was a known form of capital punishment,[69] as was crucifixion, which Herodotus and Ctesias record as a Persian form of torture and execution.[70] This portion of the narrative highlights Mordecai's allegiance to the king prior to his conflict with Haman.[71] Because of this scene, we know that Mordecai's refusal to bow to Haman was not about a rejection of the royal administration itself. This episode also recalls numerous other tales of Persian court intrigue, particularly involving plots against the king's life.[72]

69. See Num 24:4 and 2 Sam 21:6 (both use the root יָקַע); also Ezra 6:11 (מְחָא).

70. Herodotus, *Hist.* 1.128; 3.125; 3.132; 3.159 as cited by O'Collins, "Crucifixion," 1:1207–10; Ctesias F9a 1.103; F16 §66.

71. Fox, *Character and Ideology*, 40.

72. Ancient reports of Perisan royal life frequently include reports of assassination attempts on the King (Plutarch, *Artoxerxes* 29.1, 6–7; in Kuhrt, *The Persian Empire*, 650). Xenophon reports that Cyrus had 10,000 spearmen that went everywhere with him as his guard (*Cyropaedia* VII, 5.66–68; in Kuhrt, *The Persian Empire*, 582). Xenophon also attests to cup-bearers who were to prevent the king from being poisoned (Xenophon, Cyropaedia I, 3.8–9; in Kuhrt, *The Persian Empire*, 584). Ctesias mentions two separate incidents in which eunuchs were part of royal assassination plots (Persica = FGrH 688 F9a and F15(54); and in Kuhrt, *The Persian Empire*, 588).

Scene 3: The Villain Haman—His Rise, His Demise (3:1—9:17)

In chapter 3 we finally meet the story's villain, "Haman the Agagite" (3:1). His family designation invokes the narrative of 1 Samuel, in which Agag is the Amelekite enemy and ultimately the demise of Saul (1 Samuel 15). Recalling Mordecai's genealogy (2:5), this makes him and Haman part of a centuries'-long family feud. The narrator refers to Haman as "the Agagite" again in 3:10; 8:3, 5; and 9:24. In 3:10; 8:1; 9:10 and 24, Haman's name comes with the additional tagline "the enemy of the Jews." Whether Haman is called "Agagite" or "enemy of the Jews," such designations contrast with Mordecai's repeated identification as "the Jew" in Esther (2:5; 3:4; 5:13; 6:10; 10:3). By understanding their relevance, we can see why the tradition in Purim celebrations is to audibly boo and hiss when the megillah chanter reads his name! Haman gets the additional genealogical moniker "son of Hammedatha" in 3:1. Since this is an obscure reference—we only know of Hammedatha from Esther (3:1, 10; 8:5; 9:10, 24)—the gentilic identification of Haman as an "Agagite" remains more meaningful.

The very next verse after meeting Haman, we reach the primary conflict in this tale. The king, having elevated Haman, had commanded his servants to bow to this new bureaucrat at the gate (3:2). Once we get to know Haman and the king better, we might suspect that Haman wrote out this order and had the king unknowingly put his seal to it, but we do not know that to be true! Other ancient texts show that ancient Persian society was quite stratified, particularly when it came to royalty and their retinue. Thus the point of Mordecai's bowing to Haman was to acknowledge Mordecai's lower role in the hierarchy.[73] For a reason not explicit in the Hebrew text, Mordecai refuses to humble himself to Haman in this way. Notice that Mordecai never directly answers the king's servants' question in 3:3: "why do you disregard the king's command?" From 3:4, it might look like it had something to do with his being a Jew, but that is not completely clear. The LXX elaborates on this a bit in 3:8 and even more in Esther Addition B, 13:4, where it seems that something about the Jews leads them to defy kings and divide their realms. Thus this episode is reminiscent of Shadrach, Meshach, and

---

73. Herodotus, *Hist.* 1:134 in Kuhrt, *The Persian Empire*, 624 also Kuhrt's general discussion, 620–21.

Abednego's refusal to worship King Nebuchadnezzar's golden statue (Daniel 3:1–30), which that text explains as their loyalty to worship the God of Israel and no other (3:28).[74] Yet we know from the previous scene (2:19–23) that Mordecai was loyal to the king and in 8:3, Esther bows to the king herself.[75] Perhaps it all just gets back to that old family feud, and Haman being an Agagite.[76]

Haman's response to Mordecai here typifies the exaggerated actions of the Persian court in Esther. Like deposing Vashti for her single refusal to appear at the king's feast in order that all men of the kingdom would be masters of their own homes (1:17–20), Haman determines to destroy all Jews in revenge for Mordecai's singular disobedience (3:6). Making it official, in the first month of the year, as though planning his new year's resolution, he has lots cast or פּוּר *pur*, to set the date for this massacre. Based on that, it is set to occur in the month of Adar. The Hebrew here is uncertain, providing neither a clear reason for the lot casting nor the date they determined. The purpose of this messy verse is clear nonetheless: To justify the festival of Purim through its etiology in the lots (the *purim*) cast. Haman then poses his plan to the king in a way he is unlikely to resist, describing the Jews not by name, and by telling mistruths and exaggerations to portray them as uniquely disobedient to the king (3:8).

We can see how bad the situation will get in 3:10–11, where the king goes way beyond acceding to Haman's plan. He gives this cunning villain his signet ring, and with it the power of the king's seal on anything he would wish, making the king little more than Haman's puppet. Illustrating that, the language Haman uses in 3:9 to pose his plan is considerably more benign than that of the decree he sends according to 3:13, which uses three verbs to order this bloodbath: "to exterminate"

74. Bickerman points out there is no Jewish law requiring Mordecai's action, though Josephus "invents" one (*Four Strange Books*, 179). He also conjectures that Mordecai thought he should have been promoted to Haman's position after foiling the assassination plot (179–80). Fox thinks Mordecai could not have expected this (*Character and Ideology*, 43), but extrabiblical sources suggest that there were high expectations about receiving rewards from the king after helping him (see commentary and notes below on 6:1–13).

75. Crawford notes this: *Esther*, 3:923.

76. With Fox, *Character and Ideology*, 44–45. He also lists a variety of possible reasons for Mordecai's unwillingness to bow to Haman. Similarly, see Crawford, who views "racial hostility" as a likely explanation of the conflict (*Esther*, 3:894–95).

(שמד), "to kill" (הרג), and "to destroy" (אבד). He specifies that it shall include "from young to old; children and women;" and it goes on to order the looting of their possessions. He has gotten the king to decree the genocide of a people that includes his queen and the man who saved him from assassination.

The purpose of the money in 3:9–11 is not entirely clear; it seems that Haman was attempting to bribe the king to approve his plan. Comments later in the book, 4:7 and 7:4, support this interpretation. The amount is absolutely massive, and stands as yet another example of excesses in the book. In a striking reference to the escape from Egyptian slavery, and perhaps as foreshadowing that once again the people of Israel would be saved while their oppressors suffered, the king's decree about the massacre went out just before Passover (3:12; cf. 1:22; Lev 23:5).[77] They had 12 months before Haman's pogrom would occur. The end of this section telescopes the scene back to the citadel from the whole kingdom, whose subjects had received this notice in their own languages via the royal messengers (3:12–14). In the citadel, Haman and the king were banqueting again (3:15; this is banquet number five), a stark contrast to the state of their subjects, who were in chaos in fear for their lives.

At 3:13 in the Hebrew, the LXX includes Addition B, which simply inserts the decree as dictated by Haman and issued by the king. This letter oozes sarcasm, which surely would have brought a laugh to its earliest audiences. The overconfident King Over-the-top identifies himself as "master of the whole world," though he tries to temper that with humility ("not elated with presumption of authority but always acting reasonably and with kindness," Add Esth 13:2, NRSV). He goes on to proclaim his concern for peace within his kingdom and comfort of all his subjects, which would supposedly be insured by the acts of his faithful right-hand man, Haman (13:3). He would accomplish that by eradicating the kingdom of a group of malicious lawbreakers (13:4–5). This statement effects irony since one of these very people, Mordecai, has already saved the king's life by thwarting an assassination attempt (12:1–5 and 2:19–23)— in 12:1–5, that attempt implicated Haman himself. The substance of the decree comes in 13:6, ordering death for all of these people, including women and children. The letter ends with the presumption that the slaughtered would go to "Hades" (a concept that belongs to the addi-

77. Fox, *Character and Ideology*, 54; Moore, *Esther*, 43.

tions' late Hellenistic setting), thus resolving any problems of the Persian Empire (13:7). This "certain hostile people" (13:4) seemingly refers to the Jews, but the letter in Addition B never makes that explicit. That omission compounds the letter's irony: How could anyone carry out this decree without knowing whom they were to kill?

Mordecai Responds to Haman's Plan (4:1–17)

This section moves from Mordecai trying to tell Esther what to do (4:8, 13–14) to Esther telling Mordecai what to do (4:16–17). In between, they each respond to the other's concerns in ways that fit their own situations. When Esther finds out that Mordecai is wailing around the city donned in sackcloth and ashes (4:1–2), she tries to quash his traditional signs of mourning and pious lamentation before she even knows the cause of his grief (4:4).[78] Though we do not know exactly what Esther's attendants told her (4:4), her response of sending new clothing to Mordecai suggests that Esther did not know that her cousin's sorrow represented widespread anguish among her people throughout the kingdom (4:3). Apparently well separated from the masses within the confines of the palace, perhaps she was embarrassed at Mordecai's dress and behavior, and maybe she was even concerned that it would threaten any official role he had in the court (4:2).

When Esther cannot get Mordecai to change into respectable clothing, she finally tries to find out what is wrong with him via Hathach (called Hachratheus in Add Esth 4:5), one of her attendants, who acts as her messenger (4:5–8). Hathach returns to Esther with all of the relevant information, including the all-important copy of the king's decree (4:8–9). As a result of Hathach's interchange with Mordecai, Esther will learn what the reader already knows about Haman's planned massacre of the Jews in Susa, and the money he agreed to pay to enact it (4:7). Most importantly, in 4:8 we finally discover how Esther will figure in this story. Mordecai wants her to use her office as queen to intervene for her people. In Greek Esther he elaborates specifically, reminding her of her humble beginnings, and encouraging her to call on God for help in this task.

Their intermediary, Hathach, is at least one other person who knows Esther's true ethnic identity. He returns to Mordecai with Esther's

---

78. See Gen 37:34; 2 Sam 3:31; and Job 16:5 for similar signs of lament.

concern. Similar to her response about Mordecai's appearance, her reply illustrates how very different her apprehensions are than Mordecai's. "Everyone in the palace" (a phrase that either excludes or berates Mordecai) knows that if she approaches the king without being invited, she risks death. While this fact of royal life is a crucial part of the Esther narrative, we have no historical corroboration for it. We do know that kings were closely guarded, and that queens had been known to be assassins, yet the ritual with the scepter and a law against even the queen approaching the king cannot be verified.[79] Therefore, Bickerman views this as evidence for an earlier strand of the story in which Esther was a concubine but not the queen.[80] This is a reasonable insight, but we cannot be sure of its veracity. At the end of v. 11, Esther articulates another difficulty: the king has not even asked for her recently.

Mordecai's response to Esther further emphasizes his own situation, and drives home his beloved cousin's own danger (4:13). She was a Jew before she was the queen, and therefore she was not safe. Any protection she felt from wearing royal attire in the seclusion of the palace was an illusion. If Esther had been concerned before about her situation, Mordecai's response to her last comment would surely have made her more upset. Mordecai's words to Esther in 4:13 lead into what is surely the most famous line in the book, his encouragement in 4:14 that there may have been some purpose in Esther's becoming queen at that particular time: "For if you keep silence in this time, relief and deliverance will arise for the Jews from another place, but you and your father's house will perish. And who knows, maybe it is for this time that you have arrived at royal power?" Commentators of all sorts have taken much out of—and read much into—this verse. It is probably the closest thing in the book to divine activity if we read it thinking that perhaps *God* put Esther in that place "for just such a time." Additionally, some commentators have suggested that "another place" in 4:14a might be an allusion to divine activity, indicating that God would ultimately save the Jews even if Esther did not. In the end, we must read the text on its own terms, and acknowledge that it does not explicitly state any kind of divine intervention or guidance. While it may well be that the author intended it, or that ancient audiences assumed it, one of the remarkable things about the verse is that any reference to God remains absent, or at

79. Kuhrt, *The Persian Empire*, 577.

80. In *Four Strange Books*, 184.

most, implicit. "Another place" could, in fact, refer to another person or situation that would help the Jews.[81]

Notably, v. 15 omits mention of a messenger who would shuttle Esther's words back to Mordecai, a narrative feature that effectively puts the two face-to-face. Esther responds to her cousin's plea by committing herself and her attendants to a fast, and asking that all of Susa's Jews likewise fast in support of her. By calling for a fast, Esther creates a more religious atmosphere in 4:16 than we see anywhere else in the book, yet we still have no mention of God or prayer. This is the point at which Esther takes on her role as the book's namesake and protagonist, finally initiating action on her own rather than being a passive character following direction from Mordecai, the king's courtiers, or the king himself. Furthermore, starting here Esther lives into her role not as queen of Persia, but as queen of the Jews. As if to cement her newfound initiative, in 4:17 Mordecai simply follows her command to enact the fast.

At the end of chapter 4 the Greek version includes Additions C and D, 13:8—15:16. Addition C (Add Esth 13:8—14:19) consists of Mordecai's prayer to God for assistance in saving the Jews of Persia. In the tradition of prayers like that of Daniel (2:20–23; 9:4–19), Judith (9:1–14; 13:4–5), and Judas Maccabeus (1 Macc 4:30–33), he begins with a hymn of thanksgiving for God's mighty acts of power and creation (13:9–11), and then proclaims his own humility (13:12–14) before making his ultimate petition to save God's people (13:15). He clarifies here that he would not bow to Haman because only God is worthy of such honor. Like Moses and Daniel (Exod 32:11–14; Dan 9:15), Mordecai reminds the Lord that this is the same people he brought out of Egypt, as if to say, "What a waste that would have been if they were only to die now at the hands of the Persians" (13:16). Mordecai's final plea to the Lord invokes the book's reversal theme: "Turn our mourning into feasting" (13:17, NRSV). We find a similar phrase as a description of the celebration that Mordecai decreed in the Hebrew version of Esther (9:22). Notably, this sentiment also appears in a prayer of thanks in Psalm 30, and as a promise from the LORD in Amos 8:10 and Jer 31:13. At the conclusion of Mordecai's prayer, the people of Israel, fearing for their lives, join in the prayer for God's mercy.

Addition C continues with a similar, though longer prayer by Esther. Like her cousin, she praises God (14:3–5) and highlights her

81. Fox, *Character and Ideology*, 63.

own humility (14:16). She takes on an uncharacteristically dramatic role here, going beyond the usual sackcloth and ashes to putting dung in her hair as a sign of mourning (14:2), and describing her place in Israel's history as akin to that of her ancestors in faith, who were destroyed by Assyria and Babylon (14:5–7; cf. 2 Kgs 17:5–15; 24:20—25:21). Despite her role as queen, she piously acknowledges the Lord as the rightful king, a point of contention when the people of Israel first desired their own king (14:3, 10, 12; cf. 1 Sam 8:7; 12:12). Similar to Judith, Queen Esther here prays for courage (14:13; cf. Jdt 13:7) and makes clear that she has neither eaten unclean food (14:17; cf. Jdt 10:5; 12:19) nor enjoyed the bed of the Gentile king (14:15; Jdt 13:16). The prayers of Addition C exemplify the Additions' emphasis on religious observance, Israel's history, and especially God, a major shift from Hebrew Esther, in which all of these are glaringly absent. In Hebrew Esther, the triumph in the story belongs to Esther and Mordecai, and only implicitly to God. In the Greek, all the glory goes solely to God.

Esther Responds to Haman: Calls for a Banquet (5:1–8)

The first verse of chapter 5 is best read slowly and with emphasis, probably followed by a pause. That kind of reading would most effectively communicate the gravity of the scene to come, in which the Jewish queen will dare to approach her king uninvited. The fear Esther expresses for her life in 4:11 saturates this verse with expectation and suspense. In going before the king in his inner court—royal robes or not—she is doing the dangerous thing that she fears—the thing that may well be a downfall like Vashti's—or the thing that may save her and her people. The comparison to Vashti here is remarkably ironic: Vashti met her end as queen by refusing to appear before the king in royal attire; Esther risks her demise as queen by appearing before the king without invitation but most definitely donning her queenly robes. Both situations illustrate the vulnerable position of a woman, even a royal one. We must wonder how much more ordinary women suffered at the policies and whims of the men who had power over them.

The Greek Addition D (Add Esth 15:1–16) directly follows Addition C, and is a sixteen-verse elaboration of Hebrew Esther 5:1–2 where the queen dares to approach the throne, and the king welcomes her by holding out his scepter. Addition D effectively replaces those two verses, which do not appear at all in the Greek. The LXX version of the episode does have Esther appearing before the king, taking her life in her hands to plead for her people, but it contains more drama and suspense than the two-verse Hebrew version (15:1–16). The narrator notes twice that her change out of mourning clothes and into her royal finery followed her fervent supplications to God (15:1-2), and then describes Esther going with two of her maids—one to take her arm, and one to carry her train (15:2–4)—to see the king, with her beauty covering up her inner apprehension (15:5). When she gets there, she encounters a fearsome king (15:6–7a), and consequently faints onto her maid. This characterizes Esther as a much frailer creature than we see in the Hebrew text. Nonetheless, it heightens the suspense of the moment, which only resolves when God intervenes to make the king look kindly on Esther (15:8). With his newfound tenderness, he invites her to speak, reassuring her that the law about the scepter does not apply to the queen (15:9–10). He touches her with it anyway, perhaps just for good measure (15:11), almost as if the narrator were saying, "What would this story be without the king holding out the scepter to Esther?" When she finally responds, she praises the king as though he were a divine vision (15:13–14), and then proceeds to faint again (15:15). This upsets the king, whose courtiers come to her aid (15:16). Addition D ends with the dramatic scene of the queen swooning in the king's arms, surrounded by royal assistants.

In the Hebrew version, however, the narrator does not keep us on the edge of our seats nearly so long. In 5:2, the king extends his scepter to Esther right away, offering quick relief for our heroine and all those readers who are rooting for her. Numerous artists throughout the centuries have picked up on this moment of resolution, surely a turning point of sorts in the story, by depicting it in paintings.[82] The king goes way beyond allowing Esther's presence in his inner court. He offers to fulfill her every desire, further elaborating, "even to the half of my kingdom" (5:3). Apparently, even though he has not called for her in thirty days, he still thinks quite fondly of her!

The king's response here adds to his characterization in two ways. For one thing, he becomes a more sympathetic fellow for not doing what Esther and Mordecai had dreaded. Surely his enthusiastic and generous reception of her gives him a more positive cast than he had before. On

---

82. Anthuenis Claeissens, *Esther before King Ahasuerus with Haman Being Sent to the Gallows* (1577); Pompeo Girolamo Batoni, *Esther before Ahasuerus* (1738–1740). Soelle and Kirchberger, *Great Women*, 98–115.

the other hand, his response "even to the half of my kingdom" calls to mind foolish statements made by other biblical characters; words that the speaker lives to regret because they were too vague and thus fodder for manipulation by the recipient. Examples include Jepthah's rash vow to sacrifice the first person he saw coming out of his house if he could win the battle against the Ammonites (Judg 11:29–40). Centuries after Esther, we find a similarly foolish promise when Herod promises anything to his wife Herodias' daughter—she asks for John the Baptist's head on a platter (Matt 14:1–11). Herodotus' *Histories* contains a remarkable parallel to King Ahasuerus' foolishness, where King Xerxes makes a thoughtless promise that proves more problematic for him than does King Ahasuerus' pledge. Herodotus tells that Xerxes went to visit Artaynte, a woman he greatly desired. He went on this visit wearing a colorful robe that his wife Amestris had made for him. Upon seeing Artaynte, he was so taken with her that he promised her "anything she fancied as a reward for her favours." Of course, she asked for the robe. From there, the story only gets worse, and ends quite badly, especially for Artaynte.[83] Though the king in Esther does not suffer very much from his extravagant promise, his prominent official Haman eventually does. In either case, his statement here contributes to his characterization as an over-the-top doofus, or to be more technical, as a fool.[84] Because the king's poorly considered words benefit our heroine, perhaps we do not notice so much how they reflect on him.

Given the king's openhanded offer, Esther's request sounds sparse. She asks the king and Haman to come to a banquet she is hosting that day (5:4). Thus in the space of two verses we find King Ahasuerus and Haman partying again, but this time on Queen Esther's terms (5:6). The king repeats his offer of "even to the half of my kingdom" in that setting. Esther puts him off again with another opportunity to party, inviting him and Haman to a banquet the next day. We must note the comical and gender-specific effect of Esther's stringing along by their bellies the powers that be. The king keeps telling Esther that she can have up to half his kingdom if she just asks for it; she keeps inviting them to indulge on wine, a request that they happily oblige (5:6; 7:2), laying the groundwork for her big request—the protection of her people. This is one of several

83. Herodotus, *Hist.* 9.108–12.

84. Other commentators have evaluated Esther more broadly for its wisdom traits. Niditch, "Esther: Folklore," 26–46; McGeough, "Esther the Hero," 44–65.

places in Esther where the king's proclamation "that every man should be master in his own house" (1:22) mocks him. Surely ancient audiences of this tale were full of women's giggles and eye rolling at this point.

Haman Responds to Mordecai: He and Zeresh Plot against Mordecai (5:9–14)

Suspense builds. We have to wait nineteen verses before we find out what happens at the next day's banquet. In the meantime, the narrator includes two key sidebar passages. First, we learn that Haman's malice against Mordecai will not be satiated by his murder along with that of every other Jewish man, woman, and child in the kingdom (5:9–14). Mordecai's persistence in his defiance of Haman (5:9) may contribute to the intensification of Haman's hatred. Indeed, Haman's bloodlust for Mordecai becomes so unquenchable that he plots an extraordinary execution for him. Haman's wife, Zeresh, (5:10; she is named Zosara in Add Esth 5:10), whom we meet in this passage, assists him in this plan. At the same time, in 5:9 and 12 Haman shows that he is obviously flattered by Esther's inclusion of him at her banquets for the king. It is this response that highlights Esther's cleverness in inviting him. As we will see, by having Haman at these banquets she can more easily accomplish the task of saving her people from him. In that, and in Haman's plans for Mordecai's demise, the irony builds: Esther flatters Haman by inviting him to banquets that will lead to his downfall, while Haman plots a unique destruction for the man who has prompted Esther to act. Furthermore, Haman seeks instruction even from his wife (5:10, 14), perhaps subtly undermining his dominant role in the house, a position apparently so crucial in the wake of the Vashti incident (1:16–22).

Feeling newly puffed up from being included in Esther's banquets, Haman seems all the more insulted that Mordecai will not show him honor and fear (5:9). To bolster his esteem, he collects an audience to hear him list his accomplishments and acquisitions (5:10–12). At least he is master of his own ample domain, or so it would seem. As is usual with Haman, however, that is not good enough for him. He tells his entourage that Mordecai remains a thorn in his side (5:13). One might think that one of his listeners would remind him that Mordecai would meet a quick end if Haman would only wait until the month of Adar, due to the decree he so cleverly passed through the king. Instead, they tell him to devise a special fate for Mordecai that will occur no later than the next day (5:14).

This response intensifies the characterization of Haman as a villain with an unquenchable bloodthirst. Haman's cronies instruct him to construct the place of Mordecai's execution. Notably, here Haman's advisors direct him in what to do, just as he often tells the king what to do. In turn, they all expect that the king will go along with it: "tell the king to have Mordecai hanged on it." That, they say, will leave him in a good mood for Queen Esther's banquet (5:14). Indeed, the next day looks to be quite a momentous occasion.

The various translations leave some question about just how Haman intends to put Mordecai to death. The Hebrew reads, "Let a tree be made fifty cubits high, and in the morning say to the king, 'Let Mordecai be hanged upon it'" (5:14). The translation "gallows" anachronistically conjures images of the Wild West, or perhaps Victorian England. Probably in Haman's time and place, he would have erected a pointed pole on which to impale Mordecai, or he would have killed him through crucifixion, which is in fact being hanged on a tree.[85] The specification "fifty cubits high," approximately eighty feet, is yet another ridiculous detail in this tale. Not even a dramatic movie-set gallows, pole, or cross would be that tall. Furthermore, it would have been an unrealistic task to throw it together by morning.

Return to Side-Story: King Ahasuerus Wants to Honor Mordecai (6:1–13)

This second sidebar passage returns us to an earlier out-of-place episode. It serves several functions in the narrative. It marks a significant turning point in the story in which the villain Haman begins his fall from grace. It also delays the outcome of the two previous scenes so that we are left waiting to see what happens at Esther's banquet and at Haman's gallows. The first part of chapter 6 (vv. 1–13) revisits a scene that the narrator introduced in 2:19–23. In that passage, Mordecai saved the king's life by foiling an assassination plot. It was certainly heroic, but did not appear terribly relevant to the story line. Now we find that scene set the stage for one of the funniest episodes in the Bible: Esth 6:1–13.

It begins innocently enough, with the king suffering a bout of insomnia (6:1). In the Greek version, his sleeplessness is directly attributed to the Lord (Add Esth 6:1). In a historically accurate reference to the

85. Also see above commentary on 2:23.

ample archives of Persian royalty, he calls for some nighttime reading from his royal records.[86] Perhaps he assumes this will be boring enough to get him back to sleep, or maybe he finds it soothing to hear about the past goings-on of his realm. What he discovers is the loyalty of Mordecai, who saved his very life (6:2). When the king realizes that he never properly thanked or honored Mordecai for his heroism, he acts with characteristic impulse: he must ask one of his advisors what to do! Fortunately, Haman is handy; he was just on his way to tell the king to build that eighty-foot execution station (6:3–4). This coincidence, along with the king's insomnia, along with the chance that he happened to have just reviewed the incident when Mordecai saved his life presents a set of circumstances that some interpreters throughout the ages have viewed as some form of divine intervention, although it is not stated as explicitly such in the Hebrew text. It was no act of extravagance for the king to devise a means of rewarding Mordecai for his valor. Other ancient Persian documents attest to ample royal rewards for deserving subjects. In fact, Persians were known to go to great lengths to provide help and assistance to the king, specifically hoping to be rewarded with gifts and favor. Xenephon reports that this system provided the king with scores of people carefully watching the king's back.[87]

With the artful timing of a folktale, the king asks his question before Haman can make his request: "What shall be done for the man whom the king wishes to honor?" (Esth 6:6, NRSV). The vague wording allows Haman and the audience to fill in the blanks differently, for full comedic effect. Readers see this marvelous poetic justice coming to the same extent that Haman is blind to it. Being the egomaniac that he is, Haman of course assumes that the king is speaking about him (6:6). Haman enthusiastically answers the king's question, calling for an extravagant list of honors that would signal a coup attempt, were they not bestowed by the king himself (6:8–9). To wear one of the king's robes and ride one of the king's horses wearing a royal crown, led by one of the king's officials pronouncing the rider's honor represents an over-the-top scene fitting for the book of Esther. In addition, this description points to nothing less than Haman's designs on the throne, to which the king

---

86. The ancient writer Ctesias of Cnidus reported that the Persians kept careful records of all royal events (Llewellyn-Jones and Robson, *Ctesias History of Persia*, T3).

87. Kuhrt, *The Persian Empire*, 640–44; specifically Xenophon, *Cyropaedia* VIII, 2.10–12, in ibid., 644.

is predictably oblivious. The oddity of a horse wearing a crown (6:8; a feature absent in the Greek) may be one more piece of comedic effect, or it could refer to the decorations used on a royal mount. In addition, it could be a problem with an ambiguous pronoun in the text; perhaps the crown was supposed to be on the rider's head.[88] In any case, Haman has proposed an over-the-top scene of royal recognition, fully in the tradition of Esther.

Meanwhile, the audience of Esther must surely have been laughing their heads off, knowing what a hole Haman was digging for himself. He has come to the king's court in order to seal Mordecai's fate on a six-story pole; he thinks he has arrived with fortuitous timing for the king to lavish deserved honor on him. He instead receives the ultimate humiliation by having to bestow his self-tailored royal treatment on his most despised enemy (6:10–11). Crawford notes that the King Ahasuerus specifically refers to Mordecai here as "the Jew" (6:10). That not only heightens the torment for Haman, but it also points out that the king is seemingly oblivious of the decree he has issued about the destruction of the Jews (3:8–11).[89] At this point we can imagine a storyteller announcing, "Let the reversals begin!" We can imagine the response of readers and audiences upon hearing this turnabout of characters for the first time. They may have gasped, smiled, laughed, and groaned. Verse 12 effectively illustrates this role reversal. When Haman was at his height, it sent Mordecai into mourning (4:1). Now Haman is the one mourning (6:12) with his head covered. As we see throughout the book, this is only one of many places in Esther where utterly biblical reversals take effect.

Chapter 6 begins Haman's downfall, playing out in terms familiar to the Hebrew canon: the lowly are lifted up; the mighty fall (see 1 Sam 2:4–9 and "Reversals" section in the Esther introduction, above). Indeed, Haman's own wife and supporters point this out to him in religious (6:13) if not theological terms—in the Greek Haman's wife justifies his impending demise by saying, "the living God is with [Mordecai]." (Add Esth 6:13). This is a huge shift from Haman's advisors' last instruction to him about hanging Mordecai (5:14). As though they too play a part in Haman's demise, they no longer tell him what he wants to hear.

88. Berlin, *Esther*, 60.
89. Crawford, *Esther*, 3:914.

Esther's Second Banquet: Esther Reveals Haman's Plot (6:14—7:10)

In 6:14 the narrator hurries us back to the story line: Haman follows the eunuchs to Esther's second banquet in so many days. On yet the third day of their feasting together, the second day of the second banquet, the king repeats for the third time his ridiculously generous offer to Esther of "up to half the kingdom" (7:2; see also 5:3 and 6). Finally, on this third occasion Esther breaks the longstanding suspense begun in chapter 4 when she first learned about Haman's pogrom. Esther cleverly first asks the king to "let my life be given to me." Then, in a parallelism, she begs for the lives of her people (7:3).[90] The Hebrew of 7:3 can be illustrated in the following way:

> Let it be given:
> > my life—this is my request
> > my people—this is my plea

In this way Esther first plays on the sympathies of the king for his queen. Then, through what might otherwise seem an afterthought of wanting help for her people, Esther finally discloses that she is one of those people that have been consigned to destruction. Esther continues her intentionally worded explanation in saying, "for we have been sold, I and my people, to be exterminated, to be killed, and to be destroyed" (7:4). By keeping herself in the forefront, she monopolizes on her clout with the king. Furthermore, she delays exposing her ethnicity, which she might reasonably have supposed would be an unwelcome surprise to her royal husband. With humility—or hyperbole—Esther asserts that mere slavery would not have been worth troubling the king over, but their very lives are at stake. She emphasizes that with three different words for the looming genocide: "exterminate," "kill," and "destroy" (7:4). These verbs repeat Haman's profoundly bloodthirsty language in his decree in 3:13, and foreshadow Mordecai's counterdecree in 8:11.

Esther's explanation in the Greek version comes out very differently. That description of her people's looming fate notably omits the verbs "exterminate" and "kill." Though "destroy" and "plunder" remain (Add Esth 7:4, NRSV), her comment about slavery has a very different meaning in the Greek. In the Hebrew her point was that slavery would

90. Ibid., 3:918.

not be enough of an offense to complain about; in the Greek slavery appears to a major part of their fate (Add Esth 7:4).

Many have speculated about why Esther does not make her request of the king the first time she had the opportunity. After all, in the meantime, Haman has been plotting to kill Mordecai, and just might have succeeded if not for a coincidental bout of kingly insomnia foiling his plans. Some logical explanations exist, such as that she is buttering up the king and Haman before she pleads for the lives of her people, or that the suspense she creates makes him all the more willing to respond positively. It probably makes more sense, however, to view this threefold approach and delay as an effective narrative strategy. It makes for a better story if Esther has an audience with the king three times before popping this question, and if he offers her "up to half the kingdom" three times before she takes him up on it. The narrative is much more gripping if her request is delayed by more than a chapter while Haman begins his fall from grace and Mordecai commences his ascent as the king's favored. And Esther is nothing if not a marvelous story. The trope of threes is popular in folktales for good reason; it works here just as well.

Esther's carefully planned and worded petition absolutely pays off in a royal response that surely makes Haman shake in his sandals (7:5–6). If he thought he was in a bad situation when he had to parade Mordecai around town in a royal get-up, he must have feared that his doom was sealed now. The fate foreshadowed by his advisors and his wife (6:13) most surely awaits. The king wants to know who is responsible, and Esther's accusation comes with breathtaking force (7:6), equal to Nathan's "you are the man" accusation of King David (2 Sam 12:7). Esther has three words to describe Haman: "foe," "enemy," and "evil." This is no ordinary scene. It is a stand-up-and-cheer kind of scene, something a filmmaker would supply with rousing music, pregnant pauses, and close-up shots. We can imagine Esther pointing her trembling finger in Haman's flushed face, while the king looks on in shock. This confrontation dramatically highlights Esther's ascent over against Haman's fall. Esther's indictment effectively puts Haman in his place. She and Ahasuerus are royalty, Haman is not. Haman is rightly "terrified" (7:6).

The king makes an odd move and retires to the garden, leaving Haman to plead his life from Esther (7:7). The one who would have destroyed her is now at her mercy. The narrator describes the scene:

"Haman was falling upon the couch that Esther was on" (7:8). When the king returns, it appears instead that Haman has yet again crossed a line with the queen. Whether or not he was trying to rape her (or succeeding) has provoked debate among commentators. Whatever the case, the king assumes the worst. His very words, which function simultaneously as question and accusation, "covered Haman's face" (7:8). Ordinarily, we find the verb "cover," or חפה *hph*, where it describes a gesture of mourning through veiling one's head, as we saw after Haman honored Mordecai in 6:12 (also see 2 Sam 15:30; Jer 14:3, 4). This phrase illustrates the king's power over Haman, something we see first in 6:1–11, and will see even more dramatically in the coming verses.

Shortly before this scene, Haman was plotting the execution of Mordecai (5:9–14). By the end of chapter 7, Haman is executed at the time, in the place, and by the means that he had devised specifically for Mordecai (7:10). It is one of the book's chief reversals. When Harbona (Bugathan in Add Esth 7:9), one who presumably would have been bowing to Haman only days earlier (3:2; 5:9), suggests this handy and ironic method for Haman's execution, it secures the villain's downfall. Haman has lost any status he had ever held. In turn, we see that no matter how much power Haman thought he had amassed as a royal official, and no matter how much the king behaved like a "doofus," the king still had the status and the title that mattered. Haman's glory was tenuous and fleeting, and Mordecai had saved the king's life (7:9). Nonetheless, the king does not suddenly become a great leader here. After all, hanging Haman is not in fact the king's idea.

Chapter 7 ends with a narrator's comment that parallels 2:1: "the anger of the king abated" (7:10). Haman's death triggers that emotional release here, and it marks the end of the Haman story line. In chapter 2, Vashti's demotion had the same effect; there the statement signaled the close of the Vashti episode.

Esther and Mordecai Get Haman's Place and Power (8:1—9:19)

Chapters 8 and 9 of Esther provide continued resolution and reversal. Finally, the king knows what readers have known all along: that his queen is related to the man who saved his life (8:1). Not only that, but he knows that she is a Jew and thus part of a group that he allowed to be targeted for extermination. Fully in the spirit of the book, reversal goes to the extreme here, even becoming outlandish. The rise-and-fall theme in Esther would not be complete simply with Haman's death. We will see his genocidal plot do a posthumous about-face; we will see Esther and Mordecai ascend to the kind of royal power Haman had held and craved, and kill those who would have annihilated them. In giving his signet ring to Mordecai (8:2), the king hands over an important symbol of Haman's fallen rule. The narrator notes in 8:2b that Esther was the one who "set Mordecai over the house of Haman," illustrating the queen's newfound power as well as property.

In 8:3 however, the narrator immediately undermines that power. There we find Esther prostrate and weeping, imploring the king to spare her and her people. This essentially repeats her request of 7:3–4, reminding us that Ahasuerus never resolved the trouble; he only eliminated the troublemaker. When the king again holds out his scepter to Esther in 8:4 (reminiscent of 5:2), she seems to regain her composure and eloquently states her case (8:4–6). The king replies in vv. 7–8 that he has vanquished their foe; the rest is up to them. This section (8:3–8) reminds us of a quirk of Persian law, according to Esther, that once a decree had been made and signed by the king, it could not be rescinded, even by him. Apparently the king could give Esther up to half of his kingdom, but somewhat absurdly, he could not void his own law. Not only does this seem absurd to most readers today, but we have no ancient corroboration for it.[91] However, it serves an important function in the story, which is to provide the basis for the counterdecree in 8:9–12, laying the legal groundwork for the bloody events of chapter 9.

Thus we find Esther and Mordecai dictating to the king's secretaries in 8:9–14. The section opens with a chronological problem, a delay of three months in issuing the decree, from the month of Nisan (3:7) to Sivan (8:9).[92] Greek Esther solves the problem by referring to Nisan in 8:9. Commentators have proposed various solutions to this problem, but we cannot be sure of the best answer. Date ambiguities notwithstanding, the language in this passage effects full reversal by closely mimicking 3:12–15, which narrates the creation and dissemination of Haman's edict. Haman's obscene use of three verbs to describe his pogrom— "exterminate," "kill" and "destroy" (3:13//7:4)—fittingly return here in Mordecai's counterdecree for the Jews to fend off their attackers. We also

91. See 1:19 and comment on it above.
92. See Crawford's discussion, *Esther*, 3:925.

see repeated the inclusion of women and children in the raids, as well as booty (3:13//8:11). The word-for-word repetition of phrases from that section here highlights the differences between this passage and the previous ones: Mordecai rather than Haman issues the decree; "the Jews" are included in the list of who will be notified about this edict in their own language and script (3:12//8:9).

Haman's three verbs did not all appear in the Greek of 3:13 or 7:4 (those verses only read "destroy") and neither do they return here in Add Esth 8:11, where the king's order to the Jews is "to observe their own laws, to defend themselves, and to act as they wished against their opponents and enemies" (NRSV). The Greek does not present Haman's threats with such intensity as the Hebrew; its self-defense scenario is similarly tempered. In the midst of the letter's dictation, Greek Esther includes the whole letter as Addition E after 8:12. The Greek of 8:9 departs from the Hebrew by omitting Mordecai as the named composer of the edict. Thus Add Esth reads as though the king himself might have written it, though ultimately it is ambiguous. The letter begins with rather extensive circumlocutions alluding to persons who had been treated respectably within the Persian court, yet who nonetheless acted disloyally and maliciously (16:1–8). These comments lead to an assertion that the kingdom will hereafter be "quiet and peaceable" (16:8), a place of "equitable" judgment (16:9). Eventually it becomes clear that the subject of these verses is not just some nameless infidel, but Haman himself (16:10). The edict's rhetorical delay before unveiling Haman as the villain, recalls Esther's series of banquets before she revealed Haman as her people's nemesis (5:4; 7:1–8).

The letter describes Haman's crime first as betrayal of the kindness of the Persian court (vv. 1–11), by v. 14 explains his intent to destroy Mordecai and Esther, and ultimately his plan to overthrow the Persian kingdom in a coup for his own Macedonian people. Greek Esther departs from the Hebrew in its emphasis on Haman as a Macedonian with his people's interests in mind. The Hebrew identifies Haman as "the Agagite" five times (Esth 3:1, 10; 8:3, 5; 9:24), and Greek Esther refers to him as "the Bougean" (12:6; 3:1). "Macedonian" may, like "Bougean" simply be another way of saying that he is an enemy foreigner.[93] Or, it may allude to the historical reality that the Macedonians

---

93. See note above on 12:6.

(as the Greeks) ultimately did conquer the Persians, in 332 BCE.[94] As is the case throughout Greek Esther, the language abounds with exaggerated descriptions, lifting the hero and heroine onto high pedestals, and painting the villain as pure evil.

Finally in 16:17, the edict contains an actual command, "not to put in execution the letters sent by Haman." This directive does just what the king says could not be done and rescinds the previous decree (1:19), rather than creating a new decree of self-defense to protect the Jews. This may explain why, as we saw above, the battle scenes are more diminished in Greek Esther than in Hebrew. Addition E goes on to explain that Haman's death was ultimately accomplished by divine retribution (16:18). The next command instructs that the edict should be posted, and that Jews—with the help of "reinforcements" must be allowed to "live under their own laws," and "defend themselves" (16:19–20). The edict then instructs that this should mark a celebration for the Jews (16:21) and for "you" (16:22–23), that presumably being the "governors" of 16:1. Levenson points out that this inclusive note could indicate an originally Gentile origin of Purim, or it might be a way of commanding wide respect for the festival.[95] On the other hand, it could just be an editor's oversight. The final verse of Addition E threatens something like a curse to any regions who would not heed the edict, ending with the dramatic flourish that even the fauna would suffer (16:24).

The story line shared by both MT and Add Esth returns in 8:15–17 with a scene reminiscent of Haman's unwitting elevation of Mordecai (6:10–11). The newly appointed Jewish leader Mordecai appears in 8:15 looking like royalty, and he has as much power. With this Jewish royal figure standing guard, the following verses contain effusive descriptions of joy and celebration. Assuming a pre-Maccabean diaspora setting, we can almost imagine the story's audiences shedding tears of nostalgic longing for a time when they really *did* have a Jewish king standing triumphantly before them. Readers rooting for the book's namesake, however—maybe especially the women in the audience—might wonder what has happened to Queen Esther in this triumphant scene. Her absence in 8:9–17 (and continuing on through 9:11) could be another

94. Crawford, *Esther*, 3:966.

95. Levenson, *Esther*, 114.

indication of the book's earliest forms as a Mordecai story and then an Esther story.[96] Or, it could betray the androcentric bias of the time.

Celebration of this turnaround results in—of course—a banquet (8:17a; the eighth one of the book). The final, hyperbolic note of astonishing triumph comes in 8:17b, in which non-Jews were so frightened of the newly powerful Jews that they claimed to be Jews themselves. The LXX goes so far as to say that many Gentiles became circumcised! It seems likely that this turn of events would have been received by a group of persecuted Jews as downright hilarious, particularly if they were living in the time of Antiochus IV Epiphanes, who tortured and killed Jews for upholding the Abrahamic covenant through circumcision (1 Macc 1:60–61; 2 Macc 6:10; 4 Macc 4:24–26).

Chapter 9 opens on "the big day": the thirteenth of Adar. The narrator begins by reminding readers that it was to have been the day of the Jews' very demise, but instead becomes the day when the Jews triumph over those who would have killed them. It is the ultimate reversal. The narrative emphasizes how fearsome Mordecai and the Jews had become to the inhabitants of Ahasuerus' kingdom (9:2–4), and it illustrates that by numbering and cataloging the dead. In 9:5, the Hebrew even includes two of the three verbs that Haman used to threaten the Jews: "kill" and "destroy" (cf. 3:13//7:4). This indeed is poetic justice. In the citadel alone the dead are reported at 500, including the ten sons of Haman, who are listed by name (9:6–10).

As for the booty, the MT and LXX differ notably here. In the Hebrew text, the Jews followed the rules of "the ban," or *herem* (חרם) which generally required total destruction of captives and plunder (9:10, 16; see Deut 13:6–19; 20:16–18; Josh 6:18) so as to not be swayed to idolatry by foreign gods or peoples (Judg 8:22–27). This is odd because it contradicts the allowance for booty in Mordecai's edict in 8:11 (also cf. 3:13). Nonetheless, it makes a striking connection to the misdeed of King Saul in 1 Sam 15:1–35, where he did not "utterly destroy" (*herem*) his Amelekite enemy. In that way, the Jews here are able to undo that ancestral error by decimating the Amelekites in this story, Haman and his sons. In stark contrast, LXX states that the Jews "indulged themselves in plunder" (Add Esth 9:10, NRSV).

---

96. See the Text Criticism section, above, for discussion of Esther's possible editorial history.

King Doofus' response to the deaths of hundreds of his closest subjects in his very own citadel is to ask what happened outside of the citadel, and to ask Esther what else he can possibly do for her, using the same absurdly accommodating words that he used at her banquets (9:12; //5:3, 6; 7:3). She responds by asking for more of the same on the following day (9:13). She also asks that as for "the ten sons of Haman," he "let them be hanged on a tree" (9:13, NRSV). In the Hebrew version, this seems redundant, since 9:7–9 listed their names as having been killed along with the other Jews in the citadel. The Greek version clarifies that their dead bodies will be hanged (perhaps impaled, or hanged on crosses), a practice that makes more textual sense as well as historical, according to customs of ancient warfare and humiliation of an enemy. Of course, the king agrees to Esther's requests, so the sons of Haman are hanged, and the killing of the enemies of the Jews continues, with 300 dead in Susa (9:15) and 75,000 in other provinces, according to the Hebrew version (9:16). The various texts in vv. 17–19 suggest some amount of editing through their confusion about the dates and location of the killings, the celebration, and the remembrance of the events. It also seems to have been the case that the festival took place at different times in different places.

Scene 4: The Point of the Story: Purim (9:20–10:3)

Significantly, this section presents the establishment of Purim. First we find its date (v. 21), a concise etiology (v. 22a), and the nature of the festival (v. 22b), all announced by Mordecai (20, 23). In notable contrast with the Persian banquets, this celebration was not solely about partying, but included giving gifts to one another and to the poor (9:22).[97] Mordecai's final decree apparently resolves the previous date confusion of vv. 17–21 by calling for a holiday of remembrance on both the fourteenth and fifteenth of Adar (9:21 MT and LXX). A brief interlude in 9:24–28 legitimizes the celebration of Purim by rehearsing the preceding events, while vv. 29–32 establish the festival with yet another letter. Esther features prominently in 9:29–32, with the section even concluding that "her word set the matters of Purim" (32). In 9:20–32 we find repeated decrees to establish Purim from Mordecai (vv. 20–23), Esther

---

97. The language in 9:22 is comparable to what we find in Psalm 30; Amos 8:10; and Jer 31:13.

and Mordecai (vv. 29–31), and Esther (32). Those make for a redundant narrative, and those who attribute the section to editing and solve it with emendations have some clarity to offer.[98] In any case, the final form of MT 9:20–32 emphasizes Purim's authenticity.

The last three verses of the book (10:1–3) act as a brief encomium to Mordecai, referencing "the Annals of the kings of Media and Persia" as the place where his history was recorded. With 9:29–32 primarily about Esther, and 10:1–3 lacking any mention of her, we see again the possibility that early strands of the story had to do solely with either Esther or Mordecai individually. Even so, 10:1–3 gives the impression of a patriarchal bias, omitting our heroine from the grand finale. Linda Day connects this to the "male aggrandizement" of the book's opening, in that case about King Ahasuerus (1:1–4).[99] Though the book is named for Esther, and her character has distinctive moments in her own right, we must notice that at times she seems consigned to the fate that the king dictated in 1:22: Ultimately, she is not master of this house. Whether that master was the king or Mordecai could serve as commentary on the status of all diaspora Jews in this time, especially the female ones.

After 9:24—10:3, which is common to both versions, LXX resumes the dream sequence from Addition A (11:2—12:6). This final Addition, F (10:5—11:1), explains the imagery of the dream in Addition A. The dream came true, in that the "little stream that became a river" was Esther (11:10; 10:6), the fighting dragons were Haman and Mordecai (11:6; 10:7), and most significantly, God came to the aid of the people in response to their pleas (11:10; 10:9–12). While Hebrew Esther contains a closing encomium to Mordecai (10:1–3), Greek Esther appropriately directs that song of praise to God (10:9–12). It is just what we have come to expect from this version of Esther.

Addition F continues with the colophon of Greek Esther. It includes statements dating and authenticating the book. Unfortunately, none of those statements provide us with reliable information, as the exact identities and dates of the individuals named are unclear. We cannot historically place the individuals Dositheus and Lysimachus. The colophon refers to "the letter of Purim," which was presumably some form of the Greek Esther. It was apparently available for delivery (most probably to Egypt—this phrase is added in NRSV) in "the fourth year of the reign of

---

98. See Fox, *Character and Ideology*, 123–27.
99. Day, *Esther*, 165.

Ptolemy and Cleopatra" (11:1). Because there were a number of Ptolemy and Cleopatra ruling pairs who might fit this description, this does not clarify the date. It could have been as early as 171 BCE or as late as 48, depending on the rulers to which the text refers.[100] Bickerman concludes that 77 BCE is the most likely date, given all the possibilities.[101] In any case, the Greek expansion of the Hebrew Esther could not have been much later than mid-second to early first century BCE.

Notably, chapters 9 and 10, with the battle scenes and justification for Purim, do not appear in the Alpha Text.[102] It seems likely that these were later additions, possibly for the sake of encouraging a downtrodden people, and for giving the etiology of a popular festival. That possibility may resolve some of the ethical dilemmas of these sections for contemporary readers.

Conclusion

The book of Esther intersects with the contemporary life of faith in numerous ways. Readers throughout the ages have found much in it to question and consider, from its theology—or lack thereof—to its ethics. Like all biblical books, Esther remains relevant because it tells a story that remains true in many ways, both providing comfort and disturbingly mirroring our own lives.

Because the book of Esther does not mention God, it invites a unique kind of theological reflection. How do you talk about God's role in a book that does not name God? What kind of power does God have, and how is that power manifest to humankind? If God's power does not operate in the traditionally conceived manners—particularly direct intervention—then what is the role of humankind in working with or for God? Might God's relationship to humans be so subtle as to warrant no mention at all? Or is God so obviously immanent that any attempt to name the divine should be viewed as redundant or blasphemous?

---

100. See Levenson, *Esther*, 136 and Crawford, *Esther*, 3:970–71 for helpful summaries. Bickerman rules out 171 BCE as an early date because there were actually three rulers during that time. I am unconvinced that provides effective grounds for his conclusion ("The Colophon," 536, n. 38). In contrast to all of these commentators on the identification of Cleopatra and Ptolemy here, see Whitehorne, "Cleopatra," 1:1064. On the various Ptolemies and Cleopatras, see Brown, "Egypt," 2:370–71.

101. Bickerman, "Colophon," 537.

102. Crawford, *Esther*, 3:929.

Because it raises these thorny questions, Esther is a vital and engaging theological dialogue partner, one we might not expect to find in the biblical canon.

John J. Collins compares God's action in Esther to the theology of the Wisdom literature, that of "the midwife behind the scenes of history."[103] It is tempting to quibble about this assessment as interpretive rather than strictly descriptive of the text, and about the fact that any midwife is arguably more present at a birth than God is in Esther. Yet it is crucial to acknowledge that the ancient Israelites who were Esther's earliest audiences would have assumed God's presence whether or not they named it. Though at face value Hebrew Esther characterizes God as absent or hidden, there are places in the text that suggest a divine presence to some readers. Most of these arise in chapter 4, where Mordecai comes to Esther greatly troubled about Haman's planned pogrom, and Esther struggles over the dilemma this poses for her. Mordecai encourages Esther to take action with his famous line of 4:14: "For if you keep silence in this time, relief and deliverance will arise for the Jews from another place, but you and your father's house will perish. And who knows, maybe it is for this time that you have arrived at royal power?" Based on the beginning of that verse, we could speculate that "another place" providing "relief and deliverance" could in fact be God. Similarly, we could view Esther's fortuitous rise to power at "this time" as having been divinely directed. Yet again, those interpretations are not plain in the text. The fasting and lamenting named in the book is the closest that it comes to expressing blatant religiosity (4:3, 16; 9:31). The fast Esther calls in 4:16 could in fact be viewed as a turning point in the story, where that act of piety signals Esther's rise and Haman's demise. Finally, Esther's theological dilemma can be solved easily enough by turning to the Greek version of the book. God's absence from Hebrew Esther is surely one reason the Additions arose.

While many interpreters focus on the theological implications of Esther, the book contains even more to consider for what it says about human beings. Esther and her people may fast in supplication, and they may believe that God will eventually come to their aid, but the story ultimately emphasizes Esther's action and power, not God's. Mordecai implores in 4:13 that Esther should not expect to escape Haman's violence just because of her royal place, but rather that she herself must act.

103. Collins, *Introduction*, 542.

His words are reminiscent of Martin Niemöller's post-Holocaust reflections on inaction in the face of an oppressive regime, as expressed to interviewer and author Milton Mayer in the early 1950s:

> Pastor Niemöller spoke for thousands and thousands of men like me when he spoke (too modestly of himself) and said that, when the Nazis attacked the Communists, he was a little uneasy, but, after all, he was not a Communist, and so he did nothing; and then they attacked the Socialists, and he was a little uneasier, but, still, he was not a Socialist, and he did nothing; and then the schools, the press, the Jews, and so on, and he was always uneasier, but still he did nothing. And then they attacked the Church, and he was a Churchman, and he did something—but then it was too late."[104]

Esther did something, risking her life, and averted the eradication of her people. The book of Esther, like Niemöller's poignant statement, challenges contemporary audiences to act in the face of oppression, even when it involves risk.

The end of Esther makes the point repeatedly that the reason for the book is to tell the story behind Purim. That is the reason the book retains such a prominent role in contemporary Judaism. It is not only a matter of celebrating a fun chaos-festival, akin to Holi in Hinduism or Mardi Gras in Christianity. There is a distinctly bittersweet tone to the hilarity and craziness of Purim celebrations. It is laughing so that you don't have to cry over the countless Hamans and the repeated pogroms throughout history. From persecution of Jews in fourteenth-century Egypt and Europe in the Middle Ages to pogroms in nineteenth-century Eastern Europe to the Holocaust of the twentieth century, the Second Purims have continued, which is why it must be remembered annually. Amid the partying, Purim is a way of remembering that there has always been and always will be some villain, casting lots for the demise of a people. It is a call to vigilance against further Purims. It calls for a festival because heroes like Esther put their lives on the line to foil those evil designs. Sometimes, just like in the story, the underdog does become the victor, and that is certainly reason for a party.

Yet this leads to one of the most troubling features of the book: The high death toll at the end of Esther. Many of us do not like the idea of so much blood on the hands of one of the Bible's great heroines, no matter

---

104. Mayer, *They Thought They Were Free*, 168–69.

the reason. It only makes sense to me to understand that aspect of the story in its probable historical context. That is, as a self-defense fantasy of the oppressed and scattered Jews; a vision of turnabout for a diaspora people who had no hope of decimating their enemies because they were barely surviving themselves. Adele Berlin writes that this "make-believe victory is the safety valve for Diaspora Jewry that permits the continuation of the belief in the security of their lives and their community. To put the world right, as the book of Esther does, requires the removal of evil, of the enemy."[105] Berlin calls this ending of Esther "farce," and cites Eric Bentley in saying that "in farce, as in dreams, one is permitted the outrage but is spared the consequences."[106] Indeed, that is what good stories do: They make the world "right" when we cannot. Thus we can rightly view the bloodshed at the end of Esther as catharsis for the diaspora Jews and all since then who have been threatened, saved, and killed; those whose very survival relies on an over-the-top self-defense fantasy like we read in Esther.[107]

Nonetheless, this does raise the question of whether the liberation of one group requires the oppression of another. While the killings at the end of Esther are appropriately interpreted as a healthy fantasy, they also stand as a caution that the oppressed may become the oppressor all too easily; any group that undertakes self-defense runs the risk of vengefully turning into the villain they once feared. The significant challenge that the Bible poses to its readers is to grapple with the way it mirrors ordinary human traits, even in its depictions of extraordinarily evil—or good—characters. In this case, the book of Esther summons its readers to scrutinize their fear of the other, and to ask the extent to which they allow that fear to drive their own behavior. Whether through negative stereotypes of particular ethnic or national groups; whether through self-segregation in housing or friendship groups; whether through support of international policies that unfairly single out particular national or ethnic groups—we all have a little bit of Haman in us. The book of Esther calls us to consider to what lengths we will take our own fears, and perhaps, egotisms. What neighborhoods will we consider living in?

105. Berlin, *Esther*, 82.

106. Ibid., 81.

107. Wills notes that the story could be viewed as more of an "embarrassment" if it were from the Hasmonean period, when Jews did in fact forcibly convert and kill their enemies (*The Jewish Novel*, 99 n. 13).

What places of worship will we consider attending? What children will we consider as playmates for our own children? What laws will we support regarding employment, marriage, or housing? What policies and politicians will we support? What will we have to say about international conflicts? Haman, the diabolical villain, with whom most readers are loathe to relate, rightly haunts us as we fear the villains of our own time, and as we face the villains within ourselves.

Perhaps we simply must grapple with the fact that our ancestors in faith were fearful and angry unto the point of wishing violence on their enemies. This may be an uncomfortable reality to admit, but is it so far from our own feelings about our enemies? Indeed, plenty of us from all faith backgrounds have literally enacted violence out of defense as well as revenge, most often in a publicly sanctioned manner called war. Some of those situations have been more justified than others. While we must look back on those episodes to judge and learn from our past actions, we must not pretend to stand on higher moral ground now. Human beings will always struggle to live in peace. The book of Esther challenges us to consider our own tendencies toward violence in the face of danger. Rather than being embarrassed that our scriptures tell of a people whose need for self defense apparently turned into a desire for revenge, maybe this story confronts us with the fact that those people are us.

THREE

Song of Songs

Introduction

THE SONG OF SONGS teems with delightful and passionate imagery. Song marvelously combines the seriousness of romantic love with its other key feature—playful flirtation. However, in numerous ways the reader cannot help but wonder what is going on in this book. The characters do not have proper names, and we cannot be sure if they are the same individuals throughout the whole book. The scenes often have a dreamlike quality to them, which on the one hand enhances the overall poetic effect of Song; on the other hand it complicates our ability to make sense of the book. The purpose of Song is maddeningly elusive. It is neither explicitly religious nor do these songs narrate a clear plot or story line. The Hebrew words at times prove nearly impossible to decipher or translate. Even where the language is not such a puzzle, the text presents many literary gaps in which we do not have enough information to know quite what is happening. In those cases, we fill in the blanks, guessing the details according to the context and our own assumptions about the book. If we knew for certain the genre of Song it would help, but that matter also remains perplexingly debatable.

In the end, the Song of Songs allows for so many different interpretations, dates, structures and understandings that in reading Song commentaries, we may learn more about its interpreters than about the book itself. It may be impossible not to read this book out of one's own experiences.[1] It has this in common with the book of Ecclesiastes, which

---

1. This idea was suggested to me by the Reverend Alecia Schroedel.

is similarly open to interpretation; consequently, it has been said that Ecclesiastes is a "Rorschach test for the interpreter."[2] In turn, we might view the Song of Songs as a *Freudian* Rorschach test for the interpreter. Having conceded this, I boldly undertake my own interpretation below.

Interpretations

The Jewish liturgy assigns the Song reading to Passover as a celebration of God's love for the Hebrews in the saving act of the Exodus. The Christian Revised Common Lectionary includes only 2:8–12 of the Song of Songs. It is an optional reading with the Psalter for Proper 9A/Ordinary 14A/ Pentecost +8 and an optional Old Testament reading for Proper 17B/ Ordinary 22B/Pentecost 13. Other than in weddings, the book receives little exposure overall in contemporary Christian liturgy.

It was not always this way. Early Christian writers penned numerous volumes on Song. "During the later patristic period and the rest of the Middle Ages, Christian interpreters wrote more books on the Song of Songs than on any other individual book of the Old Testament."[3] Reading the book at face value would rightly cause us to wonder how such a sexual book could have such popularity in religious circles. The answer lies in reading the book allegorically, an approach practiced by figures including Origen, Gregory of Nyssa, Teresa of Avila, and Martin Luther.

A pervasive tradition about Song interprets it as allegory, which circumvents the problem of sexual poetry about an unmarried couple. Both Jewish and Christian allegorical interpretations flourished well through the Middle Ages and persisted even up until the modern era of biblical criticism. In this view, the book's lyrics about a man and woman's romantic union represent the spiritual unions of God and the believer, YHVH and Israel, or Christ and the church. At the end of the first century CE, Rabbi 'Aqiba famously stated that "Whoever sings the Song of Songs with tremulous voice in a banquet hall and (so) treats it as a ditty has no share in the world to come."[4] This statement illustrates both the early prevalence of an allegorical interpretation, and simultaneously its intrigue on a literal level. *Canticles Rabbah* interpreted the kiss

2. Dr. Julie Duncan, personal communication and class notes.

3. Murphy, *Song*, 21.

4. Cited in ibid., 13 n. 53.

of 1:2 as the communication of the commandments to each Israelite.[5] The Targum correlated the "companions" in 1:7 with "the children of Esau and Ishmael," while the Midrash identified the "shepherd" in verse 8 with Moses and the "flock" with the Israelites.[6]

The third century CE Alexandrian Origen gave us a remarkable and influential example of allegorical interpretation, as demonstrated in his surviving three Commentaries and two Homilies on Song.[7] Origen's work on Song has been called "the first great work of Christian mysticism."[8] Indeed, for every passage Origen interprets, he explains its "mystical meaning" at length. He identifies Song as "a marriage-song, which Solomon wrote in the form of a drama and sang under the figure of the bride, about to wed and burning with heavenly love towards her Bridegroom, who is the Word (λογος *logos*) of God."[9]

Explicating the shepherding imagery of 1:7, Origen first notes that the verse shows the male figure in Song to be both a king and a shepherd.[10] Yet he goes on to detail the mystical meaning of the verse. To do so, he correlates the Bridegroom to the Lord, the companions to the angels, "some souls who are associated with the Bridegroom in a nobler and more splendid sort of love" to the queen (i.e., the female figure in Song), while the sheep—especially those belonging to another shepherd—are "inferior and last of all" in his schema.[11] Furthermore, he associates the "companions" in 1:7 to "another shepherd." He expounds, "So perhaps the flocks of the Bridegroom's companions may be all those nations that are divided up like herds under angel shepherds; but those are to be called the Bridegroom's flock, of whom He Himself says in the Gospel: *My sheep hear my voice.*"[12] This example helps illustrate how Origen and other interpreters in his time understood a text such as Song.

Origen was adamant that Song's meaning was utterly spiritual, and that only the most mature Bible readers were to study this book—even

5. Cited in ibid., 28–29.

6. Cited by Pope, *Song,* 332.

7. He originally wrote the *Ten Commentaries* in Greek. Only fragments of the original Greek remain, along with Latin translations of the Greek.

8. Lawson, in Origen, *Song,* 6.

9. Origen, *Song,* 21.

10. Ibid., 119.

11. Ibid.,120.

12. Ibid., 122.

then, they should take it on as the last of all scriptures. In other circumstances, Origen considered the text potentially dangerous, lest it "seem
to be the Divine Scriptures that are thus urging and egging him [sic] on
to fleshly lust!"[13] Indeed, he includes a prayer in his *Prologue* that the
meaning of Song would lead to "chastity."[14]

Even in the eleventh century CE, Bernard of Clairvaux enlisted the
allegorical method in his 86 sermons on the Song of Songs. For this
mystic whose constant focus was love (or, like we see in older translations, "charity"), "one can find no names more apt to express [the] mutual relationship of the Word and the soul than those of Bridegroom and
bride."[15] To that end, his sermons on Song do much more to reflect on
this relationship than on the text of Song. Where he does reflect on Song,
it is on the basis of this allegory, explaining that the "kiss" in 1:2 is about
the "mystical kiss from the mouth of Christ."[16] When he reflects on 1:7,
his conclusions are similar to Origen's, as we saw above. The "bride," or
the one who follows Christ, seeks the safety of the pastureland of the
shepherd, who is the "Bridegroom," or "Christ." The danger lurking is
the "friends" ("companions," NRSV) who lead Christ's "flock" astray.[17]

During the Reformation period, Luther viewed Song as a political
treatise, in which the male figure was God or the Word, and the female
the "populace of the Solomonic Kingdom."[18] By the eighteenth century,
the allegorical view was waning, with the onset of modern biblical criticism. As early as Erasmus in the sixteenth century, we find a literal interpretation of Song as "the marriage of Solomon to an Egyptian Princess."[19]
Not since Theodore, bishop of Mopsuestia in Ciclila from 392–428 had
a prominent figure proposed such a non-spiritual interpretation. More
than 100 years after his death, Theodore received an official condemna-
tion by the Council of Constantinople for this view, among others.[20]

On the one hand, Song itself gives us no basis for an allegorical
interpretation. The Hebrew Bible does elsewhere refer to the relation-

13. Ibid., 22; also 23, 44.

14. Ibid., 24.

15. Halflants, "Introduction," 2:xxv.

16. Bernard, of Clairvaux, *Works*, 2:16.

17. Ibid., 142–43.

18. Murphy, *Song*, 34.

19. Ibid., 37.

20. Ibid., 22.

ship between God and Israel as a marriage. Isaiah 62:4–5 and Hosea 1–2 are notable examples of this. However, unlike those passages, Song never identifies the spouses as divine and human covenant partners. Also unlike those passages, Song presents a radically mutual—even equitable— picture of gender roles in love. J. Cheryl Exum notes that this aspect of Song makes it poorly suited as an allegory of the relationship between God and human.[21]

Like the book of Esther, Song never mentions God at all. Yet the book very likely had an early tradition as religious literature in order for it to have been included among the scriptures. Though explicitly absent from the text, the allegorical interpretation, along with its attribution to Solomon, may have been a reason for Song's canonization. It provided for a deeply religious view of Song, despite its outwardly secular appearance.[22]

Many historical-critical analyses in recent centuries have ridiculed the allegorical interpretation as naïve. Yet several post-modern interpreters such as David Carr and André LaCocque insightfully point out that while the text gives no indication that a theological interpretation was the original author's intent, there are nonetheless ample reasons to consider it as a viable interpretive response. For instance, early allegorical interpretations of Song were "radically reimaging the divine-human, male-female relationship."[23] Furthermore, the passionate feelings expressed between lovers in Song are at least analogous to the feelings of a faithful person for her or his God. One Bible study participant in a class I taught said just that—Song struck her as a perfect description of how she felt about God as a "new Christian."

One strategy for interpreting Song allegorically is to use inner-biblical interpretation to show how a passage in Song may have deeper meaning than it seems. For instance, Isa 43:2 has some key vocabulary and a similar sentiment as Song's paean to love in 8:6–7. In Isaiah, however, the praise is for YHVH's enduring help and presence. Neither "fire," nor "waters" can harm Israel, nor can "underground rivers" "overflow" God's people. All four of these terms also appear in Song 8:6–7, where they describe love.[24] Using the connection between the two passages as

21. Exum, *Song*, 77.

22. For a more in-depth discussion on this, see Fox, *Song*, 250–52.

23. Carr, "Gender," 245; LaCocque, *Romance*.

24. Pope, citing Robert, *Song*, 674.

a hermeneutical lens gives rise to an interpretation that links human love as described in Song to the divine love described in so many other portions of the Hebrew Bible.

Structure and Outline

One of the many debatable factors about Song is its genre, or literary type. It would seem that the opening explanatory line, or superscription (1:1) identifying this book as "The Song of Songs" would dispel any questions about that.[25] The ample imagery throughout the book surely gives it a lyrical and poetic quality, like the lines of a song. The title "The Song of Songs" does not necessarily identify it as a collection of songs, as the plural form may seem to indicate, but specifically as the best song among all songs. Beyond these things, we know relatively little. Indeed, numerous variables contribute to the mystery about Song's literary type.

For instance, we do not know the proper names of the figures in this book. For that reason among others, we cannot even be sure whether or not the man and woman are the same individuals throughout the book. We do find some consistency in "pet names" for the man and woman (or men and women): The female character(s) often call the male(s) *dodi* דּוֹדִי (doe-DEE), or "my beloved,"[26] and the male character(s) use *ra'yati* רַעְיָתִי (rah-yah-TEE), "my love" as a term of endearment for the female(s).[27] Because we find these words used throughout the book, it could indicate that we have the same two characters consistently using these pet names for one another. On the other hand, *dodi* and *ra'yati* could simply be typical names for the male or female in a form of love song unknown to us now, but standard at the time.

These ambiguities about whether we have one or several couples in the book relate to a central debate about the book's literary form. Song's author(s) has artfully combined repetition, rhyme, alliteration and simile with carefully chosen vocabulary to create a masterpiece of the Hebrew language. Despite the manifold ambiguities about Song's genre, these features firmly place the book into the category of poetry, and I

25. See the interpretation of 1:1 below for explanations of the title "Song of Songs" rather than "Song of Solomon."

26. 1:13, 14, 16; 2:3, 8, 9, 10, 16, 17; 4:16; 5:2, 4, 5, 6 (twice), 8, 9 (four times), 10, 16; 6:1 (twice), 2, 3 (twice); 7:10 ,11, 12, 14; 8:5, 14.

27. 1:9, 15; 2:2, 10, 13; 4:1, 7; 5:2; 6:4. NIV uses "beloved" for the female voice and "lover" for the male.

will categorize it as such throughout this chapter. Of course, poetry in-
herently raises questions for the interpreter, as it intentionally blurs the
line between literal and metaphorical language, between accurate and
exaggerated descriptions. We find a beautiful illustration of such poetry
in 1:15–1:16a. This section provides such features of Hebrew poetry as
repetition, parallelism, and alliteration.

> Ah, you are beautiful *ra'yati*;
> ah you are beautiful; your eyes are doves;
> ah, you are beautiful *dodi*; truly lovely.

הנך יפה רעיתי
הנך יפה עיניך יונים
הנך יפה דודי אף נעים

> *hinnak yaphah ra'yati*
> *hinnak yaphah 'enayik yonim*
> *hinnak yapheh dodi 'aph no'im*

The three "ah, you are beautiful" phrases unite the lovers' words into a
tiny poem ornamented with " *ra'yati*," "doves" and "*dodi*."

To further parse its designation as poetry, Song could consist of
one long love poem, or it could be a collection of love poems. The consistency in vocabulary, such as the terms of endearment used throughout, speaks to the former. In contrast, we could view it as a collection
of love poems enlisting typical nicknames and phrases. Neither view is
conclusive. There is simply not enough information in the text to tell
us definitively whether the book refers to the same couple throughout,
or to various lovers, singing their hearts' truest feelings about each
one's own beloved. Persuasive views exist all along the spectrum, from
Marcia Falk's analysis proposing a collection of separate love songs to
Exum's view that we have here two consistent characters who develop
"distinct personalities" throughout the book.[28] Michael V. Fox makes a
helpful contribution to this debate by arguing that the burden of proof
lies with those who would argue that Song consists of many separate

28. Falk, *Song*, 8. Of the unity of the book, Exum writes, "My intention when I
began writing the present commentary was to interpret the Song both as a unity and
as a collection of disparate poems, in what I hoped would be a creative tension . . . The
further I got into the book, however, the more difficult it became to isolate independent
units, on the one hand, and, on the other, to find genuine difference or distinctiveness
among the smaller units . . . I therefore abandoned, fairly early on, the attempt to read
the parts as discrete poems" (37).

songs rather than being a unified work, a view with which most con-temporary commentators agree.[29] To support his thesis, he carefully analyzes the many repetitions throughout the book, from single words to whole blocks of text.

Fox's work arguing for Song's unity appears in his extensive research on *Ancient Egyptian Love Poetry*, which provides historical context and literary comparison so we can see the ways in which Song is both con-ventional and unique as love poetry in its time.[30] As part of that study Fox points out that the lovers in Song would have been teens; an unmarried couple sneaking away for trysts, which in that culture would only have happened between unmarried youth. Through his comparative work, he shows such a scenario to be rather commonplace in the context of ancient Egyptian romance writings. He therefore finds that setting likely in Song as well. Thus, throughout his commentary on Song, Fox refers to the couple as "girl" and "boy," designations that helpfully contribute to our understanding of these two main characters.

I will refer to *ra'yati* (her) and *dodi* (him) throughout the commen-tary below, assuming that they are the same persons and that the songs are consistently about these two. However, I do so willing to concede that those assumptions could be wrong. By assigning the two these names, I admittedly detract from the text's ambiguity, and portray it as a decidedly unified text with consistent characters throughout. Furthermore, I must reiterate that the text itself neither uses the terms *ra'yati* and *dodi* consis-tently throughout, nor does it present them as proper names. To moder-ate my bending the text in this way, I will refrain from capitalizing these names. I have chosen to use these names for the sake of keeping track of the two characters in a way more personal than "woman" and "man," and a more differentiated way than their English translations, "my love" and "my beloved." The Hebrew designations also continually remind us that the book is a work of Hebrew, not English. These informal lovers' names function somewhat analogously to the rather contrived designa-tion "Qohelet" for the author or persona of Ecclesiastes.[31] Furthermore,

29. Fox, *Song*, 202. Also see Murphy, *Song*, 76–91; and Exum, *Song*, 35.

30. Fox, *Song*.

31. The superscription of Ecclesiastes (1:1) reads, "The words of *qohelet*, son of David, king in Israel." *Qohelet* is simply a transliteration of the Hebrew, which means "one who assembles a group." For lack of any other name to assign the author of Ecclesiastes, many scholars simply refer to "Qohelet." In addition, Michael V. Fox has argued persuasively that the author of Ecclesiastes has developed a "persona" through-

Exum argues that the relative anonymity of the lovers—who she thinks are the same throughout—makes them "archetypal," allowing most anyone to identify with their romantic songs.[32]

In addition to *ra'yati* and *dodi*, we find some other possible characters in Song, including a king and the daughters of Jerusalem. The royal figure (or figures) appears first in the opening line, or superscription, which identifies the book as Solomon's. Tradition claimed this idea forcefully. Perhaps the Solomonic superscription was an important factor in validating the highly controversial book for the sake of canonization. This feature also allowed for the traditional idea of grouping the three books that bear Solomonic attributions in their opening lines: Proverbs, Ecclesiastes, and Song. The view was that Solomon wrote Song as a young man, Proverbs as an adult parent, and Ecclesiastes as an old man.

The superscription's suggestion of Solomonic authorship, which was likely a late addition to the rest of the book, remains persistently planted in the mind of the reader. Additional passages supplement this royal setting, including 1:4, 5, 12; 3:7, 9, 11; 7:5; 8:11, 12. For those reasons, many Song readers have gladly filled in the book's literary gaps with this scenario, determining that it is all about King Solomon and one of his brides.[33] However, that solution to the book's vagueness is probably too good to be true. Solomon is a third party in the book; he is someone the other voices discuss or fantasize about, perhaps even as a point of comparison or idealization (3:6–11; 8:11–12). Furthermore, the recurrent themes of the lovers' pursuit of one another (2:14, 16–17; 3:1–4; 5:2–6; 7:10—8:3), and their talk of secret trysts (1:4a; 2:8–10a, 14; 3:6–11; 4:8), do not at all suggest the life of a king. If a king wanted a woman, he would take her. It was that simple, crass and unromantic, as we see in 2 Sam 11:2–4. King Solomon is never identified as the male lover (*dodi*) in Song. Rather, royal imagery appears throughout as part of the lovers' fantasies, sometimes as a compliment or term of endearment for the man in these love poems (1:4, 12; 3:6–11; 6:12; 7:5). Indeed, such use was not unusual in ancient Near Eastern love poetry.[34]

---

out the book. Fox refers to that persona as "Qohelet," although the word in the superscription is a title, not a proper name. See Fox, *Qohelet*; and Fox, *A Time.*

32. Exum, *Song*, 8.

33. Nelson, *Song.*

34. Fox, *Song*, 123–24.

We also hear collective voices in Song, namely the "daughters of Jerusalem/Zion" (1:5; 2:7; 3:5, 10, 11; 5:8, 16; 8:4). They frequently—if not always—serve as the audience for the female voice(s) in Song, in particular for the woman/women's four refrains: 2:7; 3:5; 5:8; 8:4 (see outline). While these women clearly act as interlocutors for the woman or women singing the love songs, we do not know exactly who they are, any more than we know exactly who the other characters are. In the outline and commentary below, I often refer to the "daughters" as *ra'yati's* "girlfriends," since they appear to fulfill that role in conversation. They do not seem to have any more formal role than to banter with *ra'yati* about *dodi*; to prod and listen to her about him.

Throughout Song, the Hebrew grammatical forms help us to understand who is speaking and who is being spoken to throughout. We can ascertain whether the speaker is singular or plural, and in some cases whether the voice is female or male. If the speaker uses pronouns, those indicate both gender and number. The book effectively paints a heterosexual scenario throughout; from there, we can presume that when one voice speaks about a male character or male characteristics, a woman is speaking, and vice versa. In other cases, pronouns and other grammatical forms indicate when the audience is a group.

For instance, in 1:13b the reference to "my breasts" allows us to presume a female speaker addressing "my beloved" in 1:13a. Based on context and grammar, we can tell that some group is speaking in 5:9. The final verb has a plural ending, and the preceding verse refers to the daughters of Jerusalem. Yet despite the helpfulness of grammar, in many cases the speaker(s) and audience remain elusive. For example, 1:8 uses the second person feminine verb form in the first line, indicating that it addresses an individual woman. However, it does not clearly indicate who is speaking. We are left to surmise from the preceding section (1:2–7) that 1:8 contains a response from the daughters of Jerusalem, whom the woman addressed in 1:5. They could be referring to the woman's query about her beloved, who "grazes" in 1:7, suggesting that she follow the man's "flock" in 1:8. However, we could also make an argument that 1:8 relates to the following verses, in which the man compliments the woman, making the man the respondent in 1:8.

Despite the ambiguities in speakers and audiences, it could be possible to categorize Song as a sort of poetic drama. This could assume a single male and single female character throughout, or could even be a collection of various acts between different couples. One feature that lends itself to this is the absence of a narrator in Song. The characters simply address each other with poetic words of romance and longing. Perhaps if we saw their words acted out on a stage, they would lose some of their dream-like nature, and make more sense. Of course, huge differences exist between Song and other romantic plays, from the absence of a clear plot line in the biblical book to its lack of well-defined—or even named—characters.

Other interpreters have proposed that Song should be understood as a collection of wedding songs. Yet the wedding scene in Song 3:6–11 contains the book's only reference to marriage. To apply that scenario to the book as a whole would be purely speculative. The frustrating reality is that we cannot know precisely how that passage relates to the rest of Song; perhaps it is a fantasy of the couple or other characters in the book (see below). Neither the word "wife" (literally "woman," אִשָּׁה, *'ishshah*, with a possessive suffix) nor "husband" (literally "man," אִישׁ *'ish*, with a possessive suffix,) appear anywhere in Song. In fact, we find the word "woman" infrequently (1:8; 5:9; 6:1 "most beautiful of women," נָשִׁים *nashim*). The lyricist(s) of Song rarely uses the word "man" (אִישׁ *'ish*); it is only in 3:7 and 8:7, which refer not to *dodi*, but to Solomon's attendants and a hypothetical man, respectively. In any case, a close and faithful reading of the text does not indicate that the book contains wedding songs—much less a series of them—or even that it has to do with marriage.

Some commentators have understood the book as a set of marriage songs, in which the lovers are a bride and groom. We should read those as an interpretive framework; the text itself does not articulate that setting. Indeed, based on verses in which the couple (or couples) pursues and longs for one another (2:14, 16–17; 3:1–4; 5:2–6; 7:10—8:3), it seems quite likely they are not married. Michael V. Fox asserts, "Within Canticles sexual intercourse does not consummate marriage. Rather, marriage will consummate sex: the lovers are already enjoying sexual pleasures, but they want public acceptance of their union in marriage as well."[35] Othmar Keel offers a similar perspective. "But fertility was apparently not the purpose in the relationships described in the Egyptian love songs and in Song—relationships that had no official sanction. The limited possibilities of birth control may have favored a substitution of

---

35. Fox, *Song*, 313–14.

oral eroticism and petting for genital eroticism—a tendency that would have grown stronger the more strictly the patriarchate punished pregnancy outside marriage and emphasized the value of virginity (cf. Deut. 22:13–22)."[36] This aspect of the text has posed a problem for those within Christian tradition who have an ethical problem with sexual content applied to an unmarried couple—and in the Bible, no less! Since such a book could have undermined church teaching against sex outside of marriage, it was (and remains, for some) in the interest of certain church authorities to make clear the book was about an officially wed couple.[37]

J. Cheryl Exum strikes a helpful balance within this debate, categorizing Song as "lyric poetry." As such, she argues that we should not be too quick to try and discern narrative development or structure in it. It wanders about, using sketchy dialogue and rather unpredictable repetitions, having neither clear starting-point nor closure. Indeed, she suggests that "rather than trying to tame the poem, why not take pleasure in its otherness, its imaginative flights of fancy, and its highly charged symbolism?"[38] Such an approach departs from the usual ways that we read the Bible. Nevertheless, it remains true to the plain sense of the text better than most other interpretations.

Another helpful way to think about the genre of Song is by looking at its context within the canon. The Hebrew canon, the Tanakh, groups Song with the books of Ruth, Ecclesiastes, Lamentations and Esther in the Five Scrolls, or Megillot; it falls after Ruth and before Ecclesiastes. Since Song is so difficult to categorize, we could use that environment to help determine its literary category. Thus a short story that ends with a significant, royalty-producing marriage (see the chapter on Ruth) precedes Song. That context might tempt us to interpret Song as a narrative about a king's wedding.

In contrast, Ecclesiastes follows Song, and contains tradition-challenging, perplexing, journal-like poetic reflections on life by a sage most scholars refer to by his title, Qohelet. That particular context could make us more likely to understand Song as a collection of love poems about a couple or couples who are trying to "suck the marrow out of life"[39] through a relationship that eludes comprehensible description.

36. Keel, *Song*, 246.

37. Nelson's *Song* is an example of this; he applies it to contemporary married couples.

38. Exum, *Song*, 46. She discusses Song as lyric poetry on 11–12, 42–46, *et passim*.

39. Thoreau, *Walden*, 101.

Indeed, Renita Weems suggests, "as meditations of a woman's heart, Song of Songs might have been viewed as the feminine counterpart to a book like, say, Ecclesiastes."[40] Given the prominence of the female voice in Song and the similar content noted above, that point has validity. Nonetheless, Song certainly expresses more hopeful and sweet sentiments than does Qohelet.

While the standard list of Wisdom books includes only Job, Proverbs and Ecclesiastes, occasionally an interpreter will include Song in that classification. Wisdom literature generally uses a particular vocabulary, including "wise/wisdom," "righteous/righteousness," "fool," "know," "understand," and "teach," signifying the pedagogical and didactic stance central to wisdom literature. None of the Wisdom books contain references to the history of Israel. While Song does not refer to Israel's history, it also does not contain any of the usual teaching vocabulary. It does, however, share its Solomonic superscription with the other Wisdom books. Those who have understood it as one of the Wisdom books have relied on this, and on its interpretation as a way to teach about love—either romantic love, or the love between a human and God, or a human and Lady Wisdom.[41]

A final way to understand Song in terms of genre has to do with a literary form referred to by the Arabic word for "description," or *wasf*. A *wasf* describes the body part by part, using simile and/or metaphor. We find this literary form in writings as early as the third millennium. It was used in Egyptian and other ancient Near Eastern writings. The older Egyptian examples were paeans to the deity; they later appeared as love songs rather than cultic literature.[42] This categorization may help us to understand why one reader found these poems not only "nice, and romantic," but also "anachronistic"—so clearly from another time that it makes little sense now.[43]

Song contains at least four *wasf*s, identified as such in the outline below. The poems in 4:1–7; 5:10–16a; 6:4–10; and 7:1–9 fall into this ancient genre. In them, a man compares his lover's "eyes" to "doves" (4:1), and her "cheeks" to "pomegranate halves" (6:7). In turn, a woman compares her beloved's "lips" to "lilies" (5:13) and his "legs" to "alabaster

40. Weems, "Song," 5:364.

41. Murphy provides a helpful discussion on Song as wisdom literature (*Tree*, 106–7).

42. For a helpful discussion on this literary form and its roots in various ancient Near Eastern literature, see Keel, *Song*, 20–29.

43. Frederick Focke Mischler.

columns" on bases of "gold" (5:15). In these cases, the *wasf*s make sense even in English. Similarly, the prominent food references (pomegranate: 4:3, 13; 6:7, 11; 7:12; 8:2; apple: 2:3, 5; 7:8; 8:5; fruit: 2:3; 4:13, 16; 7:13; 8:11, 12; fig: 2:13; all NRSV) led one reader to respond "I could just eat her up," which may well be the intended effect.[44]

While these similes sound fairly complimentary, others may come off as rather strange to our contemporary sensibilities. For instance, he likens her "teeth" to "ewes" in 4:2//6:6, and her "breasts" to "fawns" in 7:3. The illustrations move to downright bizarre when he croons "your neck is like the tower of David / built in courses; / on it hang a thousand bucklers, / all of them shields of warriors" (4:4, NRSV) and "your nose is like a tower of Lebanon, / overlooking Damascus" (7:4b). One artist has created a tongue-in-cheek rendering of this *wasf* in cartoon form, titled "The Song of Solomon Illustrated (for our literalist friends)." The drawing illustrates the absurdity of taking the passage literally,[45] The drawing also provides a message about overly literal readings of the Bible as a whole.

Many readers find it difficult to relate to the *wasf* imagery. The content of this love poetry may seem so foreign that it actually alienates contemporary readers from the ancient text. One helpful way to overcome this chasm is to consider ways we currently talk about women and men's bodies that are equally odd. I have found Bible study groups remarkably successful at identifying examples of this. One person mentioned that in some fairly contemporary U.S. cultures, one would compliment an exceptionally buxom woman by saying "she's built like a brick outhouse" (or a slight variation of that using a more coarse term than "*out*house"). Another Bible study participant mentioned that someone with beautifully toned stomach muscles is said to have "six-pack abs."[46] Venturing further into the realm of slang, we find the paradoxical affirmations "You 'da s---" (with the last word being a fecal reference), and in appreciation of a woman's curvaceous derrière, "junk in the trunk." These compliments from our own time and place surely rival the peculiarity of

44. Thanks for this goes to my brother-in-law, William Joseph Mischler. Athalya Brenner also has an article on this subject: "The Food of Love," 101–12.

45. Cited 8 November 2010. Online: www.acts17–11.com/snip_song.html/ or a search on this title.

46. This was suggested to me by Burt Jones at David's UCC in Kettering, Ohio.

those in Song, and therefore may help us to better understand its ancient romance poetry as less alien to our own culture.

Another important consideration for understanding the *wasf* is the original cultural context of the poetry. We can attribute part of our disconnect from this genre to our unfamiliarity with the imagery. A twenty-first century North American person has little contact with goats (4:1//6:5), shields (4:4), pomegranates (4:3//6:7), or gazelles (4:5//7:4). Thus, the more we know about these items of comparison, the better we can relate to these apparently odd love lyrics. For instance, we discover the sheer value—if not the appearance—of a woman's hair, like goats on a hillside (4:1//6:5). Goat's hair was woven into such treasures as tabernacle vestments (Exod 25:4; 35:26). Whether or not such cultural information is available about the imagery, another option is to think about the *wasf*s as secrets between lovers, as inside jokes or compliments that could only be understood within the intimate bounds of a romantic relationship.

Biblical scholars have gone to great lengths in both research and speculation to understand the meaning of the *wasf*s, particularly the imagery that makes little sense to us today. One proposal suggests that instead of trying to untangle these poems, we should read each one as "a celebration of the joys of life and love and at the same time an invitation to share that joy."[47] That comment points to the observation that "if we look closely enough . . . no 'description' is actually obtained: by the end of the poem we still have no idea what the loved person looks like, in the sense that no *complete* image is communicated."[48] Yet the descriptions have not only to do with joy, and surely we have *some* idea of physical appearance from the *wasf*s, though it may be sketchy and even obscure. In addressing each separate *wasf* below, I will propose various ways for understanding the strange imagery, both in its own cultural context, and as compared to our own.

These numerous possible Song genres help illustrate the difficulty of outlining the book. Commentators over the years have probably produced as many different outlines for Song as they have devised ways to describe its literary type.[49] It might seem that the repetitions throughout

47. Soulen, "The *wasf*s," 224.

48. Brenner, "'Come Back," 235.

49. Exum has compiled a helpful table of the different ways various commentators divide the book (*Song*, 39).

the book would serve as cues to understanding its structure. For instance, a refrain, or repeated phrase directed to the daughters of Jerusalem appears in 2:7; 3:5; 5:8; and 8:4. While these are not all exact repetitions, they are strikingly similar. These refrains often effectively pause the dialogue, rather than continuing its flow. We find that repetitions not uncommonly serve to structure other Hebrew poetry, particularly the beginning and end of sections, as in inclusios.[50] All of these reasons make the daughters' refrain a plausible source of structure for an otherwise rather unstructured book. In the end, however, these repetitions do not provide significant structuring for the book, though they certainly give it some unity. I have chosen to highlight the refrains in my outline, but also to integrate them into the larger sections. Another repetition in the book is the "*refrain to dodi*" in 2:16; 6:3; 7:10. I do not assign this a structural function either, though it is still worth noting.

In many cases, it seems that we Bible scholars are simply casting about for a way to give structure—and in turn, hopefully meaning—to an otherwise perplexing book, simply because that is what we do with books. Hence many of these efforts, perhaps including my own, appear rather contrived, and outlines of the book vary significantly from one commentator to another. Nonetheless, true to the practices of my field, I offer an outline below. I have opted to view the book as two fairly large sections (1:2—3:11; 4:1—8:7), with the headings of those sections loosely describing the content therein. Very short sections open and close the book (1:1; 8:8–12; 8:13–14). In order to track the individual speakers throughout the book, I have divided these large sections into many small sections, each of which notes the shift in dialogue. What seems most crucial in the outline below is the simple identification of speakers. Additionally, these small blocks of text, separated according to the speaker, find much more agreement among interpreters than do the larger divisions.

Whether lyric poem, love songs, or ancient romance poetry, we have in Song a dialogue of sorts between a male voice (or voices) and a female voice (or voices). What development takes place over the course of their interchanges—if any—is obscure. The one thing a reader can reliably do to understand Song is to track the speeches of the characters, such as they are. As mentioned above, I have decided to identify the

---

50. Examples of inclusios include Ps 118:1 and 29; 150:1a and 6b; Eccl 1:2 and 12:8; Song 2:8–9 and 17.

characters as *ra'yati* ("her") and *dodi* ("him") for the Hebrew pet names they repeatedly (though not exclusively) use for one another. When I use those names in the below outline, it does not necessarily indicate that they are so named in a particular passage, but rather that the grammar indicates a woman's or man's speech. In a few cases, the text is unclear about the speaker, so I have hypothesized about which of the characters is speaking. I will detail those ambiguities in the commentary portion of this chapter.

Outline

1) 1:1 Superscription

2) 1:2—3:11 We Meet *ra'yati* and *dodi*: Songs of Flirtation and Fantasy

    a) 1:2–8 *ra'yati* and her girlfriends sing about *dodi*

        i) 1:2–4 *ra'yati* sings to and about *dodi*

            (1) 1:2a *ra'yati* sings about *dodi* to her girlfriends

            (2) 1:2b–4a *ra'yati* sings (as though?) to *dodi*

            (3) 1:4b *ra'yati* and her friends sing about *dodi*

        ii) 1:5–6 *ra'yati* defends herself to the daughters of Jerusalem (or to her brothers)

        iii) 1:7 *ra'yati* sings to *dodi*

        iv) 1:8: *dodi* responds (this could be the daughters)

    b) 1:9–11 *dodi* sings *ra'yati's* praises and promises her gifts

    c) 1:12–14 *ra'yati* sings about their attractive smells

    d) 1:15—2:3 *ra'yati* and *dodi* sing compliments to one another

        i) 1:15 *dodi* sings

        ii) 1:16a *ra'yati* responds

        iii) 1:16b–17 *ra'yati* compliments (or fantasizes about) the setting of their love affair

        iv) 2:1 *ra'yati* sings of herself, alluring him

        v) 2:2 *dodi* responds

        vi) 2:3 *ra'yati* responds

    e) 2:4–6 *ra'yati* reminisces and fantasizes about *dodi*

    f) *2:7 Refrain to daughters of Jerusalem*

    g) 2:8—3:5 *ra'yati* sings about *dodi*

        i)   2:8–17 *ra'yati* fantasizes about and longs for *dodi*'s love song to her

           (1) 2:8–10a *ra'yati* sees *dodi* approaching

           (2) 2:10b-15 *dodi*'s love song, quoted by *ra'yati*; he longs for her

           (3) 2:10b–13b he sings, "Come away with me in spring-time" (section marked by inclusio)

           (4) 2:14 he sings of finding her

           (5) 2:15 something foils their love (uncertain which of them is speaking)

           (6) 2:16–17 *ra'yati* claims him; longs for him [2:16 <u>refrain to *dodi*</u>]

        ii)   3:1–4 *ra'yati* seeking the love of her life

        iii) *<u>3:5 Refrain to daughters of Jerusalem</u>*

    h) 3:6–11 *ra'yati*'s dream wedding fantasy told to the daughters of Jerusalem

3) 4:1–8:7 *dodi* and *ra'yati*: Songs of Longing for One Another

    a) 4:1—5:1 *dodi* sings to *ra'yati*: how precious you are

        i)   4:1–7 *dodi* sings a *wasf* to *ra'yati*: you are as precious as the land of milk and honey

        ii)   4:8—5:1a *dodi* sings to *ra'yati*: come away with me, for you are the destination

           (1) 4:8 The invitation

           (2) 4:9–15 *dodi*: you are as a treasure

           (3) 4:9–11 how precious you are: emotions, tastes, smells

              (a) 4:12–15 you are as precious as a garden

              (b) 4:16 *ra'yati* responds: calls on creation, that her garden would be his garden

              (c) 5:1a *dodi* accepts her invitation and basks in her garden

           (4) 5:1b *ra'yati* invites her girlfriends to share the joy

    b) 5:2–8 *ra'yati* sings about *dodi*—he is out of reach

        i)   5:2a *ra'yati* sings of hearing *dodi* at the door

        ii)   5:2b *dodi* asks to be invited in

        iii) 5:3–6 *ra'yati* can't get to him soon enough (or can she?—vv. 4–5)

        iv) 5:7 *ra'yati* laments about the sentinels

   v) <u>5:8 *ra'yati* calls on her girlfriends for help (variation on the refrain)</u>

  c) 5:9—8:7 *ra'yati* and *dodi* long for each other; her girlfriends join in

   i) 5:9—6:3 *ra'yati* sings to her girlfriends about *dodi*

    (1) 5:9 her girlfriends respond (to v. 8), encouraging her to sing about *dodi*

    (2) 5:10–16a *ra'yati* responds, singing a *wasf* for *dodi*

    (3) 5:16b—6:3 *ra'yati* continues to sing about longing for *dodi*

     (a) 5:16b *ra'yati* claims *dodi*

     (b) 6:1 her girlfriends offer to help find *dodi*

     (c) 6:2 *ra'yati* responds, she knows where he is after all: in his garden

     (d) 6:3 *ra'yati* summarizes: <u>refrain to *dodi*</u>

   ii) 6:4–10 *dodi* sings a *wasf* for *ra'yati* (note repeated phrases from ch. 4 *wasfs*)

   iii) 6:11–12 *ra'yati* sings of *dodi*

   iv) 6:13—7:9 *dodi*'s songs about *ra'yati*

    (1) 6:13a song about *ra'yati*

    (2) 6:13b *dodi* responds, defending *ra'yati*

    (3) 7:1–9 *dodi* sings another *wasf* for *ra'yati*

   v) 7:10—8:4 *ra'yati* invites and longs for *dodi*

    (1) 7:10–13 *ra'yati* invites him [<u>7:10 refrain to *dodi*</u>]

    (2) 8:1–3 *ra'yati* wishes for him

    (3) <u>**8:4 *ra'yati*'s refrain to the daughters of Jerusalem**</u>

   vi) 8:5–7 song about *dodi*

    (1) 8:5a her girlfriends are watching them

    (2) 8:5b–7 *ra'yati* asks for *dodi*'s pledge of love; sings to the power of love

4) 8:8–12 *ra'yati* Sings of Her Brothers

  a) 8:8–9 *ra'yati* quotes her brothers taunting her

  b) 8:10–12 *ra'yati* comes back at them

5) 8:13–14 Parting Songs of Longing

  a) 8:13 *dodi*

  b) 8:14 *ra'yati*

Language

While Song seems unclear and difficult to understand in English translations, the Hebrew original is a greater puzzle yet. In some verses, even
the greatest Hebrew linguists remain stumped. The book contains the
highest number of *hapax legomena*—Hebrew words used only once in
the whole Hebrew Bible—of any other book from Genesis to Malachi.[51]
In those cases, we have little if any basis for knowing how to correctly
translate a word, since we cannot find it in any other context. Other
ancient Near Eastern languages may provide some help in our understanding, but the uncertainty remains. A good way to get a sense of this
linguistic dilemma is by looking at an English translation that includes
translator's footnotes. Those highlight the number of places in which
the team of translation experts was stumped. For instance, the NRSV
includes translators' notes that read "Meaning of Heb[rew] uncertain."
My particular copy of the NRSV has that note on all but two pages of
Song. In contrast, contemporized translations and paraphrases attempt
to make the meaning as clear as possible. They have done so by largely
eliminating difficulties and ambiguities, producing what can be a decep-
tively clear and smooth reading.[52]

In many cases, Song contains explicitly sexual language. In other
places, the imagery remains ambiguous. Since the wider context does
include rather erotic references, an interpreter faces the dilemma of determining whether seemingly innocuous verses in fact consist of sexual
innuendo. In many cases, we may wish that we could see the facial expressions or gestures of the singer, or hear her inflections in order to
know her intent.

Some passages rightfully call forth a stereotypical, pre-adolescent,
Beavis and Butthead laughing fit, as in "*heh-heh*, he said *gazelles*!" Since
dodi directly compares "gazelles" to breasts, they have every reason to

---

51. Greenspahn's analysis concluded that Song has the "highest percentage of its
total vocabulary comprised of 'absolute *hapax legomena*'" (In Murphy, *Song*, 75.)

52. Petersen's *The Message* is a good example of this. He makes some commend-
able efforts at contemporizing Song's most perplexing poetic imagery. However, readers
should be aware of the great extent to which this version relies on hypothesizing about
the meanings of Hebrew words and ancient metaphors. The *Contemporary English
Version*, which is more a translation than paraphrase, also clarifies ambiguous passages,
but it helpfully provides translator's footnotes, including the frequent caveat, "One possible meaning for the difficult Hebrew text."

giggle.[53] Other words could conceivably produce a similar response, but in those cases a sexualized interpretation is less clear ("mountain of myrrh" and "hill of frankincense" in 4:6 are good examples; see discussion below). Since *Beavis and Butthead* are notorious for sexualizing anything, they would easily prove the above point about Song being a Freudian Rorschach test for the interpreter. Another illustration of how apparently innocent language can be sexualized is from the "Nudge Nudge" sketch in *Monty Python's Flying Circus*.[54] Two men sit in a bar, and one asks the other, "is your wife a *goer*? Eh? Know what I mean, know what I mean? Nudge, nudge, wink, wink, say no more, say no more; a nudge as good as a wink to a blind bat . . . ," and on *ad infinitum*. Even with the nudges, winks, and inflections, the other man remains a bit perplexed until he is able to clarify: "are you *insinuating* something?" The other stalls, but finally replies, "Well, yes!" We may rightly find ourselves in the position of wondering whether the singers of Song would be nudging, winking, or explicitly gesturing. Since we cannot know, we should question our own readings, whether we are inclined to read like Beavis and Butthead, Monty Python, or Origen.

Amid this conundrum of words however, we find some of the most beautiful poetry in all of the Hebrew Bible. Song consists of repeating themes and vocabulary that knit it together into a more or less unified whole.[55] It is like a magnificently created interior design that you marvel at, thinking simultaneously "I never would have thought to put those patterns and colors and styles together" while in awe of how well it works. In addition to the motifs and key words throughout, Song contains other elements of good poetry, including alliteration, rhyme, simile, metaphor, and inclusio.

Date

Song is notoriously difficult to date. Debates about this have raged for many years, and continue today. Linguistic arguments exist suggesting that it is a late—and early—text. A number of authors point out the "late," even "mishnaic" features in its language, while others show how

53. *Beavis and Butthead*, directed by Mike Judge (MTV, 1993–1997).

54. Episode 3, Season 1.

55. Murphy asserts, "with the exception of Ecclesiastes, no other book of the Bible so amply displays verbal and thematic repetitions" (*Song*, 76).

these same features occur within older biblical texts as well. [56] Still others see linguistic features distinctive to much older texts.[57] Yet late linguistic features could have been added to an older text by an editor. We know that Song must be at least as old as the first century CE, since fragments of it were found among the Dead Sea Scrolls cache. The only remotely historical reference in the book is its Solomonic superscription (1:1). Yet, as we will see below, that is more likely an added literary tool than a sign of date or authorship. Ecclesiastes and Proverbs contain similar Solomonic superscriptions; nonetheless most commentators assign them late dates. The current critical consensus is to place Song in the Persian (ca. 538–333 BCE) or Hellenistic (333–63 BCE) periods of the postexilic era. Admittedly, this is a huge span of time.

Some commentators argue that the social setting of Song marks it as an early text.[58] Richard S. Hess bases this on the scene in 3:1–5, in which the woman is alone on the street looking for her lover. He asserts that could not have happened in later biblical times due to laws restricting women's movement.[59] Carol Meyers views the largely egalitarian relationship between the lovers in Song as an indication of premonarchic times, in which time she argues that gender roles were rather unrestricted, compared to the later monarchic period.[60] However when it comes to Song, what some view as social setting others may justifiably interpret as lovers' fantasies or poetic devices.

It may be that J. Cheryl Exum has the voice of reason on this matter in her conclusion to a discussion of dating Song. "Would knowing when it was written help us understand the poem? Probably not very much . . . Love poetry, like love, knows no season."[61] While my own tendency, due to the language of Song, is to assign it a late date, I am ultimately inclined to call myself an agnostic on that particular topic. This is due to the ambiguities that plague that effort, and the relative fruitlessness of settling on one particular date rather than another.

56. For instance see Fox, *Song*, 188–89; Murphy, *Song*, 74 notes that the linguistic data suggest a late date, but are not necessarily conclusive of that.

57. See Murphy's summary of Song as compared to Ugaritic texts (*Song*, 4).

58. For instance Hess, *Song*, 18–19, who cites Keel's work. Also see Meyers, *Discovering Eve*, 178–80.

59. Hess, *Song*, 18.

60. Meyers, *Discovering Eve*, 180.

61. Exum, *Song*, 67.

Superscription (1:1)

This opening line serves as an introduction—perhaps as a title page—to the book. Superscriptions are a standard ingredient found particularly in the poetic and prophetic literature of the Hebrew Bible books, and may indicate a book's purpose, literary type, author, dedication, setting, time period, or in the case of the Psalms, liturgical instructions. For example, see Eccl 1:1; Prov 1:1; Jer 1:1, Hos 1:1; and numerous Psalms (e.g., the opening phrases of Psalms 3–9; 11–32, found prior to verse 1; English translations traditionally do not assign a verse number to the Psalms' superscriptions).

The repetitive title "The Song of Songs" (שִׁיר הַשִּׁירִים *shir hashirim*) expresses the superlative form, and thus could be translated "the greatest song." This is comparable to "Lord of lords" from Deut 10:17; Ps 136:3, familiar also from New Testament citations (1 Tim 6:15; Rev 17:14; 19:16) and made famous in Handel's *Messiah*. The Latin Vulgate rendered the title "Canticum Canticorum," and some, mostly older reference works thus called the book "Canticles." The title "The Song of Solomon," based on the end of the superscription (literally translated, "the song of songs, *which is of/to/for Solomon*"), has been another commonly used designation. This term may erroneously promote the idea that King Solomon was its author. That attribution is historically misleading. The Hebrew preposition related to Solomon has a range of meaning, which could indicate anything from a dedication of sorts to an authorial attribution. Ascribing a book to a famous figure was commonplace in ancient literature. Solomon may have seemed a fitting pseudonym for this book because of his affiliation with other poetic literature (Eccl 1:1; Prov 1:1), and his long list of wives (1 Kgs 11:1–3), which may have made him seem an appropriate figure to envision in this courtship, love, and sexuality. Furthermore, his name may have helped legitimate Song for canonization. Yet the language of the superscription itself does not clearly express Solomon's relationship to the book, as my literal translation above shows.

We Meet *Ra'yati* and *Dodi*: Songs of Flirtation and Fantasy (1:2—3:11)

In 1:2–7 we hear *ra'yati*'s voice almost exclusively, with a brief response— perhaps from *dodi*—in 1:8. This section effectively introduces us to our female character and the object of her love, as she sees him. It seems that her audience here largely consists of her girlfriends, though at times she may be singing directly to *dodi* (1:2b-4a). Here she swoons over him (1:2–3), and either recounts or fantasizes about a tryst with him (1:4a).

In 1:2, *ra'yati* compares *dodi*'s love to wine, and the wine loses. The theme of wine runs throughout Song, often over against love (1:2, 4; 4:10; 5:1; 7:2, 9 [Heb 7:10]; 8:2). In fact, the same comparison appears as early as 1:4, in which *ra'yati*'s girlfriends join her in this compliment. Notably, ancient Egyptian love songs also tend to mention a beverage, though in those texts beer is a frequent choice.[62] Sarah McLachlan provides a contemporary analogy to this type of romance lyric in her song "Ice Cream," in which she sings, "your love is better than ice cream . . . your love is better than chocolate."[63] These tasty, alluring foods effectively illustrate these women's (*ra'yati*'s and Sarah's) desire for their love interests.

In addition to the wine in 1:2b and 4b, this section teems with sensual imagery. In 1:2a it is touch, with kisses; in 1:3a it is smell, with anointing oil, and perfume. The reference to "king" in 1:4 may conjure visual imagery such as clothing, furniture and other finery. The second half of verse four strangely shifts to the first person plural: "*we* will exult . . . *we* will extol" (NRSV). Presumably, the group speaking includes *ra'yati* and her girlfriends; these may be the same as the "young women" (NRSV has "maidens") in 1:3b. Perhaps they are affirming *ra'yati*'s praise for *dodi* with their comparison of his love to wine in 1:4b, echoing her opening remark in 1:2. The final phrase of 1:4 shifts voice again, apparently here *ra'yati* in turn confirms her girlfriends' remarks about *dodi*.

In 1:5–6, *ra'yati* proclaims—and apparently defends—her beauty and her self-determination. These verses give us much of what little information we have with which to characterize *ra'yati*. Furthermore, 1:5 stands as a blatant example of the way biblical translation has been affected by the biases of culture, and the social location of translators.

Until the NRSV appeared in 1989, English translations had almost exclusively rendered the conjunction in 1:5a "I am black *but* beautiful." This occurred despite the fact that the Hebrew prefix -וְ, or *v-*, can mean either "and" *or* "but." The prevailing translation "but" relies on the Vulgate, and apparently ignores the textual record of the Septuagint, which has "and" (καί *kai*). That conjunction almost always suggests

---

62. Fox, *Song*, 80. Dr. Betsy Bryan, personal communication on November 3, 2006.

63. Sarah McLachlan, "Ice Cream."

connectivity ("and"), not contradiction ("but"). The following phrases in 1:5b–6 do not necessarily indicate whether this should be the conjunctive or disjunctive particle, though 1:6a may suggest that dark skin would have been seen as a distracting—rather than alluring—feature. If that is so, however, may that not have been all the more reason for *ra'yati* to declare she was "black *and* beautiful"? At issue is whether her tone in 1:5a is defensive (in which case "but" would be appropriate) or confident (indicating "and").[64]

In all likelihood, the racial assumptions of biblical translators over the centuries dictated their choice to use "but" rather than "and." Once academia and biblical studies became open to persons from social locations other than European, American, male, and Protestant, voices of African and African American women and men showed how this bias had dominated translations to the detriment of people of color and all English readers. Readers and commentators who can personally relate to having dark skin and being female have said in essence, "Why would you assume that 'beautiful' contradicts 'black' rather than accentuates it?" The implicit answer to that question points to the stereotypes and biases of white translators.

On the other hand, it would also be faulty to suppose that a contemporary race critique can resolve our misconceptions of this Hebrew phrase. We can make few assumptions about the ancient Near Eastern world based on modern constructions of race. In the ancient world, ethnicity and nationality had much more to do with categorizing individuals than did skin color. For instance, in 1:5b *ra'yati* compares her complexion to the royal tents, likely a complimentary association. Furthermore, 1:6 indicates that *ra'yati*'s skin color did not have to do with race or clan, but rather with spending a great deal of time outdoors, perhaps working. That she points out these things herself may seem to indicate a defensive tone, yet elsewhere in Song the daughters and *dodi* (1:8a, 10, 15; 2:14; 4:1–7; 6:4–7, 10; 7:1–7) compliment her looks. In addition, Exum plays on the ambiguity of the conjunction, and suggests that readers are to consider both "and" and "but" here, noting furthermore that such multivalence belongs particularly well in poetic literature. She also notes

64. Weems offers her rationale for translating "black *and* beautiful," in *What Matters,* 32–34; and in "Song," 5:382–83.

that we miss a key feature in 1:6a because we do not know precisely what kind of looks *ra'yati's* girlfriends are directing to her.[65]

In 1:6b the "wine" motif resumes, something we had first seen in 1:2 and 4. Here, rather than "wine" *ra'yati* sings of "vineyards." Apparently, her work in the vineyards somehow relates to her brothers' being "angry" with her. We cannot be exactly sure of her meaning when she says she has not "kept" her "own vineyard." It may be that we have here our first encounter with Song's notorious use of double entendre. The earlier comparison of "wine" to "love" (or "caresses," as Exum translates 1:2 and 4), combined with its uses in Song 6:11//7:12 [Heb 7:13]; and 8:12 could imply that "vineyard" refers to *ra'yati's* sexuality rather than grape arbors. Pope argues that not keeping her vineyards indicates her "promiscuity."[66] This possible interpretation remains disputable. Another feasible understanding would read 1:6b with 1:5–6a in a tone of confidence. In that case, her statement in 1:6b could be asserting, in effect, "You've told me what to do, and I'll do what I want!" Of course, the problem is in not knowing what "what to do" means here. While it could refer to guarding her own sexuality, it also could mean more broadly minding the rules of the patriarchal household, or "that she has not been able to tend to her own needs as a woman."[67] In the end, we do not know precisely what 1:6b means, other than that there is some rift between *ra'yati* and her brothers.

As *ra'yati* sings to *dodi* in 1:7, Song's setting apparently turns pastoral. It seems that *dodi* has sheep to tend. Yet NRSV and NIV insert the word "flocks" here because the Hebrew provides no object for "graze." This omission creates the enticing possibility that the object of *dodi's* verbs is *ra'yati*, rather than any sheep. As we will see, the language for "pasturing" (רעה *r'h*) elsewhere may have a euphemistic meaning as well (2:16; 6:2–3).[68]

A motif of the lovers seeking one another appears in 1:7 for the first of many times (2:17; 3:1–4; 4:8; 7:10–12; 8:13). *ra'yati* coyly proclaims that she does not want to be hidden from *dodi* in any way "as one veiled," or "covered." Whether the reference to being veiled had any further

---

65. Exum, *Song*, 103–5.

66. Pope, *Song*, 326.

67. See Exum, *Song*, 106, who helpfully summarizes the various views on this, including Fox's, which is articulated in the final suggestion (Fox, *Song*, 102).

68. With Exum, *Song*, 107.

connotations to Song's early hearers, we cannot know for certain. Most likely *ra'yati*'s point is about being unknown to *dodi*, not about disguising herself. The comparison made by Marvin Pope to Gen 38:14—and thus to *ra'yati* posing as a prostitute here—has little weight because that uses a different Hebrew word for "veil."[69]

In 1:8 we find a response about how *ra'yati* can find *dodi*. She need only "follow the flock," and in this verse unlike v. 7, "flock" (צֹאן *tso'n*) does appear in the Hebrew. The text does not make clear whether this reply belongs to *dodi* or the daughters. Weems points out that *ra'yati* did not ask the daughters, she asked *dodi*, and thus the answer likely belongs to him.[70] Exum on the other hand notes how *ra'yati* is called "fairest among women" here, which is the daughters' nickname for her elsewhere in the book (5:9; 6:1).[71] In any case, the response seems to indicate a pastoral setting for *ra'yati* like we saw for *dodi* in the previous verse. However, this scenario is somewhat unexpected for a woman. Perhaps the language is metaphorical or as I suggested above, euphemistic, though we cannot rule out the possibility that she helped care for her family's flocks.

While we cannot be sure if *dodi* was speaking in 1:8, in 1:9 we clearly hear his voice for the first time in the book. His strange compliments to *ra'yati* in 1:9-10 have much in common with the *wasf* form, though this brief section is not usually grouped with the longer *wasf*s. *Dodi*'s song here highlights his lover's physical beauty and allure. While a horse may sound like a strange way to describe a woman, a "mare among Pharaoh's chariots" in 1:9 has great significance. To distract and confuse the male horses of the Egyptian cavalry, enemy troops would release a female horse into their ranks.[72] In that case, the illustration would refer to *ra'yati*'s sexual appeal. *Dodi*'s praise of her bejeweled face and neck may also relate to the ornamentation sometimes placed on horses. In 1:11, he promises to add to her jewelry. Unfortunately, we cannot be sure who "we" entails, at the beginning of the verse. Possibilities include *dodi*'s friends, *ra'yati*'s girlfriends, or a jeweler.

69. Pope, *Song*, 330–31.

70. Weems, "Song," 5:386.

71. Exum, *Song*, 108.

72. Pope, *Song*, 336–43 and Weems, "Song," 5:386–87; Fox disagrees with the war scenario (*Song*, 105); Exum reviews the possibilities without ruling out any (*Song*, 108–9).

In a short section of text, the lovers have filled our ears with sensual songs. We tasted *ra'yati's* mouth-watering lyrics about her beloved, and smelled his fragrance (1:2–4); *dodi's* song brought our gaze upon his love's head-turning looks and charms (1:9–11). In 1:12–14 *ra'yati* directs our noses again to their attractive smells. Nard, the plant-based perfume from India, does not appear outside of Song in the Hebrew Bible, so we are limited in what we can know about this reference, but such an import item would surely have been costly. Because she speaks of "*my* nard," it may well be that *ra'yati* here speaks euphemistically of her body's own sensual, precious fragrance.

The smells continue in 1:13–14. This time *ra'yati* provocatively describes *dodi* as a necklace sachet of myrrh resting between her breasts. This ointment, from Arabian tree sap, was used as perfume (Ps 45:8; Prov 7:17), cosmetic (Esth 2:12), and for sacred anointing (Exod 30:23); it re-appears throughout Song in 3:6; 4:6, 14; 5:1; and 5:5 (twice). She follows this with a simile comparing his fragrance to that of the white henna flowers found in En-gedi. This town lay on the western shore of the Dead Sea, and was known for its natural spring water, agriculture, and security as a military outpost. Of relevance to this passage, excavation of the site shows that it may have been a production site for perfume.[73] It does not require much imagination to view the lyrics of these two verses as descriptive of a sex scene. Verse 13 paints a rather clear picture of the couple's intimate position; that continues in v. 14, particularly if we recall that "vineyard" connotes female sexuality.

If 1:13–14 is *ra'yati's* exceedingly brief *wasf*, then perhaps *dodi* responds in turn with his own one-liner in 1:15. This verse begins a section in which the couple exchanges kind words with one another. In 1:15 *dodi* sings a repetitive refrain about *ra'yati's* beauty, and for the first time he uses the metaphor of "doves" (יוֹנִים, *yonim*) to describe her eyes. He will use that metaphor again in 4:1; *ra'yati* uses it of *dodi's* eyes in 5:12. In 2:14 and 6:9, *dodi* even makes "dove" a pet name for *ra'yati*. In 1:16a *ra'yati* echoes her lover's compliment, which begins with the same words as 1:15a.

The topic next turns to the lovers' surroundings. The description in 1:16b-17 could indicate a cedar and pine house with a green couch; on the other hand, it could mean that their tryst takes place in a wooded

---

73. Hamilton, "En-Gedi," 2:502.

area or garden. We again cannot be sure if *ra'yati* is fantasizing here, or singing of their actual house and décor.

Ra'yati next turns the focus on herself in 2:1; *dodi* picks up the banter, using her own word, "lily" (שׁוֹשַׁן, *shoshan*) in 2:2. *Dodi* accentuates his love's uniqueness by calling her a "lily among briers." *Ra'yati*'s turn is next, and she moves from the "lily" metaphor for herself to describing *dodi* as an "apple tree among the woods" (2:3).[74] In 2:2–3a, each lover in turn uses the same structure of vocabulary and word order to express these compliments, making 2 and 3a tightly knit pair. Following this parallelism, *ra'yati* continues her "apple tree" metaphor about *dodi*, sensually describing his close presence; provocatively telling of his taste.

In 2:4–6, *ra'yati* extends her reminiscence—or fantasy—about *dodi*. This time the setting is the "wine-house," which returns us to that ongoing metaphor. She apparently turns her speech to him in 2:5, asking for delicacies of the wine-house. The plural Hebrew form of the opening verb in 2:5 indicates a wider audience than just *dodi*; perhaps she is including her girlfriends here, or her song at this point may be fashioned to draw in the audience.[75] Raisins would be an obvious treat at this place featuring other grape products. With the mention of "apples" in the second phrase of 2:5, we might guess that *ra'yati* intends to receive additional or alternate sustenance from her lover, since she told us in 1:3 how she delights in his "apples." This pair of verses (2:4–5) both end emphasizing "love" (אַהֲבָה, *'ahavah*).

A translation difficulty complicates 2:4, where the Hebrew reads "his *banner* upon/concerning/over me was love." Various emendations and interpretations attempt to make sense of this odd phrase. Elsewhere in Song (6:4, 10) the root for "*banner*" appears in a military context. A minimal change in the vowel markings, which is supported by some of the ancient versions, allows for the reading "he looked upon me [with] love." The Akkadian gives the basis for NRSV and Fox's "his *intention* toward me was love," which points to an act that may have had sexual meaning.[76] Even aside from that translation, the phrase could be figurative or euphemistic for the couple's sexual encounter, relating "banner" to his "shadow" and "fruit" in 2:3b. The interpretation of this verse relates to 2:6, which could represent *ra'yati*'s fantasy, or the actual position

74. The fruit may in fact be apricots, as Fox argues (*Song*, 107–9).
75. Exum suggests this (*Song*, 116).
76. Fox, *Song*, 108.

of their embrace. The Hebrew is truly ambiguous; English translations must choose the subjunctive (NRSV), past (JPS) or present (NIV).

Next, *ra'yati* rather abruptly addresses her girlfriends with a refrain we find irregularly placed throughout the book. "Refrain to daughters of Jerusalem," as I named it in the above outline reads in 2:7 and 3:5, "I implore you, daughters of Jerusalem, by the gazelles or the wild does; do not arouse or awaken love until it is ready." This refrain also appears in 5:8 and 8:4 with slight variation. In 2:7 and 8:4 the refrain is paired with the lyric about the couple's embrace (2:6; 8:3), making for a lengthier repetition. Furthermore, 5:8 opens the same as the other three refrains, though *ra'yati* has a different message for the daughters there. Unfortunately, the meaning of this refrain is not entirely clear. Despite the repetition of the line, it does not have a clear or consistent structural function. In some cases, it seems to conclude a section (3:5), and in others it apparently divides units (2:7).

The refrain opens with *ra'yati* demanding that her girlfriends take an oath. She invokes animals that have significance elsewhere in Song (gazelles, צְבָאוֹת *tsva'ot*, 2:7, 9, 17; 3:5, 4:5; 7:3 [Heb 7:4]; 8:14; doe אַיָּלָה *'ayyalah* 3:5; in masculine form [אַיָּל *'ayyal*] 2:9, 17; 8:14). Perhaps she is prompted to name these animals in this vow due to some symbolism regarding love. Many commentators have noticed that the Hebrew words for these animals sound like the divine appellatives "hosts" (צְבָאוֹת *tsva'ot*) and "El" (אֵל *'el*), references that would have heightened the effect of the swear. The meaning and translation of this refrain vary, with two interpretations of the verse predominating. The most widely accepted is that *ra'yati* here asks her girlfriends to swear not to stir up or rouse love as general advice. This understanding of the refrains would restrain the physical urgency conveyed in the rest of the book, yet it is not to suggest that *ra'yati* is advocating the avoidance of physicality—her actions certainly do not evidence that. Renita Weems suggests understanding this repeated verse in the sense of Qohelet's poem about appointed times in Eccl 3:1–8: "a time to love, and a time to wait for love."[77] Exum sees a powerful paradox between these refrains in which love is "virtually personified," and Song's poignant statement in 8:6–7: Love must not be rushed; love is as strong as death.[78] If this is the case, then perhaps the message is that the lovers' embraces (2:6; 8:3), nurtured

77. Weems, "Song," 5:390.
78. Exum, *Song*, 117–19.

in an unhurried environment (2:7; 3:5; 8:4), can lead to an everlasting form of love (8:6–7). A small number of commentators accept a quite different scenario in interpreting this verse, in which the girlfriends' oath would be not to interrupt the couple's lovemaking.[79]

Ra'yati Sings about *Dodi* (2:8—3:5)

The first song in this section, 2:8–17, comprises a fairly discrete unit. The pair of words "mountains" and "gazelle" in 2:8–9 and 2:17 act as an inclusio—a repetitive way of providing bookends to a section, often indicating the beginning and end of a poem in Hebrew. This song also includes the repetition of the refrain "Arise, my love, my fair one, and come away," which we saw first in 2:10 and 2:13b. A structure comprised of *ra'yati*'s introduction (2:8–10a) and conclusion (2:16–17) surrounds this section. In the middle is *dodi*'s love song, quoted by *ra'yati*. This fascinating piece of poetry leads the audience to think they have heard *dodi*'s words (2:10b-15); closer scrutiny shows that *ra'yati* is the voice for her beloved's sentiments here.

The motif of the lovers' separation and longing for one another appears prominently in 2:8–9. *ra'yati* sees dodi from afar, and then peeking in at her from a close but unattainable distance on the other side of the wall. The term "gazelles" appears again in 2:9 as it did in 2:7; here and coming up in 2:17 it is *ra'yati*'s simile for *dodi*. Along with "stag" (2:9, 17; 4:5, 7:4; 8:14) the significance of these animals in a mountainous setting appears to be their ability to traverse difficult terrain. Presumably, *ra'yati* hopes that *dodi* will similarly be able to overcome whatever barriers keep him from her. It is impossible to know exactly the intent or scenario in these verses, other than that *dodi* appears to be out of reach to *ra'yati*. That, in turn, leads to her apparent fantasy about his song to her.

Dodi's love song in 2:10b-15—whether *ra'yati*'s fantasy or memory—is surely one of the most beautiful poems in Song. His lyrics begin in 2:10b with, "Come away . . . ," a phrase that contemporary singer Norah Jones also croons to her lover.[80] *Dodi*'s plea is that *ra'yati* would "come away with me in springtime;" the imagery of 2:11–13 vividly il-

---

79. An example of this view is Fox, *Song*, 110.

80. Jones, "Come Away." Jones also mentions "springtime" in this song, providing a further connection to this passage.

lustrates that setting. The singer allows us to see, hear, and smell this season of love's renewal. Winter in the near East means rain, but that ends in spring. In all likelihood, the spring song has another layer of euphemistic meaning as well, indicated particularly by the "vines" in 2:13b. As we saw above, the vineyard has sexual overtones (1:6). The singer here experienced love like the gift of spring, full of sensual delights that supersede the "rainy" past, perhaps of one who had been brokenhearted. Anyone who has experienced the pain of separation or disintegration from love, only to find renewed love where it once seemed impossible, can relate to *dodi's* tender words in 2:10b-12. What better gift could there be for one once alienated or separated from love?

Love may have been fulfilled in 2:14, though we cannot be sure—he may simply be longing to find his "dove." According to 2:15, something or someone apparently seeks to foil their love. Yet that is only one meaning we can glean from the obscure language of this verse. We cannot even be sure who is speaking here, or to whom. Numerous other interpretations exist, including Exum's, in which she relies on the likely sexual innuendo of "foxes" and "vineyards," to conclude that *ra'yati* here desires to find in *dodi* a good catch among the eligible men (foxes) who can freely "play the field," or rather, "vineyard."[81]

Ra'yati resumes speaking in 2:16–17, where she claims and longs for her beloved, beginning with a lovely, concise rhyme: דּוֹדִי לִי וַאֲנִי לוֹ *dodi li va'ani lo*. A very wooden, literal translation allows us to practically see *ra'yati* gesturing—even grasping her beloved's hand—as she sings these dear words: "my beloved [is] to me, and I [am] to him."

In 2:16b the pastoral scene re-appears with a likely sexual euphemism. *Ra'yati* wishes that *dodi* would "shepherd among the lilies." Like in 1:7, "shepherd" here has no object—NRSV adds "flock," resulting in "pastures his flock among the lilies." A better translation for this intransitive verb is "graze," or even "feed." Based on references throughout Song (2:1–2; 4:5; 5:13; 6:2–3; 7:2), "the lilies" likely refers to *ra'yati's* pleasure spots. Thus "graze in the lilies" may indicate *dodi's* sensual exploration of her body's "flowers," perhaps using the same analogy between flowers and female anatomy as Georgia O'Keeffe painted millennia later.

This scene—or fantasy, we cannot be sure—ends much as it began, though with a more ambiguous verse. Is it nighttime or morning in 2:17a? Could 2:17a further describe the anticipation of spring, thus

---

81. Exum, *Song*, 129–30. For other views, see Murphy, *Song*, 141 and Fox, *Song*, 114.

summarizing and paralleling 2:11–13? Might it metaphorically indicate awaiting love's right time, as in the refrains of 2:7; 3:5 and 8:4? Is *ra'yati* sending *dodi* away or beckoning him closer?[82] She apparently calls on him to spend the whole day deftly overcoming the geographical obstacles between them ("cleft mountains," NRSV 2:17b)—or could she be asking him to deftly explore her own "cleft mountains," in yet another double entendre?[83] We will have cause to struggle again with this perplexing verse, as 4:6 and 8:14 repeat parts of it.

Ra'yati's next song again revolves around the theme of searching for her beloved. This section, 3:1–4, contains movement and resolution, comprising an unusually coherent passage compared to the rest of Song. Nonetheless, the episode wafts between reality and dream, beginning as it does in *ra'yati*'s bed.[84] If this song had a name, it would be "Seeking the Love of my Life," or just "Love of my Life," a phrase that repeats in each verse (the first two open with the verb "seek"). We heard this nickname for *dodi* first in 1:7. It describes him as "the one–who–my spirit / life / self / soul [Heb נֶפֶשׁ *nefesh*]–loves," thus "Love of my Life," or "him who my soul loves" in NRSV.

The repetition of the root "seek" (בקשׁ *bqsh*) four times in two verses (3:1–2) emphasizes the intensity with which *ra'yati* searches for *dodi*. In 2:9 and 14 he was seeking her, for apparently she was lost to him; now in 3:1–4 he is the one lost to her. As *ra'yati* seeks her beloved, she moves from a setting of comfort and safety to one of risk and danger and back again; she shifts from private space to public space, finally returning to private. The scene opens at her bed (3:1), where she begins

82. Exum makes sense of these difficult verses, and equally remarkable, contextualizes them within the whole book: "The similarity between 2:17 and 8:14 invites us to look more closely at how, in its poetic unfolding, Song 2:8–17 might offer a clue to the meaning of the Song as a whole. Song 2:8–17 ends as the Song ends, with the woman seemingly sending her lover away and calling him to her in the same breath. It is followed in 3:1–5 by a second "story" in which the woman seeks and finds her lover. This pattern indicates that the paradoxical sending away and calling for(th) is a prelude to the lovers' union, a union that throughout the Song is simultaneously assured, deferred, and, on a figurative level, enjoyed." (*Song*, 133)

83. Many possible translations and interpretations exist for this difficult phrase. Fox translates "mountains of Bether," which are near Jerusalem. In his view, the barrier is geographical, but *dodi* glides over it with ease (*Song*, 116). Exum instead renders the ambiguous Hebrew as "cleft mountains," and understands it as double entendre (*Song*, 132).

84. Some ("many"—Murphy, *Song*, 61) interpret this section as a dream sequence.

searching. She continues to look for him, venturing out of the house and into the various locations of the city, first the more enclosed areas and then the open spaces (3:2). Even as she encounters strangers—the city's guards—she still seeks the love of her life (3:3). *Ra'yati* has ventured to ever increasing places of vulnerability. By describing *ra'yati* in these places where a woman would not likely have gone alone, the text illustrates the risks she will take for the love of her life, which in turn depicts the depth of her love for him.

This vignette of 3:1–4 has told of a romantic "hide and seek," though the tone is much more serious than a children's game. The fourfold repetition of "seek" (בקש *bqsh* 3:1a, b, 3:2a, b) finds balance in the fourfold repetition of "found" (מצא, *mts'*), 3:2b, 3:3a, 3:4a). The first two instances of "found" appear in the negative—she *cannot* "find" him. The third occurrence marks the episode's climax, where *ra'yati* is found, but by the guards rather than her beloved. Finally there is resolution when in 3:4 *ra'yati* "finds" *dodi*. She at last embraces the love of her life, and draws him into an arguably more intimate space than her bed, where her search began. The two phrases in 3:4b express this in parallelism: "mother's house // chamber of the one who was pregnant with me." The full meaning of this is uncertain. Strangely, it seems that they end up in her mother's bedroom. Depending on how we understand the Hebrew, there may be a double entendre here indicating her mother's womb, where *ra'yati*'s life began.[85] While this is a literal absurdity, it is meaningful in the scheme of this episode about seeking and finding: What could be a safer place?[86] Furthermore, this could figuratively relate to the time elsewhere in Song where *ra'yati* longs for *dodi* to be like her brother (8:1).

The reference to her "mother's house" in 3:4b (בֵּת אֵם, *bet 'am*), rather than the more common phrase "father's house" (בֵּת אָב, *bet 'av*) also appears in 8:2a, which parallels this reference. This phrase also recalls Ruth 1:8, in which Naomi sends each of her daughters-in-law back to their "mother's house," refusing their offers to return with her to Bethlehem. The only other place we find this phrase is in Gen 24:28

---

85. Meyers writes that "it is not simply a bedroom, it is the 'chamber of her that conceived me,' an amplification highlighting the mother's procreative role" ("Returning Home," 104).

86. The idea of returning to the womb is used poetically as the cyclical completion of life in Job 1:21.

where Abraham's servant, seeking a wife for Isaac, meets Rachel at the well; she tells of that encounter at "her mother's house."[87] Carol Meyers suggests that the reference to "mother's house" indicates a focus on relationality rather than on patrilineal succession.[88] In addition, Meyers has argued that this feature indicates female authorship and point of view. In other words, only a woman would talk of returning to her mother's house.[89]

This section concludes with the refrain to *ra'yati's* girlfriends in 3:5, an exact repetition of 2:7. In both of these instances, the verse may function as a section divider. Both here and in 2:7 the refrain makes an abrupt shift in the song, just when we might have thought the couple would be able to satisfy their love. Still, we remain unsure of *ra'yati's* meaning here. Just as we wondered with 2:7, we ask again: Is she advising restraint, or requesting privacy so that their passions would be uninterrupted? These contradictory interpretations, along with the couple's hiding and seeking, beckoning and sending away, and verse that is simultaneously erotic and tame, will tease us throughout the book.

Ra'yati's Dream Wedding Fantasy Told to the Daughters of Jerusalem (3:6–11)

The final episode in this section of "flirtation and fantasy" (1:2–3:11) shifts to an entirely new setting. Like some of the previous scenes, we read this starkly independent unit tentatively, since it hovers between dream and reality, building suspense by gradually releasing details. It begins abruptly, with "Who is that?" It beckons us to look another way— from *ra'yati's* "mother's house" (3:4) to the "wilderness" (3:6). We cannot be sure who is speaking here, though based on the context, since *ra'yati* was just speaking, this may be her voice as well.[90] Furthermore, according to 3:10–11, the audience seems to be the "daughters of Jerusalem/ Zion"—*ra'yati's* girlfriends, whom *ra'yati* frequently addresses.

87. At least one woman in Egyptian love poetry refers to her "mother's house" as well (Fox, *Song*, 119).

88. Meyers, "Returning Home," 179–80.

89. Ibid., 103–6.

90. With Exum, who reviews the possibilities and concludes by process of elimination that the speaker is the woman (*Song*, 143).

Contributing to the dream-like atmosphere is the description of a royal procession coming from a distance, looking like a hazy, palm-tree shaped mass (NRSV and NIV have "column of smoke"),[91] smelling of the same erotic spices that tantalize our noses in other portions of Song (1:13; 4:6, 14; 5:1, 5, 13; 8:14), and the exotic scented powders of far-off travelers. Between the smoke, the powder and the many fragrances, this song allows us to smell the scene before we have seen it.

Soon enough, however, we have something remarkable to behold, and quite a sight it is: Solomon's chaise, clearly portable in this instance (3:7). Surrounding that are three score of "Israel's mighty men" (גִּבֹּרֵי יִשְׂרָאֵל, gibbore yisra'el), or "warriors." This term for "mighty men" should be somewhat familiar from the book of Ruth, in which Boaz is referred to with the adjective for "mighty," or "great" (גִּבּוֹר, gibbor; see section on Ruth 2:1). The presence of this entourage suggests that a royal procession of some kind is approaching, perhaps even a war party. The following verse (3:8) emphasizes that possibility, with its two mentions of "swords" surrounding the word "war." The verse ends with dread of night, a time of risk elsewhere in the book as well (3:1, 5:2).

The scene continues in 3:9–10, apparently with background information about King Solomon's ornate transportation. The Hebrew word that NRSV translates "palanquin" is different than the one rendered "litter" in 3:7. In this case, the word appears only here, so we remain rather uncertain of its precise meaning. Fortunately, the narrator of this scene goes on to provide a full description, including the various building materials. Surprisingly, the text tells not only what it was made of, but also poetically notes the spirit in which it was made: it was "arranged with love." Even this seemingly romantic comment is surrounded by uncertainty. Because the context tells about the royal décor, and the word for "love" as an adverbial abstraction is unique, many other translations have been suggested. Minor emendations turn this into "ebony," "leather," and "stones," among others.[92] Some similarity exists between this stanza and that in 2:4, where "his banner over me was love." Though the word there occurs in a more grammatically acceptable way, it has a similarly figurative sense. If this phrase indeed suggests emotion rather than ornamen-

91. Incidentally, the vocabulary for "column of smoke" has no commonality with that of the divine "pillar of fire" or "pillar of smoke" in Exod 13:21, 22; 14:19, 24; 33:9, 10.

92. See Exum, *Song*, 149–50, for a summary of the various interpretations.

tation, it provides the first indication of this scene as something other than a war party. This sense is accentuated in the following verse (3:11), which refers to Solomon's wedding day.

We do not know the meaning of the "crown" in 3:11, whether it was a royal diadem, or a wedding garland. The fact that Solomon's mother places it on him is similarly obscure, though it suggests the interesting possibility of some connection to "mother" in Song 1:6; 3:4, 11; 6:9; 8:1, 2, 5. On those occasions, the mention of *ra'yati's* "mother" may suggest familial rather than hierarchical structures; perhaps the author is suggesting something similar here in regard to Solomon.

At the end of this scene we finally discover that what at first looked like a war party is apparently a groom's party (3:11); the king is not filled with blood lust, but with the mirth of love. He is not dressed for battle, but for his wedding. The suspense of this scene climaxes with a view of the king himself. We, with the daughters of Zion, hear *ra'yati* getting our attention, calling "Look!" (3:11). The verse ends the scene with a powerful parallelism: "on the day of his marriage // on the day of his heart's joy."

Throughout its interpretive history, this passage has contributed to the notion that Song is a book of wedding lyrics. Yet a close reading of 3:6–11 shows only one reference to marriage, in v. 11. Indeed, that verse is somewhat separate from the rest of the pericope. We cannot conclude that "King Solomon" in this passage equals *dodi*, particularly since *ra'yati* does not speak directly to him anywhere in this pericope, nor is it even clear whether *ra'yati* is the one speaking. In other parts of Song however, *ra'yati* more clearly refers to *dodi* as king. For instance, in 1:4 and 12, she has been singing about *dodi*, and in 7:5 [Heb 7:6], she has been praising him in a *wasf*. Similarly, in 4:9–12 *dodi* uses bridal imagery in a song about *ra'yati*.

In light of that, we remain uncertain about the role of this pericope in the book. What purpose does this scene serve? What does King Solomon's wedding party have to do with *ra'yati* and *dodi*? It seems likely that this song consists of *ra'yati* conjuring for her girlfriends her dream wedding, in which she spoke of her lover as "King Solomon." Yet, as usual, we cannot be sure. The abrupt inclusion of this passage amid a couple's love songs to one another keeps us guessing.

Dodi Sings a *Wasf* to *Ra'yati*: You Are as Precious as the Land of Milk and Honey (4:1–8)

This section begins a longer portion of Song (4:1–8:7) in which the couple sings songs of yearning for each other. *Dodi's* voice predominates from 4:1 to 5:1, and he opens the section with the first *wasf* of the book (4:1–7; see Introduction for an explanation of *wasfs*). My title for this *wasf*, "you are as precious as the land of milk and honey," refers to the many allusions to the landscape, flora, fauna, and even architecture of Israel. Of course, this is much more than a song about a beloved land. With what turns out to be the imagery of a fantasy world, *dodi* poetically caresses his beloved's body—beginning with her eyes, and moving downward. He leaves the reader wondering whether he is only able to gaze at or long for *ra'yati*, or whether his hands follow his words along her body's contours.

This *wasf* begins and ends with *dodi* calling *ra'yati* "beautiful" (יָפָה, *yephah*). He pairs that word with his pet name for her, "my love" or "*ra'yati*" in both 4:1 and 7, creating a poetic envelope or inclusio around the section. *Dodi* used these same words for his lover in 1:15, where he also included the phrase that follows them here, "your eyes are doves." The dove was among the first domesticated birds, and may have been kept as a pet. Furthermore, the dove was known for its faithfulness to its mate, and its inclination to hide flirtatiously in rock crevices.[93] These features seem fitting as *dodi* describes *ra'yati's* dove-like eyes hiding behind her veil, an item of clothing that ironically should provide modesty, but which obviously prevents neither *dodi's* gaze nor his desire. With the first half of this verse, *dodi* has begun his *wasf* of *ra'yati* by admiring her eyes; from there he moves more or less downward to her hair, her teeth, her lips, her neck and her breasts.

Dodi admires *ra'yati's* hair by way of an apparently odd comparison to female goats (4:1b). He may have been saying that her tresses were silky and wavy, as was likely the look of a flock of the long-haired creatures moving along a Gilead hillside. The hair of female goats was valuable and attractive. Among other pricey offerings such as precious stones and metals, YHVH commanded the people to bring goat's hair to be used for yarn in the creation of the tabernacle (Exod 25:4; 35:26).

---

93. Botterweck, "יוֹנָה," 6:37, 39.

Heightening the compliment, *dodi* poetically describes these goats as luxuriously grazing in the pastoral refuge of the Transjordan Mountains.

Moving from her hair to her mouth, the next comparison (4:2) also involves a flock, this time clean-shaven with bright, bare skin. The note that each has a twin—no animal is bereaved of her child—presumably indicates that the woman has all of her teeth. In our culture, we take a full set of white teeth for granted even in someone we might not consider otherwise attractive; in ancient times a gapless smile would have been much less frequent and thus far more remarkable. In 4:3, *dodi* continues to describe his love's attractive mouth, with lips drawn in a scarlet line. Like in 4:1, in this verse *dodi* mentions *ra'yati*'s veil, again only as an afterthought to what he knows—or fantasizes—lies behind it. This time, he sings longingly about her face, which has the blush of pomegranate halves.

As *dodi*'s description of *ra'yati* moves further down her body, he describes her neck in 4:4 in ways that seem rather bizarre; some have even called this analogy "grotesque."[94] He sings, "Your neck is like the tower of David, built in courses; a thousand shields hang upon it, all the armaments of mighty soldiers."[95] It appears that the tower's rows of stones or bricks have been decorated with the warriors' weapons—a beautiful sight, as described in Ezek 27:11. The more recent colloquialism "she's built like a brick outhouse," used to describe a substantially buxom woman, may be an apt comparison for such a strange description. Or, it may make more sense to assume that *dodi* is commenting on the adornment of his love's neck—her jewelry. In this case, imagine a necklace of shiny beads or hammered metal, composed of multiple strands. Examples of such jewelry have been found on ancient figurines and sculpture.[96]

On the other hand, the lyric may draw on the qualities of David's tower: regal, unique, valuable, warranting the utmost protection. This verse paints a picture of something staggering and awe inspiring. Indeed, it may well have been something that a man in particular would find

94. Black, "Beauty," 302–23.

95. We do not know with certainty the meaning of Hebrew word for "courses." However, this translation is currently the most convincing and thus enjoys the scholarly consensus. For a detailed description of the relevant issues, see Pope, *Song*, 454, 465–68.

96. For illustrations of necklaces that apparently resemble this description, see Pope, *Song*, 467–68; Plate III and Fig. 7.

impressive. If so, this description could be analogous to a man today who might compliment his lover by comparing her to his favorite sports car, motorcycle or fighter jet. Perhaps we need only look to seductive photography that places beautiful—even naked—women on or in such vehicles in order to imagine this ancient singer's intent with such an apparently odd comparison.

From *ra'yati*'s neck, *dodi* moves on to sing about her breasts (4:5). Here, like in 4:2, *dodi* invokes the imagery of twins as part of his paean to her. This time, they are "stags, twins of a gazelle," the same words *ra'yati* used for *dodi* in 2:9, 17, and 8:14. Unfortunately, because "stags" occurs only here in the Hebrew Bible, and "gazelle" appears only a bit more frequently, we do not have much information about their significance or meaning in this *wasf*. Presumably, these similes would play on the lovely, lithe, swift and well-toned attributes of these creatures.

The description moves to the rather peculiar statement that the animals signifying her breasts "graze among the lilies" (4:5b). That statement is familiar from 2:16b, though in that case the "lilies" may have erotically referred to *ra'yati* (see above). Here, the "lilies" may again suggest *ra'yati*, possibly just by painting a word-picture of her whole body as a woodland scene. Or, foreshadowing the imagery of *dodi*'s lips as lilies (5:13), this lyric could picture the couple in an intimate embrace, with his lips kissing her breasts. Could he be responding to her song in 1:13, which describes him lying between her breasts like a sachet necklace?[97]

In v. 6a *dodi* repeats part of 2:17, where *ra'yati*'s poetry seemed to entice her beloved to spend a whole day seeking her. Creating a sense of unity for the book, here "the man responds to the woman's exhortation of 2:17."[98] We cannot be sure if the *wasf* genre continues into 4:6 or if it ended in 4:5. Nothing in 4:6 explicitly indicates the description of a body part, though a number of commentators have suggested that "the mountain of myrrh and the hill of frankincense" provide a parallelism with the previous verse about *ra'yati*'s breasts, indicating physical rather than geographical features. In that case, perhaps *dodi* is saying that he will seek and enjoy intimacy with his love until morning—or night. The dilemma about the time of day indicated in this phrase is still as elusive as it was in 2:17.

---

97. Dobbs-Allsopp, "Delight," 263.

98. Exum, *Song*, 167.

If 4:6 does not refer to *ra'yati*'s body, then we must wonder what else it could mean. If the "mountain of myrrh" and "hill of frankincense" refer to actual geographical locations, we do not know what or where those places are, nor do we know their significance for *dodi* and *ra'yati*. Complicating rather than solving matters, the word for "frankincense" (לְבוֹנָה, *levonah*), sounds and looks a great deal like "Lebanon," a geographical theme in the up-coming section.[99] Like any good poem or lyric, the meanings in this book are multilayered, with each signification hinting at another, which could be implied or explicit, either in this phrase or in the next thought.

Whether or not 4:6 was technically part of the *wasf* that *dodi* began in 4:1, 4:7 surely acts as an ending for the section. Bookended with 4:1, 4:7 makes an inclusio, repeating the initial phrase of the pericope about *ra'yati*'s beauty, heightening that compliment and concluding the song by going on to call her "unblemished."

Dodi Sings to *Ra'yati*: Come Away with Me, for You Are the Destination (4:8—5:1a)

Dodi's singing to *ra'yati* continues in 4:8–5:1b, where he invites her to come away with him (4:8), luring her with extravagant compliments (4:9–15). *Ra'yati* responds with her own invitation in 4:16, which *dodi* accepts in 5:1a, and *ra'yati* tells about in 5:1b. This section is reminiscent of 2:10b-15, where *ra'yati* quoted *dodi* as wanting her to come away with him—now he speaks that desire in his own voice.

In 4:8, *dodi* uses a new pet name for *ra'yati*: "my bride." He applies that appellative to her in every verse of 4:9–12, and again in 5:1. In verses 9, 10 and 12, *dodi* adds the term of endearment "my sister," making "my sister, my bride" his most elaborate name for her. Notably, neither "sister" nor "bride" literally identifies *ra'yati*. Rather, they indicate *dodi*'s desire for closeness with her—both literally and figuratively. Indeed, such terms were not unusual in ancient Near Eastern love poetry.[100]

Dodi's invitation in 4:8 seems to suggest that his love is far away from him, yet that for some reason she would have to depart from sev-

99. Weems, "Song," 5:403.

100. Exum quotes ancient Sumerian texts in which "sister" is clearly used by a man as a term of endearment for his lover (*Song*, 174–75). Fox points out that Egyptian love songs include "sister" as an appellative for one's lover (*Song*, 136).

eral locations in order to reach him. In a repetitive parallelism, he asks, "with me, from Lebanon, bride, with me, come" (4:8b). This awkward rendering follows the Hebrew word order, which emphasizes their togetherness. *Dodi* follows the verb at the end of the first phrase with another verb, pleading that she "journey" from the tops of Amana, Senir, and Hermon; from the lairs of lions and the dens of leopards.[101] What are these places, and why would *dodi* talk about *ra'yati* being there? Surely he cannot mean that she was literally in all of these locations, but if not, what is his meaning in mentioning them? The locations refer to the mountains in southern Lebanon/northern Palestine. The three mentioned are different peaks in that range. *Dodi* probably invokes all three mountain tops for the sake of poetic parallelism. Lebanon itself has rich meaning in the Hebrew Bible, where it illustrates beauty and bounty (Ps 72:16; 92:12; Hos 14:5–7). As mentioned above, "Lebanon" may in part be significant as a pun with the Hebrew word for "frankincense." To that extent, it would here provide a connection with the previous section, as well as suggesting that Lebanon may be *ra'yati* herself. "Lebanon" also was the source of the wood for "Solomon's chaise" in 3:9. In 5:15 *ra'yati* compliments *dodi* by invoking Lebanon, and in 7:4 *dodi* takes on this imagery for his love one last time.[102] All of those references build on each other to provide content for the imagery in 4:8.

In the second half of 4:8, *dodi*'s mention of wild animals in their hiding places illustrates a backwoods setting. His intent may be to express how out of reach and distant his love seems to him; as far as he is concerned, she must travel from a dangerous wilderness to be with him. Another possibility is that *dodi* sees *ra'yati* –or his fantasy of her— as a bit wild. In other words, this could be a "*ra'yati* as *Xena: Warrior Princess*" motif—imagery that could also relate to her neck as compared to an armed tower. Perhaps he wants to indicate the risky nature of their relationship, or her breathtaking effect, like that of snowcapped mountains, looming from afar, or the heightened senses attained both from fear and from passion.

101. The Hebrew has "mountains of leopards," but Exum, *Song*, 154, and Fox, *Song*, 135 make a minor emendation to read "dens," which makes more sense in the context, and follows the parallelism.

102. See Exum for a lengthier analysis of Lebanon and its meaning in the Hebrew Bible (*Song*, 170).

Dodi croons to *ra'yati* about how the smallest features of her appearance—her eyes and a single facet of her necklace—have enamored him of her, almost sounding like a mini-*wasf* (4:9). He goes on to pick up on her own words of praise for him, saying that her love is better than wine (1:2, 4; 4:10a; cf. 1:2). He surpasses that compliment by saying how good she smells (4:10b, 11b), and provocatively describing how the inside of her mouth tastes (4:11a). His reference to Lebanon at the end of this portion of the song connects with 4:8.

The tastes and smells of 4:8–11 shift to imagery of *ra'yati* as a secret, exotic, luxurious garden in 4:12–15. Similar descriptions of a lover as a garden can be found in other ancient Near Eastern love poetry, though interestingly Song does not make what would seem an obvious connection between such fecundity and procreation, as we find in other ancient examples.[103] The lovers' bountiful garden in Song serves no purpose other than the pleasures of love. Though *dodi* describes this garden as tantalizingly off-limits, it is nonetheless a more domestic setting than that of 4:8 and the mountain wilderness. Here resides not wildness and danger, but deliciousness and delight, provided through the most delectable fruits and fragrances. In fact, it may be that 4:12 indicates a self-sufficient, spring-fed garden, as opposed to one that needs irrigation.[104] To that end, he paints a picture of a lush and coveted secret garden just out of his view.

Much of this section depends on the meaning of the opening noun in 4:13, yet we do not know for sure what that word indicates. Nonetheless, it clearly has the possessive suffix; whatever the word, *dodi* plainly tells *ra'yati* it is "yours." NRSV translates it "channel," with the note "Meaning of Hebrew uncertain," NIV renders it "plants," and JPS uses "limbs." The meaning could be anything from "roots/shoots" to "watercourses." Despite the ambiguity, we hardly need a wink and a nod to get the impression that *dodi* is erotically referring to *ra'yati*'s body. Indeed, both trees/roots and water/wells have sexual connotations elsewhere in biblical and other ancient Near Eastern literature.[105]

---

103. Exum, *Song*, 174–75.

104. Keel, *Song*, 174.

105. See, for example, Prov 5:15–20. For numerous examples of this, including citations of ancient texts and illustrations in which "canal" euphemistically indicates vagina, see Keel, *Song*, 170–78.

The closing imagery of fragrances, spices and unguents in 4:13–14 marks this not only as an opulent garden of exotics, but as a garden of mythic proportions. As numerous commentators point out, the list of luxuries represents import items from far and wide—they would not have been found all together in any garden, much less one in Israel.[106] This imagery suggests tastes and smells practically to the point of over-stimulation; the erotic connotations here abound. Finally, in 4:15 we find an inclusio enclosing this longer section with the mention of "Lebanon." Its wildness flows from 4:8 and through to this very garden; there *dodi* will find "the water of life" (4:15). For that among other reasons, this garden connotes the first garden, an allusion that Phyllis Trible relies on in her description of Song as "Love's Lyrics Redeemed"—redeemed, that is, from the disobedience of Genesis 2–3 that results in a forbidden garden. As we have seen, the garden motif illustrated divine blessing, fertility, sexual intimacy, and romantic love throughout the ancient Near East. Could it be that the mythical garden of love here in Song undoes the curses and chaos of another garden myth, that of Genesis 2–3?[107]

Now that *dodi* has built suspense on suspense from wilderness to garden almost to its breaking point, *ra'yati* responds, though disjunctively, by addressing the winds in 4:16a. Perhaps her intent is that these winds would stir up her fragrances—the ones *dodi* listed in 4:13–14— drawing him to her scent. Soon enough, that turns into an indirect summons to her beloved: "let *dodi* come to his garden, and eat its excellent fruits" (4:16b). Notably, she gives a nod to their status as a couple by calling him to this, "*his* garden." Furthermore, the verb and preposition choice, "let him come into" (from the root בוא, *bv'*) is a transparent euphemism for sex, even in English.[108]

Dodi's response to this in 5:1a consummates both lovers' fantasies to the detail. He opens with the same suggestive verb with which *ra'yati* summoned him, announcing "I come" (בוא, *bv'*). He repeats his own descriptions of her: "wine," "spice," "honey" and "milk" (4:10, 11, 14). Emphatically he claims *ra'yati*, as she invited him to do in 4:16b. The

106. For an informative description of the various plants and spices listed in 4:13–14, see Exum, *Song*, 177–80.

107. Trible, *God and the Rhetoric*, 72–143.

108. For instance, Gen 6:4; 16:2; 19:31; 30:3; 38:8 9; 39:14; Deut 22:13; 25:5; Judg 15:1; 16:1; 2 Sam 12:24; 16:21; 20:3; Ezra 23:44; Prov 6:29. In contrast with this list, our example in Song 14:16 uses the preposition – ל *l-*, whereas these are paired with אל *'el* or על *'al*.

long "i" sound of the first person singular verbal form or possessive suffix ends every word but one in 5:1a: בָּאתִי *bo'ti* "I come," לְגַנִּי *legani* "to my garden," אֲחֹתִי *'ahoti* "my sister," אָרִיתִי *'ariti* "I pluck," מוֹרִי *mori* "my myrrh," שָׂמִי *sami* "my spice," אָכַלְתִּי *'akalti* "I eat," יַעְרִי *ya'ri* "my honeycomb," דִּבְשִׁי *divshi* "my honey," שָׁתִיתִי *shatiti* "I drink," יֵינִי *yeyni* "my wine," and חֲלָבִי *halavi* "my milk." Thus his song creates a rhyming sound effect that bespeaks his joy in their union. *Dodi*'s repeated verbal claim for his love expresses the constancy and depth of his desire for her, as though he had pinned her, offered his class ring, gotten on his knee to propose, carried her over the threshold, and made love to her through the whole honeymoon.

By this point it seems clear that *ra'yati*'s elusive, distant, wild, tasty, fragrant sexuality has not remained off-limits to *dodi*—responding to each other's mutual enticements, they have indeed delighted in one another. All of the verbs in 5:1 suggest such intimacy, though some are more evocative than others. In any case, we can be relatively certain that the singer in this verse intends to describe himself as a lover, not a gardener, who wants to feast with—and on—his love.

We cannot be sure who is speaking in 5:1b, or to whom, but the imperative verbs ("eat, drink, be drunk") suggest either a mixed or a male audience. Perhaps *dodi*, in his bliss, has gone to sing love's praises to his friends, or perhaps these are *ra'yati*'s girlfriends, chiming in with encouragement for the young lovers.[109] Though, as we have seen, the lovers hardly need encouragement. As it stands, this closing comment reinforces the passion of the lovers for the sake of the readers, drawing us into the scene by fanning the flames of love for audiences across the millennia.

Ra'yati Sings about *Dodi*—He is Out of Reach (5:2–8)

The song in 5:2–7 describes a distinct scene, though as usual in Song, we are unsure if we are hearing about a fantasy, dream, or real events; we struggle to know whether to understand the lyrics literally or figuratively. The episode is at once vivid and obscure. In 5:2b–6aα we might think that *dodi* and *ra'yati* have attempted a rendezvous, or even consummated

---

109. Exum argues for this by asserting that Song really only has three "characters" who participate in the dialogue: *dodi*, *ra'yati*, and the "daughters of Jerusalem." Thus, unless we assume that the book suddenly adds new characters here, the daughters must be the audience in 5:1b (*Song*, 182–83).

their love in a suspense-filled nighttime tryst. Yet according to 5:6aβ-7 and even 5:3, it seems that something has actually foiled the couple's union. Perhaps *ra'yati*, undressed and bathed for sleep, just could not get to the door in time (5:6). Or, maybe the mores of society conspired to keep them apart, or to subdue *ra'yati* into a more stereotypical female role (5:7). Exum rightly notes the marvelous way in which the lyricist simultaneously describes the couple's distance and their intimacy through the use of double entendre, which is suggestive yet not fully allegorical.[110]

One question this raises is whether the vocabulary in this section is full of sexual imagery—or not. Several words and phrases suggest as much since they function as euphemisms elsewhere in the biblical text. Yet other language in the passage cannot be identified as sexually suggestive elsewhere in the canon. Nonetheless, based on the sexually charged context of Song as a whole, this section hints at physical intimacy and even passionate lovemaking. The pericope opens with *ra'yati* describing her state of partial sleep (5:2). As though summoned by *ra'yati*'s half-awake heart, we are suddenly roused with her by the sound of her beloved, *dodi*. And then he speaks, or we might assume that he shouts, as though through a door that is not named in the lyric, but implied by his knocking. He addresses *ra'yati* with a verb that will repeat throughout the section: "Open." As though he needs to clarify, he pleads in this imperative sentence, "Open *to me*." Notably, "open" has no object; this intransitive verb will continue to tease the reader throughout this song.

The eager *dodi* goes on to use some of his favorite terms of endearment for his love: In 5:1 he resumed (as in 4:9–12) calling her "my sister"; this time pairing that name with *ra'yati* rather than "my bride," which he used in the preceding section. His gushing continues with him claiming her as "my dove" (cf. 1:15); he completes his extravagant address of 5:2a by deeming her "complete," or "perfect." At the end of 5:2, we finally get a little more information about the scene: Apparently his journey to *ra'yati* took long enough that he became covered with the night's dew.

In 5:3, *ra'yati* extends her narration from 5:2a. Here, she either explains why she cannot get to the door, or she euphemistically describes their lovemaking. Does her nakedness (5:3a) prevent her from seeing

---

110. Exum writes, "This slippage from one mode to another, the blurring of distinctions between the more literal level of wishing, dreaming, desiring and the figurative level of consummation is one of the poetic techniques that makes the Song so sensual" (*Song*, 190).

dodi, or does it enable their intimacy? Do her "washed feet" (5:3b) indicate that she has retired for the night, or does that refer to their sexual union? As we saw in Ruth, "feet" is frequently a euphemism for "genitals" in the Hebrew Bible (Deut 16:24; Judg 3:24; Ruth 3:4, 7, 8, 14; 2 Kgs 18:27; Ezek 16:24). Furthermore, in 2 Sam 11:8–11, using the same Hebrew words as in this passage, David tells Uriah to "go to your house and wash your feet." Confirming the euphemism, Uriah replies to David, "Why should I lie with my wife when all the other warriors are on the battlefield?" Thus, there is precedent in the Hebrew Bible for this phrase at least as a male double entendre for sex. As usual, the singer of Song leaves the passage beguilingly open to interpretation; we cannot be sure exactly what these lyrics describe.

If that were not intriguing enough, the next verse (5:4) considerably ups the ante. There, *ra'yati* sings that "my beloved stretched out his hand into the hole, and my insides stirred for him." The combination of the same Hebrew words for "hand" and "stretch out" occurs in Deut 25:11. There, the wife of a man in a fight "grabs" his opponent's "genitals" (NRSV); in that case, the Hebrew word for "hand" euphemistically represents "genitals." Furthermore, "hole" in 5:4 certainly sounds like a euphemism, given the context. However, it is not used euphemistically elsewhere in the Hebrew Bible. Finally, "insides" in 5:4 (NRSV has "inmost being;" NIV "heart;" KJV "bowels") can refer to the womb (מֵעֶה *me'eh*, Gen 25:23; Ruth 1:11; Ps 71:6). This all rightly causes us to wonder about various meanings of Song 5:4. Is *dodi* fumbling with the door while *ra'yati* listens eagerly from her bed? Does this scene graphically describe their foreplay and lovemaking, even referring to her climax, with the phrase "my insides stirred for him?" Does the songstress want to tease us with both possibilities without offering a clear resolution? Again, Song fascinates us precisely because of such intriguing ambiguity.

At the beginning of 5:5, *ra'yati* sings, "I arose to open to *dodi*." We might assume that she is getting out of bed, based on 5:2a and 3, but the text does not specify that. Nor, as we saw above, does it offer an object for the verb "open." She "arose to open" what? The door? Herself? This question persists in 5:6 with another instance of "open" used as an intransitive verb. Some English translations (NRSV, NIV) heighten this word play by rendering "hole" in 5:4 as "opening," though that does not represent the same root as "open" in 5:5.

We also find in 5:5 a parallelism about the myrrh that dripped and flowed from her hands. Are her hands for some reason dripping with myrrh, or is she euphemistically describing her own sexual excitement? Perhaps she was in the middle of applying this fragrance to her body (Song 1:12; 4:13–14) or bed (Prov 7:17), and had it all over her hands. Another possibility is that she had actually anointed the door, something we find in some ancient settings.[111] Again, the poetess may be using wordplay here. As we saw in 5:4a, the word for "hand" in 5:5a refers to genitalia in some instances (for instance, see Isa 57:8; NRSV translates the Hebrew word "hand" as "nakedness"). Finally, NRSV closes 5:5b with the phrase "handles of the bolt." Yet this is the only case in which a rather common word means "handles"—its primary definition is the "hollow, or flat of the hand, palm, sole of foot."[112] Based on that, we find a few uses that seem to indicate a hand or palm-shaped (slightly curved) object, such as a pan (Exod 37:16) or branch (Lev 23:40). We can be justified in wondering whether this lyric refers to a fragrant cosmetic and a door-latch, or to a sketchy description of sexual excitement and play.

"I arose to open to *dodi*" in 5:5 finds completion in 5:6 with the suggestive "I opened to *dodi*." Though that seems like it would be the culmination to the scene, it is foiled almost immediately with *dodi*'s unexplained departure. The song turns into a sad ballad from there on, with *ra'yati* perhaps becoming breathless, instead of beckoning to *dodi* in response (5:6bα). She goes on to search and call for her beloved, to no avail. The end of 5:6 illustrates that well with a parallelism about her fruitless hunt for *dodi*, abruptly shifting the tone from the preceding verses.

The scene deteriorates further when, instead of *ra'yati* finding *dodi*, the city guards find *ra'yati*. The pair of verbs at the center of 5:7 report that the guards "beat" and "wounded" her. What a contrast from 5:4 to 6aα. The passage began with *ra'yati* voluntarily disrobed (5:3); it ends with her forcibly unveiled (5:7). Though the Hebrew words are not the same, it nonetheless creates an inclusio effect and a striking reversal. An earlier reference to these guards as well as a similar scene of the lovers seeking one another are good reasons to consider this scene as a parallel to 3:1–6.[113]

111. Pope, *Song*, 522.

112. *BDB*, 496a.

113. Exum, *Song*, 186–202; Fox, *Song*, 143.

A variation on the refrain to the daughters of Jerusalem additionally marks the end of this section (5:8). Only its opening imperative is
the same as the other refrains (1:5; 2:7; 3:5, 10, 11; 4:16). In this instance,
it seems *ra'yati* is calling on her girlfriends for help. Illustrating priorities
that only make sense for a person in love, *ra'yati* does not call on her
friends to rescue her from the abusive guards, but instead asks them to
tell *dodi*–if they find him—that she is lovesick.

Ra'yati Sings to Her Girlfriends about *Dodi* (5:9—6:3)

Ra'yati's girlfriends do not have many lines in Song (1:8; 5:9; 8:5a), but
5:9 is surely the most poetic. In response to the familiar refrain in 5:8,
the daughters employ a lovely parallelism, repeating the phrase "how is
your beloved different from another beloved?" in 5:9aα // 5:9bα.[114] They
even use *ra'yati's* own verb from this and the other refrains, "implore."
Thus, not only does 5:9 serve as the daughters' response to *ra'yati's* refrain, it allows for a transition to *ra'yati's* *wasf* about *dodi*. Her girlfriends
ask her what's so special about her beloved, and she obliges with a song
about just that in 5:10–16a. This context sets *ra'yati's* *wasf* in 5:10–16a
apart from *dodi's* *wasf*s. While *dodi* sings his *wasf*s directly to his lover,
ra'yati sings about her beloved to her girlfriends.[115]

Ra'yati Responds, Singing a wasf for *Dodi* (5:10–16a)

In *ra'yati's* song of 5:10–16a, she describes *dodi* as most prized among
gems, precious metals, fine perfumes, and architecture of the rich and
famous. He is a luxury villa; he is an irresistibly head-turning fragrance,
music, and vision. In the opening verse (5:10), he stands out among all
others like a "banner," a theme that also appears in 2:4; 6:4, 10 (NIV and
NRSV translate this word as "outstanding"). She additionally illustrates
him as distinctively glowing, and red. By the time *ra'yati* finishes her
paean, she will have verbally painted her beloved with at least five different colors.

Renita Weems interprets the comment about *dodi's* ruddiness
(5:10) as an indication of his complexion in comparison to *ra'yati's*: he is
"red," while she is "black" (1:5). The former reads as a compliment (cf. 1
Sam 16:12, 17:42); the latter, cause for defensiveness (Song 1:6). Yet both

---

114. Murphy also identifies 5:10–15 as a response to 5:9 (*Song*, 61).

115. Exum points this out, *Song*, 203.

may have originated from outdoor labor. In the context of this *wasf*, a literal understanding seems far from certain. Nonetheless, Weems rightly raises it for consideration, wondering whether there was some kind of gender double-standard at work.[116]

That *ra'yati* comments next on *dodi*'s head (5:11) suggests that the previous verse was indeed about his face, although that is not explicit. In keeping with the *wasf* genre, this description begins with one end of his body, and moves to the other. In this portion of the song, his head and face receive much attention; *ra'yati*'s lyrics move downward from there.

In this *wasf*, *ra'yati* employs a whole palette of colors to describe her beloved. His reddish face, golden head, black hair and the milky whites of his eyes only begin the color scheme, which continues with even more brilliance through 5:15. In 5:11–12, the colors seem too abundant to make sense. How can his face be "red," and his head "gold," while his locks are "black?" *Ra'yati* describes his head as "gold" using two different Hebrew words in 5:11a; the latter specifically means "pure, refined, fine gold." Perhaps she was indicating the value or preciousness of *dodi*'s head, rather than its color, while she posed the other two descriptions more literally. Indeed, other uses of this Hebrew word for "gold" serve as a point of comparison to illustrate value (Lam 4:2; Job 28:17; Ps 119:127; Prov 8:19).

In 5:12, reminiscent of 1:15 and 4:1, *ra'yati* describes *dodi*'s eyes as doves. Perhaps he takes flirtatious peeks at her, like a dove playing hide-and-seek by a stream? She admires the milky whites of his perfectly set eyes. Imagery of milk and a spring of water return here from 4:11 and 15.

Ra'yati again explores the theme of fragrance in 5:13, explaining why she finds *dodi*'s cheeks and lips so alluring. Different vowel marks in ancient texts provide two different readings of the Hebrew in 5:13aβ: His cheeks are either "towers of perfume," or they "put forth perfume." Either of these possibilities fit, and we cannot be certain which is correct. The latter translation provides a fitting parallelism with 5:13b, in which *dodi*'s lips "drip with flowing myrrh." Furthermore, that reading reminds us of *ra'yati*'s perfumed body parts (1:12; 4:13–14). However, the translation "towers of perfume" allows for an intriguing connection to Song 4:4, 7:5, and 8:10, which use the same Hebrew word in comparing *ra'yati* to "towers." Finally, the now-familiar "lily" reappears here. Delightfully,

---

116. Weems, "Song," 5:415–16.

in this case lilies indicate *dodi*'s lips, while elsewhere in Song, they allude to *ra'yati*'s body; lilies among which her beloved's lips grazed (2:1–2; 4:5; 6:2–3; 7:2).

True to form, *ra'yati*'s *wasf* lyrics move down *dodi*'s body to describe his arms—or his fingers. *Ra'yati* opens 5:14 singing literally that "his hands are rods of gold." However, fingers or arms make more sense as rods than do hands, and this Hebrew word indicates "arm" elsewhere (see Gen 49:24). Interestingly, Isa 57:8 uses this word "hand" as euphemistic for genitals. While this allows for more intriguing innuendo and may well be a euphemistic intent, that reference would be out of place in this portion of the *wasf*. The "gold" indicated here heightens *dodi*'s value—it is the third different word for gold in this *wasf* (see 5:11). As if that weren't good enough, *ra'yati* adds that this gold is filled with precious jewels—perhaps indicating his fingernails or jewelry.[117]

Ra'yati accentuates this illustration of his arms with a parallelism in 5:14b about his jewel-encrusted body. The unusual Hebrew vocabulary apparently states, "his body is a bar of ivory, encrusted with lapis lazuli." The word for "body" has wide-ranging meaning, including references to procreation. For instance, one way to describe "offspring" is to say "the one who comes forth from his *body*" (Gen 15:4; 2 Sam 7:12, 16:11). Decorating the "bar," or "plate of ivory" are gems, which have traditionally been translated "sapphire," but are more likely lapis lazuli. In ancient Egyptian literature, these gems typically represent beautiful hair.[118] Given those points of comparison, perhaps her lyric here teasingly hints at his erection as nothing less impressive than an "ivory rod," surrounded by dark hair like precious jewels.

Whether or not this love song intended such sexual innuendo, we should note that in other parts of the Hebrew Bible, these precious materials convey even greater value than they do in English. They are the stuff of royal wealth (1 Kgs 10:18; Ezek 28:13), priestly honor (Exod 28:18, 20), even utopian and divine visions (Exod 24:10; Ezek 1:26; Dan 10:6). Similarly, other ancient near eastern literature makes equally extravagant comparisons in describing one's lover, even in describing the gods.[119] *Ra'yati* could hardly muster more glorious imagery for her beloved.

117. Gen 24:30, 47; Ezek 16:11; 23:42; Jer 38:12.

118. See P. Chester Beatty I, Group A, 31(C) cited in Fox, *Song*, 52; Exum, *Song*, 207. Keel cites additional references from other ancient Egyptian literature, *Song*, 202.

119. Exum, *Song*, 208–9, Keel, *Song*, 202–4.

Ra'yati's description continues downward to *dodi's* legs (5:15), apparently upping the ante from what she has said about his arms. Here she continues to conjure his body with highly valuable elements, including yet another mention of "gold," the same word used of his head back in 5:11. We cannot be sure what other materials poetically refer to his legs—marble, or alabaster, or some other kind of opulent surface. Nonetheless, we can be sure that from 5:11 to 14 to 15, *ra'yati* describes her beloved as a treasure fit for royalty, complete with gemstones and precious metals. He is more valuable than money could buy. *Ra'yati's* song about her beloved then shifts from luxury goods to a place of great beauty and wealth in 5:15b: Lebanon.[120] This reference further categorized *dodi* as a superb catch.

The *wasf* ends with 5:16a; oddly, it seems to return to the top of his body with praise for his mouth in v. 16aα. While that could function as a poetic echo of 5:13,[121] the intent may be something more abstract than a compliment about his smile. While this Hebrew word literally means "mouth" or "palate," elsewhere it relates to speech and even taste, as in Song 2:3 and 7:10 (also see Prov 5:3; 8:7; 24:13 and Job 12:11; 33:2). Similarly, this reference in Song could refer to his words, or voice, as NRSV translates. The adjective she uses, "sweet," can function metaphorically, but it certainly suggests his literal taste as well. Finally, this *wasf* concludes in 5:16aβ like it began in 5:9, with a summary about *dodi's* magnificence. Here, *ra'yati* calls her beloved "entirely delightful." To help get that point across the singer has composed 5:16a in order to actually *sound* sweet—it even rhymes: חכו ממתקים וכלו מחמדים (*hiko mamtaqim vekulo mahamadim*).

Ra'yati Continues to Sing about Longing for *Dodi* (5:16b—6:3)

Following the *wasf* of 5:9–16a, *ra'yati* turns to her girlfriends, reminding us that they prompted the preceding love song back in 5:9. In 6:1, they prompt her to sing even more about him. In light of her songs thus far, her response in 6:2–3 sounds like a thinly-veiled reference to their night of lovemaking together.

120. See above explanation on Lebanon, in the commentary on 4:8.

121. Exum notes that this verse "looks back to her earlier praise of his lips" (*Song*, 202).

This section opens with the lovely statement of 5:16b, which concludes and in a way summarizes the *wasf;* at the same time, it sets up *ra'yati*'s following conversation with the daughters of Jerusalem. Notably, in 5:16b *ra'yati* gives *dodi* a new nickname: "friend." This marvelously illustrates a sense of mutuality between the lovers, as she uses the Hebrew word that is the masculine version of *dodi*'s name for her: רֵעִי *re'i.*

The progression of 6:1–3 suggests an intriguing double entendre. The girlfriends take up the theme of *dodi*'s hiddenness, and seek him as though he were separated from *ra'yati*. Yet her answer indicates that he is very much with her. As we have seen, the language of "garden," "spices," "graze," "lilies" have sexual implications elsewhere in Song (1:7, 8, 13; 2:16, 18; 3:6; 4: 5, 6, 12, 14, 15, 16; 5:1, 5, 13; 6:2, 3; 8:13). Have her girlfriends been teasing her about seeking him, when she had him all the time? Is she describing having just "found" him in "her garden"? In all likelihood, this verse tells of love made, rather than love sought.

Amid all of this innuendo, we cannot lose sight of this as impassioned love poetry. *Ra'yati*'s rhyming statement of 6:3a is a good reminder of that; it is a refrain she has already sung in reverse in 2:16, and she will sing something similar again in 7:10. The phrase אֲנִי לְדוֹדִי וְדוֹדִי לִי, *'ani ledodi vedodi li*, very literally translates "I am to/for my beloved (*dodi*), and my beloved (*dodi*) is to/for me," or "I am my beloved's, and my beloved is mine." Furthermore, it provides the effect of an inclusio with the beginning of this section, 5:16b. With this near repetition, she emphatically proclaims her love for *dodi* to him, to her girlfriends, and to readers for all time.

Dodi Sings a *Wasf* for *Ra'yati* (6:4–10)

This section consists of another love poem for *ra'yati* by *dodi*, and it includes numerous repetitions from his *wasf* in chapter 4. However, this section also contains some new and unusual militaristic imagery about *ra'yati*. In fact, those particular lyrics stand out in this section not only because of their uniqueness, but also because they book-end the *wasf*. "Terrible as battle-banner-bearers"[122] serves as an inclusio, appearing as an exact repetition in 6:4b and 10b.

Ra'yati compared him to Lebanon (3:9; 4:8,15; 5:15; 7:4); he compares her to Tirzah and Jerusalem (6:4). Tirzah was a northern Israelite

---

122. 6:4//6:10 both read אֲיֻמָּה כַּנִּדְגָּלוֹת *'ayumah kannidgalot.*

city of great significance. It even served as the capital for some time, so the reference probably connotes power and prestige; grandeur and glory. In addition, the Hebrew word "Tirzah" means "beautiful," likely attributable to its location in the lush northern hill country.[123] This aesthetic quality certainly has importance in the *wasf*. *Dodi*'s parallel phrase takes his compliment over the top—he adds "Jerusalem" as a point of comparison. That southern capital city was known as *the* spectacle of divine beauty high on a hill, famed for King Solomon's lavish palace and temple. Of course, Jerusalem had great military and religious value as well. These two locations in the same lyric express something like the magnificence we might identify with the phrase "from sea to shining sea."

The military prowess associated with Tirzah and Jerusalem may relate to the third phrase of 6:4. Odd as it seems, we cannot ignore this apparently displaced statement, "terrible as battle-banner-bearers"; the exact same comment reappears in 6:10. This word for "terrible" only occurs in one other place in the Hebrew Bible, in which it refers to enemy troops (Hab 1:7). The reference to "banners" exists elsewhere in Song in various forms. Besides here and in 6:10, we find it in 2:4, where *ra'yati* sings that "his banner over me was love."[124] The same root appears in 5:10 as a verb, where *ra'yati* uses it to say that *dodi* is "distinguished" (NRSV) from all others; he provokes attention, possibly as would an army's banner. In light of this context, perhaps here *dodi* means to return *ra'yati*'s compliment from 5:10, noting her striking attractiveness. Or, we might consider the whole phrase as analogous to our contemporary use of "bad" or "dangerous" as praise for a love interest, when spoken with the right tone of voice and glimmer in the eye.

In 6:5a *dodi* appears almost intimidated by *ra'yati*'s attention. He wants her to avert her eyes because of their effect on him. The meaning of this verb ranges from "alarm" to "pride."[125] The fact that *dodi* goes on to sing *ra'yati* a *wasf* indicates that his feelings are more of awe and affection than anxiety or fright. Pope and Keel capture this well in their translations "they drive me wild" and "they make me crazy."[126] In his

123. *BDB* 953b.

124. See above discussion re: 2:4.

125. *BDB*, 923a הִרְהִיבֻנִי *hirhhivuni*; also see Psalm 138:3 for the other use of this verb in the *hiphil*.

126. Respectively, Pope, *Song*, 551, 564 and Keel, *Song*, 211, 215.

wasf of 6:5b-7, *dodi* notably repeats 4:1b–2b and 3b almost word for word from his earlier *wasf* of 4:1–7.[127]

In 6:8–10 *dodi* slightly shifts from this description song to singing *ra'yati*'s highest praises. Here he returns to the comparisons he made in 6:4, where he contrasted her with impressive cities. Now she is his "Miss Universe," not only as compared to other women (6:8), but also when pitted against the very heavenly bodies (6:10). He counts "sixty queens," "eighty concubines," and "young women without number" (6:8).[128] Those figures prepare an element of surprise when he offers his next number twice in 6:9, "one." Clearly *dodi* ranks *ra'yati* as *the* singular woman, "perfect" and "flawless." His affections for her are rivaled only by those of her mother. Even the impressive harem he listed sings her praises. Those praises of *haleluha* (הַלְלוּהָ) call to mind the Psalmists' words for YHVH (Ps 22:22, among others). The divine implications heighten in 6:10. Here, comparisons to heavenly bodies may conjure divine be- ings. The closing military reference not only recalls 6:4, but perhaps in the context even suggests the heavenly host.[129] We can also hear divinity seeping from *dodi*'s paean to *ra'yati* in his use of the same adjective for the sun in 6:10 (literally, "the heat") as for *ra'yati* in 6:9: "flawless."[130]

Ra'yati Sings of *Dodi* (6:11–12)

The following section (6:11–12) presents numerous problems. Debate abounds among commentators who weigh questions including: "Who is speaking here, and what is he or she talking about?" "What is the best way to divide the verses following 6:10?" "How should we translate the many unintelligible words in this passage?" In my interpretation, the singing shifts to *ra'yati* in 6:11–12. My justification for this view is that the verse is paired with v. 12, which I read as one of *ra'yati*'s fantasies about *dodi*. I must concede that there is no scholarly consensus on either

127. See above section on 4:1–7 for discussion on the imagery here.

128. While this harem is indeed sizeable, it does not indicate King Solomon's ha- rem, per se, which numbered "700 princesses and 300 concubines" (1 Kgs 11:3; Exum, *Song*, 221). Exum and Weems also note a possible connection between this passage and the list of "mighty men" in Song 3:7 (Exum, *Song*, 221; Weems, "Song," 5:419).

129. See Keel, *Song*, 220 for possible inferences about the goddess Ishtar in this sec- tion.

130. Exum translates this "splendid," to encompass its range of meaning from "pure" to "brilliant" (*Song*, 223).

part of this explanation, nor of its meaning. My interpretation leads to yet more questions: Is *ra'yati* describing a walk in a garden, which leads her to fantasize about being with *dodi* in a chariot? Or do her words contain enough innuendo to suggest that her "walk in a garden" is actually an erotic tryst with *dodi*, which she describes as a royal chariot-ride?

In 6:11 her adventure begins in a "nut garden." This would easily seem euphemistic for male genitalia in English, and some evidence does suggest this was also the case in the ancient world, both for male and female sex organs.[131] The word for "nut" (אֱגוֹז *'egoz*) appears only here, so we have no other basis in the Hebrew Bible for interpreting it as sexual innuendo. "The valley" (נַחַל *nahal*) in 6:11a sometimes refers to a "*wadi*"(stream bed), and can indicate a fertile place (Num 13:23–24). Her reference to "vine" (גֶּפֶן *gephen*) recalls the same word in 2:13, where *ra'yati* quoted *dodi* in another sequence rife with fecundity; this also points ahead to references to "vine" in 7:8 and 12 (Heb 7:9 and 13). Based on their own contexts, these allusions in ch. 7 increase the likelihood that *ra'yati* intends something more intimate here than a stroll in the garden. Additionally, "vine" in Psalm 128:3 indicates the fertility of a "wife." Finally in 6:11, we find a familiar fruit in Song, a "pomegranate" (רִמֹּנִים *ramonim*). While this appears in *dodi*'s *wasf* imagery to describe *ra'yati*'s cheeks (4:3//6:7), elsewhere it appears to be more sexually suggestive (4:13 and 8:2, and possibly 6:11). With so much fertility imagery and so many possible euphemisms, *ra'yati* tempts us to wonder what she has in mind here.

Ra'yati closes out this short scene with an odd statement—almost a non-sequitur.[132] "Before I knew it, my imagination put me in a chariot beside my nobleman" (6:12). This translation gives the false illusion of clarity, when in fact the Hebrew of this verse is practically incoherent.[133] The word for "my imagination" is נֶפֶשׁ (*nephesh*). Often translated "spirit," "soul" or even "self," it apparently indicates the driving force behind her fantasy here. This word would not make sense if the passage were to be read as an actual event. The verse finishes with problematic wording, which may mean "nobleman," though a transliteration of the

131. Pope, *Song*, 577–78.

132. This supports the view of Keel, who divides vv. 11–12 into separate sections (*Song*, 225–29).

133. For lengthier discussions on this verse, and the various possibilities of its translation, see Pope, *Song*, 584–92; Fox, *Song*, 156; Keel, *Song*, 225–26; Exum, *Song*, 224–25.

Hebrew could be understood as an obscure proper name, "Amminidib."[134] Despite the ambiguities, it seems that *ra'yati* could very well be talking about *dodi*.

Dodi's Songs about *Ra'yati* (6:13—7:9)

This section begins with a one-verse interchange that contains nearly as much difficulty as the preceding two verses. Again, various scholarly theories and translations abound for 6:13 (7:1 in Hebrew). I identify 6:13a as a song about *ra'yati*, though it is unclear who is singing. Verse 13a opens with the four-time repeated call to "return." These imperatives are directed at someone called "the Shulammite." This obscure reference has been read by many interpreters over the years as identifying the woman whose voice we hear throughout Song. In the context of the book so far, it would make some sense that *ra'yati* is the one being called to and looked at here. The meaning of "the Shulammite" varies from "the perfect, unblemished one" (based on an understanding of the word as a form of שָׁלוֹם *shalom*) to identifying one from Shunem (as in 1 Kgs 1:15 and 2 Kgs 4:12) or even one from Jerusalem.[135] Whatever this title means, we still must wonder who is doing the calling and looking, and why?

The grammar clearly indicates a group of voices speaking. Perhaps, based on v. 13b, some unnamed groups in two camps are watching *ra'yati* dance and thus calling her to them in 13a. Or, possibly *ra'yati's* girlfriends were calling her to return from her fantasy in the previous verse.[136] They, after all, are the usual group to speak in Song, and for that reason would make more sense than some suddenly-interjected unidentified groups of encampments. If this is the girlfriends' call, however, they have made a surprise entrance—and quick exit—in the context. In either case, 6:13b could be *dodi's* response, defending her from the apparent ogling of this group.

Because these speculations are yet again based on ambiguous Hebrew, we cannot be sure about what is going on here, or who is talking. Having dealt with these three utterly obscure verses (6:11–13

134. Keel advocates this route, and explains the meaning of Amminidib as "my uncle is noble" (*Song*, 226). KJV also translates "Amminidib" here.

135. Fox advocates "the perfect, unblemished one," and lists three additional options (*Song*, 157–58). Exum lists "Jerusalemite" as one of many options (*Song*, 226–28).

136. With Keel, *Song*, 228.

[Heb 6:11—7:1]), we must acknowledge the possibility that they are an inexplicable redaction, or awkward insertion into Song. Thankfully, in the next section we return to familiar material for the Song of Songs: another *wasf* from *dodi* for *ra'yati*.

Dodi Sings Another *Wasf* for *Ra'yati* (7:1–9 [Heb 7:2–10])

In this *wasf*, *dodi* begins his description of *ra'yati* with her "feet in sandals," enlisting one of his favorite words, "beautiful" (יָפֶה, *yph*, also see Song 1:15 [twice], 16; 2:10, 13; 6:4, 10; 7:6 [7:7 Heb]), and reminiscent of other instances where sandals were alluring (Ezek 16:10), alluring (Jdt 10:4, 16:9) or powerful (Ruth 4:7; Deut 25:5–10).[137] In a connection to *ra'yati*'s apparent fantasy about *dodi* as a "nobleman" in 6:12, he uses the same word to refer to her. Here the word for "daughter" (בַּת *bat*) precedes "noble" (נָדִיב *nadiv*), giving rise to translations such as "prince's daughter" (NIV) and "queenly maiden" (NRSV). If *ra'yati* were indeed fantasizing about *dodi* in 6:12, this provides a poetic response to that scenario. As *dodi* verbally moves up *ra'yati*'s body, he describes her curvaceous thigh as the ornamental creation of a "master worker." Only used here in this exact form, a very closely related word appears in Prov 8:30 to describe the role of Wisdom in creation.

Dodi's words gradually move above *ra'yati*'s thigh, though the exact location is uncertain—and perhaps intentionally so. The Hebrew in 7:2 [Heb 7:3] may mean "umbilical cord" (as in Ezek 16:4) or even "vulva." An Arabic cognate means "secret part," which seems more likely to indicate vulva and/or vagina—though perhaps euphemistically—than belly.[138] Furthermore, *dodi* describes this body part as a "bowl," or "basin," and then redundantly affirms its "roundness." Finally, he notes that this round bowl "never lacks mixed wine." The word translated "mixed wine" is a *hapax*, and may simply mean some kind of liquid mixture; the Arabic indicates water mixed with wine. It seems more likely that he is describing her wet genitals as ready for his lovemaking, than that he wants to drink belly shots out of her navel.[139] Other possibly sexual refer-

137. Citations from Keel, *Song*, 231.

138. *BDB*, 1057a.

139. With Pope (*Song*, 617–19) and Keel (*Song*, 234). Exum reviews the options and the ambiguities of the phrase (*Song*, 233–34). Also see Fox, who argues for this interpretation (*Song*, 158–59).

ences to wine in Song strengthen this argument (e.g., 5:1; 7:9 [Heb 7:10]; 8:2). Given the content, it is remarkable that the poet has succeeded in crafting such a lyrical and delicate verse without ever sounding crude.[140]

Perhaps in 7:2b [Heb 7:3b] *dodi's wasf* moves to *ra'yati's* belly, though euphemistic undertones persist. The Hebrew word in this instance commonly refers to "belly," and even "womb." Here, *dodi* calls *ra'yati's* belly a "heap of wheat," possibly a curvy belly—which he may or may not have viewed as attractive.[141] *Dodi* returns to one of Song's frequent images when he says that *ra'yati's* belly is "fenced about" or "bordered with lilies." Above, we saw various meanings for "lily" throughout Song, some more suggestive than others (see 2:16; 4:5; 5:13; 6:2–3 and the corresponding commentary sections). In the next line *dodi* repeats himself from 4:5a in comparing *ra'yati's* "breasts" to "gazelles."

The next stop in *dodi's* body poem is *ra'yati's* neck (7:4 [Heb 7:5]). He gave us the infamous "tower of David" comparison for her neck in 4:4, but here the immediate effect is more obviously complimentary. In this simile, her "neck is like an ivory tower." Moving further up her body, he calls her eyes "pools in Heshbon beside the gate of Beth-rabbim." Heshbon lies in a Moabite city that was sporadically occupied by various ancient Israelite tribes. Archaeological remains show evidence of a tenth century BCE, 23-foot deep reservoir there.[142] Perhaps *dodi* had seen or heard of something like this, prompting his poetry. As usual, we cannot be sure what *dodi* intended with these geographic references, but in a region like Palestine or Moab, such a reserve of water would likely have been viewed as a precious commodity. It would also have had qualities such as reflection of light; a poet might say "glimmer." Exum suggests the possible play on words between "eyes" and "spring" (both עַיִן *'ayin*).[143]

140. With Murphy, who praises the Song by noting "although the poetry is explicitly erotic in its appreciation of sexual love, it never becomes prurient or pornographic" (*Song*, 102).

141. Athalya Brenner suggests that this, among numerous other features in this *wasf*, lend it the quality of parody. She writes, "Interpreting the allusion to the dancer's obvious corpulence as an adoring remark within the present context seems to me to be conditioned by the wish to view 7.1ff. as straightforward praise, much like the other *wasfs*. If we are willing to consider the present poem as a humorous offshoot of the *wasf* convention . . . another picture emerges. The dancer is, frankly, fat, her belly in dance motion is big and quivering, much like an unstable mound of wheat" ("'Come Back,'" 247–48).

142. LaBianca, "Heshbon," 585–86.

143. Exum, *Song*, 235.

Dodi returns to familiar imagery when he gets to *ra'yati*'s nose, which he compares to the "tower of Lebanon, which looks out over Damascus" (7:4 [7:5 Heb]). This is the third tower *dodi* has enlisted in order to praise *ra'yati*'s body (4:4 (twice); 7:4a, 4b), and the seventh time "Lebanon" has appeared in Song (3:9; 4:8 (twice), 11, 15; 5:15; 7:4). Finally, *dodi* praises *ra'yati*'s hair, and her head in general. Again, he refers to a place name: "Your head is upon you like Carmel" (7:5 [Heb 7:6]). This may indicate *ra'yati*'s remarkable height or stature, an attribute to which *dodi* apparently returns in 7:8 (7:9 Heb).[144] He sings of her hair's purple-red color, which calls to mind the textiles used in the tabernacle and temple (Ex 25:4; 35:25; 39:3), as well as Song 3:10 where it is the color of the King's love seat in *ra'yati*'s fantasy. That royal reference leads to 7:5b [Heb 7:6b], where *dodi* enlists *ra'yati*'s playful flirtation of himself as king. (1:12) This time, he views himself in a strange situation for a king: "captive." Of course, it makes more sense when we read that it is *ra'yati*'s flowing hair holding him prisoner. Having worked his way from toe to head, *dodi* closes out the *wasf* here.

As in the other *wasf*s, many of these images work as deep- rather than surface-level body descriptions.[145] We do not know *ra'yati*'s measurements, though we get the impression she is attractively curvy to *dodi*. We do not know the color of her eyes, nor if they are limpid, as 7:4 might indicate, yet *dodi* may have viewed her eyes as valuable, or even as a luxury destination in a distant land. We cannot be sure of her hair color, but *dodi* apparently finds it enchanting, perhaps even regal, along with her nose and neck.

While the *wasf* may technically have ended, *dodi* has not yet finished singing about his love—and her body. The sensual poetry of 7:6–9 [Heb 7:7–10] reminds us of *ra'yati*'s words in 2:3–6, though here *dodi*'s desires are more explicitly physical. This makes 7:6–9 a fitting post script for the *wasf* he just finished. The opening verse (7:6 [Heb 7:7]) echoes 7:1 [Heb 7:2] with *dodi*'s oft-repeated compliment for *ra'yati*: "beautiful" (יפה *yph*). Calling to mind his references to "Carmel" (7:5 [Heb 7:6])

144. Keel, *Song*, 236.

145. With Brenner, who remarks about *wasf*s, "If we look closely enough, however, no 'description' is actually obtained: by the end of the poem we still have no idea what the loved person looks like, in the sense that no *complete* image is communicated. It seems that the details given are primarily designed not to supply a photograph, so to speak, but to involve the reader's sense and emotions, inasmuch as they presumably reflect the heightened emotional state of the assumed speaker" ("Come Back," 235).

and "the tower of Lebanon," he describes her in 7:7 [Heb 7:8] as tall, but also edible—like a date-palm and its fruit clusters. Elsewhere this tree symbolizes sustenance and fertility (Exod 15:27; Joel 1:12). In 7:8 [Heb 7:9] however, *dodi* goes beyond description to action—at least how he desires to act. He wants to entwine with, explore, and apparently taste the tree that is *ra'yati*.

Throughout this section, *dodi* uses imagery that is familiar from other parts of Song. He moves from "palm-date clusters" to "vine clusters" in 7:8 (Heb 7:9). These recall many other references to the "vine" and "vineyard" in Song (1:6, 14; 2:13, 15; 6:11; 7:12 [7:13 Heb]; 8:11, 12), some of which carry sexually suggestive undertones. The reference in 7:7 (Heb 7:8) is explicitly sexual, with the date-palm clusters compared to *ra'yati*'s breasts, and *dodi* desiring to climb that tree in the following verse (7:8 [Heb 7:9]). Keel counters interpreters who take this and other references in Song to breasts as indications of an emphasis on fertility.[146]

Though 7:8b–9 (Heb 7:9b–10) contains numerous translation difficulties,[147] it seems that we find *dodi* longing for *ra'yati*'s apple-scented breath, recalling 2:3 and 2:5 and looking ahead to 8:5. While the apple was as valuable a fruit as any (Prov 25:11; Joel 1:12), it was not the fruit on the tree of the knowledge of good and evil (Gen 3:3, 6 use פְּרִי *pri*, the generic word for "fruit"), lest Milton's magnificent but extra-biblical imagery lead anyone astray.[148] *Dodi*'s fantasy about tasting continues when he speaks of *ra'yati*'s mouth at the opening of 7:9 [Heb 7:10]. Here he imagines—or experiences—her mouth like "wine," inserting another oft-used image in Song (1:2, 4; 4:10; 5:1; 7:2, 9 [Heb 7:10]; 8:2). He presumably imagines her "wine" "gliding smoothly" into his mouth, though the Hebrew does not specify the "lips and teeth" in 7:9 [Heb 7:10] as "his."[149]

---

146. Keel, *Song*, 246.

147. Song 7:8 (7:9 Heb) reads "the scent of your nose." Fox retains this translation and includes discussion about nose kissing (97, 163). While "the scent of your breath" has good support (Exum, *Song*, 239; NRSV; NIV; NASB), other interpretations include Pope, who understands "your nose" (אַפֵּךְ *'apek*) as "vulva" or "clitoris" (*Song*, 636).

148. Milton, *Paradise Lost*, vol. 9 line 585. In fact, the idea that this fruit was an "apple" arises from a Latin play on words, in which "*malum*, 'apple' = *malum*, 'evil'" (Keel, *Song*, 268 n. 1).

149. Indeed, the translation "teeth" is in the Greek, Syriac and Vulgate, not the Hebrew, which has "sleeping ones." A prior difficulty in 7:9 [7:10 Heb] is that the Hebrew literally reads, "your mouth is like the best wine, going smoothly for *dodi*." Many com-

Ra'yati Invites and Longs for Dodi (7:10—8:4)

In turn, *ra'yati* responds to *dodi's wasf* and fantasies with an invitation. Using much of his own imagery, she beckons him to her explicitly and intimately, and fully within the bounds of Song's poetry. She begins in 7:10 (7:11 Heb) with the third repetition of her "refrain to *dodi*" (see outline, above). It begins as usual, אֲנִי לְדוֹדִי *'ani ledodi* "I am *dodi's* . . ." In this case, it ends with ". . . and his longing is for me" וְעָלַי תְּשׁוּקָתוֹ *v'alay tashuqato*). In 6:3a the text reads, אֲנִי לְדוֹדִי וְדוֹדִי לִי, *'ani ledodi vedodi li* "I am my beloved's [*dodi*], and my beloved [*dodi*] is mine"; 2:16a contains the reverse דּוֹדִי לִי וְאֲנִי לוֹ (*dodi li veani lo*) "my beloved [*dodi*] is mine and I am his." The change to "longing," or "desire" (תְּשׁוּקָתוֹ *tashukato*) in 7:10 (7:11 Heb) strikes numerous commentators as a significant connection to Genesis 3:16 where the woman's "longing" (תְּשׁוּקָתֵךְ *tashukatk*) for the man was part of her punishment after eating from the tree of the knowledge of good and evil. Perhaps this signals a repair of that breach.[150]

This familiar refrain leads her to summon him to "the fields," and to "pass the night in the henna" (7:11 [Heb 7:12]).[151] From there she entices him to "start early to the vineyards"—they will be looking for buds and blossoms, with 7:12 (Heb 7:13) listing no less than four different words for "bud" or "blossom." From grapevines to pomegranates, blooming fruits have appeared before in Song, with various shades of innuendo (1:14; 2:13, 15; 4:3//6:7). *Ra'yati* sang some of these same lines in 6:11b.

---

mentators puzzle over why the verse suddenly addresses *dodi* if he is supposed to be the speaker. My preference is to understand "*dodi*" based on its simple meaning "my beloved," in which case the man (whom I have identified as "*dodi*" throughout) is here referring to the woman as "my beloved," even though it is usually her pet name for him. Other options abound for how to resolve this, including omitting the word from the translation of the verse (NRSV, NIV [omits all but 9aα], RSV, Pope, *Song*, 639); reading it as an interjection from *ra'yati* into *dodi's wasf* (Fox, *Song*, 162–163); or as a reference to both *dodi* and *ra'yati* ("flowing smoothly to lovers," Exum [with Gordis], *Song*, 212, 214, 239); Pope rehearses these possibilities and more (*Song*, 639).

150. This Hebrew word (תְּשׁוּקָה *teshuqah*) appears only in Song 7:10 (Heb 7:11) and in Gen 3:16. For more on the connection between these two passages, see Weems, "Song," 5:428; Fox, *Song*, 163–164; Exum, *Song*, 241; Trible, *God and the Rhetoric*, 159–60.

151. The word for "henna," כְּפָרִים, *kepharim*, appears in this exact form in Song 4:13. However, the word can also mean "villages," a translation that appears in NRSV, RSV, and NIV. Keel makes the logical point that "villages" "would not achieve the goal of being alone" (*Song*, 254).

Furthermore, in 5:2, 5 and 6 she used the same root for "open" as we find here in reference to the grapes. In this bountiful and even romantic context, *ra'yati* proclaims she will "give . . . my love (דֹדַי, *doday*)." These verses have a similar sense as 4:16, though the vocabulary differs. At the very least, chapter 7, verses 11–12 (12–13 Heb) fantasize about or fulfill a night of making love in a lush garden; on another level they allude to the couple's actual love play, with her body as the garden.[152]

The next verse (7:13 [7:14 Heb]) opens with דֹודִי *dodi*, which here serves as a play on "my love" דֹדַי, *doday* from the close of 7:12 [7:13 Heb]. "Mandrakes" הַדּוּדָאִים (*haduda'im*) make it even more clear that *ra'yati*'s intent—or at least her fantasy—is about more than a walk in the vineyard or orchard. Besides its similar sound to "my love," mandrakes were known as the love and fertility potion of their time (Gen 30:14–16). The opening of this verse in which "the mandrakes give forth their scent" contains the same vocabulary as 1:12, except that refers to *ra'yati*'s "nard" instead of "mandrakes." Surely, the verses both indicate arousal. We cannot be certain of the meaning of something "excellent" (מֶגֶד, *meged*, probably fruit) over the "opening" (פֶּתַח, *petah*, also meaning "doorway") in 7:13 (7:14 Heb). However, the verb for "open," based on the same root (פָּתַח, *patah*) appeared rather suggestive in 5:5–6 (see above), and if we can assume "fruit" is that excellent thing hanging over the doorway, it would certainly relate to the previous two verses. In any case, *ra'yati* has "treasured up" a wide variety of these "excellent" things, apparently just for *dodi*.[153]

Following her invitation to *dodi*, *ra'yati* longs for greater closeness to him. She uses familiar imagery of kinship, food, and drink, which leads to her renewed longing for his embrace (8:1–3). She closes the section with the refrain to the daughters of Jerusalem (8:4). In 8:1, *ra'yati*'s words about her mother recall similar comments she made in 3:4 (see discussion above re: 2:8–3:5). There, the reference was to her mother's womb; here it is to her breasts. As disturbing as this apparent "family romance" might seem to contemporary readers, there are some explana-

---

152. With Exum, *Song*, 241. Also see Keel, who notes that the final phrase of 7:12 (Heb 7:13) "clarifies that the 'blossoms' and 'blooms' are to be interpreted figuratively." He compares this to 2:10–13 and 6:11 (*Song*, 254) and Fox adds a comparison to 1:13–14 (*Song*, 164).

153. Fox states emphatically that these "openings," especially with its plural suffix, "is hardly an allusion to the girl's vagina (contrary to Wittekindt)." He associates this reference to the couple's "booth in the field," as in 1:16–17 (*Song*, 164).

tions to help make sense of it. These images probably indicate *ra'yati*'s desire for access to *dodi*. Such access which would be so simple if he were only a part of *ra'yati*'s own household and family, in which case she may call him "brother" even if that were not biologically the case.[154] This would eliminate the need for their trysts and fantasies, so that they could go so far as to express their affection in public without fear of derision. In addition, "brother" was a pet name found in other ancient Near Eastern love poetry.[155] Some cultural conventions probably existed in this time that allowed for marriages within the same tribe between couples who were more closely related than contemporary standards tolerate.[156] Fox points out that *ra'yati*'s words of longing here remind us that the couple was indeed not married, but pursuing one another, and that her desire is for closeness to *dodi*, not to literally be his sister.[157]

A quick look at various translations of 8:1 illustrates confusion there. It is unclear as to what would happen if *ra'yati* were able to fulfill her fantasy and bring *dodi* into her mother's house. *Ra'yati* may assert that *dodi* or her mother would "teach me [*ra'yati*]" there. Or, she may be simply modifying the phrase about her mother's house, clarifying with the parallelism "the room of her that conceived me [*ra'yati*]." We see the latter in the Septuagint and Syriac, and it is also found in Song 3:4.[158] With that support elsewhere in Song, and the fact that "teach me" makes little sense here, most commentators and some translations choose the alternate reading.[159]

At the end of 8:2, *ra'yati* gives *dodi* "spiced wine; the sweet wine of my pomegranate."[160] This suggestive reference recalls the immediately

154. Weems, "Song," 5:428.

155. Fox, *Song*, 8.

156. Weems states that "cousins in Eastern cultures are considered ideal marriage partners." She additionally point to Genesis 28–29 as "an instance in which a matrilineal kinship-based relationship was arranged and encouraged, in this case between a son and his mother's brother's daughter" ("Song," 5:428).

157. Fox, *Song*, 166.

158. Fox and Pope also refer to 6:9 and 8:5 to support the alternate reading (*Song*, 166; *Song*, 658–59).

159. See NRSV and RSV. Relating this reading to the logic of the book Exum points out, "By this stage in the poem the lovers hardly seem to be in need of any lessons in the ways of love" (*Song*, 247).

160. MT has the singular "pomegranate," but other ancient witnesses have the plural here, leading some commentators to suggest that they indicate *ra'yati*'s breasts (Fox, *Song*, 166).

preceding section, among others in Song (5:1; 7:2 [3], 9 [10], 12 [13]). The section ends with two repetitions from earlier in the book. In 8:3 *ra'yati* longs for or enjoys a very particular embrace with *dodi*; there her words are nearly an exact repetition of 2:6.[161] Finally in 8:4, *ra'yati* returns to her oft-repeated refrain to the daughters of Jerusalem (1:5; 2:7; 3:5 10, 11, 5:8, 16).

Song about Dodi (8:5–7)

In 8:5–7, *ra'yati*'s voice continues, with an apparent interlude from her girlfriends in 8:5a, and some of Song's most powerful—and famous—verses in 8:6–7. The first phrase of 8:5 (aα) exactly repeats the opening of *ra'yati*'s dream wedding scene from 3:6. In this case, however, the words seem to be coming from her girlfriends as they see her returning from her night of lovemaking. From there, the poetry shifts back to *ra'yati*, speaking to *dodi*. In 8:5b her meaning is obscure, although the vocabulary aligns with other portions of Song. First she "awakens" *dodi*—presumably following their night of romance together—using the same verb as we find in the refrain to the daughters of Jerusalem in 2:7; 3:5 and 8:4. He had been lying under an "apple tree," reminding us of several other references to "apples" throughout Song: 2:3, 5; 7:8 [Heb 7:9]. All of this sounds ordinary enough, but then in an apparent non sequitur she turns to talking about his mother, under that same tree. What exactly his mother was doing there is open to some debate, but numerous commentators understand it to mean that she "conceived" *dodi* there, rather than giving birth to him there.[162] The significance could be *ra'yati*'s gratitude for the love(making?) that produced the one (with whom) she now (makes) love(s).[163] In addition, the reference to

161. The Hebrew gives no reason to pose the verse in the subjunctive, as in NRSV ("O that his left hand were under my head, and that his right hand embraced me!") The only verb in this verse, "embrace" (חבק, *hbq*) is an imperfect, which can mean it is currently happening in addition to happening in the future (with Fox, *Song*, 165; Keel, *Song*, 264; Pope, *Song*, 653; Exum, *Song*, 242).

162. The Hebrew (חבל *haval*) allows for either possibility. Exum (*Song*, 243–44), Keel (*Song*, 267), Pope (*Song*, 663–64), Fox (*Song*, 167–68) all translate "conceived" for (חבל *haval*) in 8:5b, though Keel only does so in the first instance.

163. See Exum (*Song*, 249) and Keel (*Song*, 268) for a similar sentiment. Exum (*Song*, 243–244), Keel (*Song*, 267), Pope (*Song*, 663), Fox (*Song*, 167–68) all translate "conceived" for (חבל *haval*) in 8:5b, though Keel only does so in the first instance.

his mother picks up on a whole list of other such comments in Song: 1:6; 3:4, 11; 6:9; 8:1, and 2.

Ra'yati's poetry becomes sublime in 8:6 when she calls for *dodi* to wear her on his heart and arm like a signet seal. Such seals were the stuff of royal narratives in the biblical world, where a king would sign his signature by pressing his engraved stone or metal ring or necklace into clay or wax. This left a unique insignia and so conferred his assent to a decree, or ownership of an object. Other biblical passages use the signet as a powerful symbol (Gen 38:18; Exod 28:11, 21, 36; Jer 22:24; 1 Kgs 21:8; Hag 2:23; Job 38:14; Esth 3:12; 8:8, 10, 12), but nowhere else in the Bible does it evoke such intimacy between lovers.[164] It was commonplace to wear such a seal as a necklace or ring, which would place it over the heart or on the arm, respectively. The symbolism of placing that seal on his heart suggests the intimacy of his embrace and his giving over of his very being; to place it on his arm or hand (זְרֹעַ *zeroʿa*) may have referred to his strength (1 Sam 2:31; Ezek 22:6).[165] This imagery suggests similar meaning as what we are familiar with in a marital ring exchange.

Verse 8:6 goes on, upping the ante by personifying love; comparing its strength to nothing less powerful than death itself, which is also personified here.[166] The verse describes love's "ardor," or "jealousy" (קִנְאָה *kinʾah*) as "fierce as *sheol*," the place of the dead. Indeed, if anything gets in the way of death, it is love—more specifically new life as the outcome of love.[167] Finally in 8:6, love's "flames are flames of fire, a powerful flame." This redundant line paints a picture of what we might call "burning love," and indeed points to passion. It may not sound as tender as the oft-sung wedding anthem to which the verse has been set,

---

164 We do find a similar non-biblical reference in the ancient Egyptian love poem "Seven Wishes" (Group B of Cairo Love Songs; no. 21C): "If only I were her little seal ring, the keeper of her finger!" (Fox, *Song*, 38, 169).

165. Pope notes that "anatomical terms are somewhat loosely used in biblical poetry, and 'arm' may be a poetic synonym for 'hand'" (*Song*, 666).

166. Notably, most of the refrains to the daughters of Jerusalem also contain a personification of love throughout the book (2:7; 3:5; 8:4).

167. Keel notes the connection between 8:5 and 8:6–7 in that "love forges the links between the generations with the same tenacity that death employs in its attempt to destroy them" (*Song*, 270). He goes on to point out the "importance of love in the transmission of life," listing numerous women in the Hebrew Bible whose love literally overcame death (Michal [1 Sam 19:9–17]; Abigal [1 Sam 25]; Maacah [2 Sam 20:14–22]; Rizpah [2 Sam 21:8–14]) (*Song*, 274).

but most anyone who has experienced love knows that such intensity often accompanies it.[168]

Ra'yati's soliloquy closes in 8:7, where she continues and then finishes her love poem. Here she goes on to say that neither "many waters" nor even the "underground rivers" could "extinguish" or "overflow" this burning fire of love. And house-sized wealth, if offered for love, would be "utterly despicable," relying on the same vocabulary as 8:1b for those who would scorn *ra'yati* if her relationship with *dodi* were public.

In 8:6b–7 we have a striking departure from the usual lyrics in Song. Rather than recounting *ra'yati* or *dodi's* experiences or fantasies, this passage makes sweeping statements about love, emphasizing its worth. Few lines of verse, from ancient to modern, can compete with *ra'yati's* description of love in 8:6–7. From a heart-seal to eternal fire, her words most certainly capture the essence of the love—and lovemaking—she has described throughout. And all lovers throughout time can say "amen" to the truth of her words.

Ra'yati Sings of Her Brothers (8:8–12)

From this moving finale, Song's ending takes a strange turn. The final section of the book, 8:8–12, abounds with ambiguous meaning. Suddenly in 8:8–9 the poet speaks in the first person plural, opening with "We have a little sister. . . ." We cannot know who exactly the implied speaker was. However, the opening phrase suggests either *ra'yati's* older brothers or sisters. Either scenario would be out of place in Song, since those voices have not sounded at all through the rest of the book. This would not be the only time *ra'yati's* brothers seem to have been harassing her (1:6). If that is the case, it may help explain *ra'yati's* desire elsewhere in the book for *dodi* as a brother (3:4; 8:1)!

Another possibility is that *ra'yati* continues to speak in 8:8–9, quoting her brothers' or sisters' taunts.[169] The passage contains a good deal

168. This popular wedding anthem is *Set Me as a Seal*, by Clausen.

169. Alternatively, Exum suggests that *ra'yati* is the speaker here, not quoting anyone, but rather "the narrator of this vignette, and the little sister of whom she speaks is fictive in the same way that Solomon's vineyard in Baal-hamon is. Both the sister and Solomon's vineyard are foils that allow the speakers to say something about themselves. They say it metaphorically . . . She says that, unlike the girl in her example, for whom preparations will be made when she reaches marriageable age, she needs no such attention, since she (a fortified city) has already surrendered to her lover. He says that his vineyard (the woman) is worth more than Solomon's and he alone will tend it" (*Song*, 255).

of militaristic imagery, referring to *ra'yati* as a "wall" with a fancy "silver battlement" and a "door" that should be "shut up with" strong and lavish "cedar boards." Such battle scenarios are not unique in Song, though previously they have appeared in the context of the lovers' fantasies and compliments about one another (3:6–8; 6:4, 10, 13 [Heb 7:1]). Perhaps in this case, the militarism suggests the protectiveness of her older brothers in a society that fortified her sexuality as a patriarchal family commodity (cf. Genesis 34; Deut 22:13–21, 23–29; 2 Samuel 13).

Whether *ra'yati* was quoting someone or not in 8:8–9, she clearly responds in 8:10. Using some of the same vocabulary, she begins, "I am a wall, and my breasts are like the towers!" Here she may be taking on both the military imagery from 8:9 ("wall") and the apparent physical put-down of 8:8 ("she does not have breasts"). We can recall easily enough that *dodi* would have agreed with *ra'yati*'s evaluation of her breasts, rather than that of the speaker in 8:8 (cf. 4:5; 7:3, 7–8 [Heb 7:4, 8–9]). While she calls herself a "wall" on the one hand, she also identifies herself as "one who brings peace" (8:10).[170] By her choice, she is no battleground to *dodi*.[171]

We cannot be so certain who was speaking in the following verses, 8:11–12.[172] Several commentators assign these verses to *dodi*, who tells of "Solomon's vineyard" and it's paid keepers, yet still claims his vineyard—*ra'yati* —as not only his, but also as more valuable than Solomon's. A common proposal suggests that "Solomon's vineyard" in v. 11 refers to his harem, while in v. 12 *dodi* would be claiming that *ra'yati* (*his* vineyard) is more valuable to him than the infamous Solomon's harem.[173]

---

170. This phrase, כְּמוֹצְאֵת שָׁלוֹם (*kemotset shalom* or "one who brings peace") may give additional credence to Fox's interpretation of 6:13 (Heb 7:1) as "the perfect, unblemished one" rather than "the Shulammite," based on an understanding of the word as a form of *shalom* שָׁלוֹם (*Song*, 226–28).

171. With Exum, who notes that this statement in v. 10 "has a sexual significance." She "surrenders" herself to him (*Song*, 259).

172. Murphy notes "they could be spoken by either the man or the woman" (*Song*, 193).

173. Exum (*Song*, 243, 255, 259–61). Murphy allows this as a possibility, and even suggests that 8:11–12 are a "boasting song . . . in which the man prizes his beloved beyond the entire harem of Solomon," comparable to 6:8–9 (194). Also see Fox (*Song*, 174–75), who supports this scenario with an alternate translation of Baal-hamon as "husband of a multitude" (175). Keel also envisions such a setting, and notes that the "keepers" in 8:11 were the "harem guards," over against *dodi*'s "vineyard," which is his alone (v. 12a) (*Song*, 280–82).

These verses resume the vineyard metaphor from throughout the book (1:6, 14; 2:13, 15; 6:11; 7:8, 12 [Heb 7:9, 13]; 8:11–12), and especially echo the initial appearance in 1:6, "my vineyard I have not kept." The verb in 1:6 is נטר *ntr*, the same root as in 8:11 for "keepers." This raises the possibility that *ra'yati* is speaking in 8:12, claiming that—in direct contrast to her own words in 1:6—she finally does get to keep her own vineyard. In turn, the verse implies that she gives it to whomever she pleases, in this case *dodi*.[174] If it is *ra'yati* speaking in 8:12a, she firmly asserts her autonomy, her sense of protecting herself in her own way, and her commitment to *dodi*.[175] If *ra'yati* is the speaker in 8:12, we might gather that she has resumed the fiction of *dodi* as Solomon (cf. 1:5; 3:7, 9, 11) in 8:11,[176] claiming that her beloved owns the most valuable vineyard in the land—her. In this scenario as in others, it becomes difficult to sort out how it explains all the details of v. 11. Of course, a final possibility is that vv. 11–12 belong to two separate speakers. For instance, Duane Garrett assigns v. 11 to the "chorus" and v. 12 to the "soprano."[177]

The mention of Baal-hamon is obscure. Translated, it means "possessor of abundance," which may indicate Solomon's wealth.[178] Whether 8:11–12 poses *ra'yati* or *dodi* as the speaker, the conclusion remains that *dodi* and *ra'yati* belong to one another, with *ra'yati* being the most prized vineyard of all, more so even than literally King Solomon's vineyard, or figuratively all the money such a vineyard would be worth.

Parting Songs of Longing (8:13–14)

The final verses of Song close out the book with unifying themes and imagery. Furthermore, with *dodi* speaking in 8:13 and *ra'yati* in 8:14, each of the lovers has the opportunity for a brief final statement in Song, articulated through a parting lovers' dialogue. A question 8:13 raises is,

174. Murphy concedes this possibility, though sets it against "the disdain expressed for the bride-price in 8:7b" (*Song*, 200).

175. Pope writes, "If the groom speaks, declaring dominion over his spouse's body, it is classic male chauvinism. If the female here asserts autonomy, this verse becomes the golden text for women's liberation" (*Song*, 690).

176. Contra Murphy, who simply asserts that "Solomon is meant literally here, because he was rich enough to possess such a valuable 'vineyard'" (*Song*, 199).

177. Garrett and House, *Song*, 258.

178. With Fox (*Song*, 174), and Exum (*Song*, 260). Weems suggests it may more specifically refer to "a well-known private vineyard owned by King Solomon" ("Song," 5:433).

who are the "companions?" Pope reminds us that we also found "companions" (חבר *haver*) in 1:7, in which case *ra'yati* was talking about *dodi*'s "companions."[179] In 8:13, *dodi* calls these "companions" "his," so perhaps they are indeed the same group as there, analogous to *ra'yati*'s "girlfriends."[180]

In the final verse of Song (8:14), *ra'yati* has her turn, in which she calls on familiar similes and metaphors. She beckons *dodi* with her oft-used animal similes of him as a "gazelle" or "young stag" (2:7, 9, 17; 3:5).[181] She invites him to mountains that, like she has implied before, may well be physical rather than geographical (see 2:8, 17; 4:6 and above discussions on these verses). As many commentators have pointed out, these verses do not serve as terribly effective closure for the book. Based on this dangling ending, at least one scholar has argued that the ending of the book must have been lost.[182] Nonetheless, closing Song with such familiar imagery provides a sense of unity for a frequently confusing book. Furthermore, the two lovers' parting sentiments of longing for one another recalls their earnest and passionate desire for one another, which has played and replayed as the ongoing theme of Song as a whole.[183] The ending is much like the beginning and middle, with the lovers longing for one another.[184] Layers of meaning throughout the book suggest they may have found one another from time to time, but this suggests there was nothing enduring to those trysts. A tease, the poet will not finally resolve the pursuit for us, even in the ending, leading us to wonder how long the couple themselves lived in that state of anticipation and limbo in their quest for a sanctioned—rather than secretive—relationship.

---

179. Pope, *Song*, 693.

180. Exum, *Song*, 262.

181. The opening verb in v. 14 is ברח *brh*, which primarily means "flee." Most commentators explain this as fleeing to *ra'yati* (Fox, *Song*, 177; Pope, *Song*, 698; Keel, *Song*, 285).

182. Ehrlich, cited in Fox, *Song*, 176.

183. Indeed, Weems suggests that *ra'yati* "is hurrying her lovers' sexual climax" in vv. 13–14, lest they be caught lovemaking in the garden ("Song," 5:433). Pope suggests that the opening verb of v. 14 may be double entendre for "screw" (*Song*, 697–98).

184. Fox (*Song*, 176) and Exum (*Song*, 25–263) both view the end as leading the reader back to the beginning of the book.

Conclusion

Interpreting the Song of Songs into the parlance of contemporary religious life poses many challenges. Not only does the book fail to mention the divine name, any religious acts, or Israel's history, it is ultimately about sex.[185] The church has had longstanding anxiety about sexuality, even when expressed within the bounds of marriage. Song complicates the problem by presenting a couple that has no marital tie. They are a young woman and young man deeply in love, pursuing each other feverishly despite numerous barriers. Since the early history of Song, interpreters have circumvented these problems by understanding the book allegorically. That remains a viable option for contemporary readers, even backed by scholarly voices.[186] Nonetheless, the challenge for today is whether a person of faith can embrace Song of Songs on its own terms. Will Song "preach" without being presented allegorically? I see several possibilities for this.

First, many persons today will admit without hesitation that unabashed and mutual romantic love expressed physically has its place in the life of faith. Surely there are ways to articulate this appropriately through homiletics, barring the children's sermon! Perhaps Song can encourage healthier understandings of both sexuality and romance, and even serve as a biblical jumping-off-point for communities of faith to struggle with these difficult and controversial issues.

The dilemma for most preachers may arise primarily in the fact that Song's sexual content relates to an unmarried couple. Yet that dilemma may pose an excellent opportunity to address the issue of marriage itself, a topic extremely pressing for most communities of faith. For instance, many Bible readers erroneously conflate their understanding of contemporary civil marriage with that of biblical marriage. Song is one of many biblical opportunities to correct that error. In addition, most denominations spend little time these days discussing the sexuality of single people, other than in their youth groups and in debates about gay marriage. Yet it is a relevant—even pressing—topic for unmarried people of all ages and orientations. As biblical erotic love poetry about

185. Actress Maggie Smith emphatically makes this point in a scene with Rowan Atkinson in the 2005 film *Keeping Mum*.

186. Carr, "Gender," 245; LaCocque, *Romance*. See discussion above in "Interpretations" section.

an unmarried couple, Song presents an opportunity to eradicate the taboo on that subject.

Many faith communities have spent countless hours and meetings debating a related topic, which is, who exactly may be married? Who deems a union legitimate, on what terms, and with which individuals? This issue has arisen in regard to the matter of gay/lesbian/bisexual/transgender marriage, both of clergy and of laypersons. Though Song is explicitly about heterosexual love, the fact that *ra'yati* and *dodi* are single raises the subject of legitimacy among all kinds of unmarried lovers. Song boldly celebrates romance and the physical love that accompanies it, despite the absence of cultural approval. It raises the question of whether a state or even religious sanction is necessary to legitimate love, or whether love itself does that.[187] All indications in the book are that *ra'yati* and *dodi* were condemned by their communities. Their affair persisted nonetheless, and has continued indefinitely through the immortal text. Perhaps this can inspire couples today whose love receives no sanction from society. Ironically, those are likely persons who find minimal welcome in faith communities, and who may wrongly assume that their stories appear nowhere in the Bible.

Song, however, is not only about sex and whether or not it is approved by the community. In Song sex arises in the context of love and romance. That in itself has contemporary relevance. For instance, popular culture arguably suffers from an overabundance of romance at the expense of practicality. The opposite seems to be the case in the culture represented by the biblical literature, where we find little to no indication of romance other than in Song. A marital relationship in biblical times was primarily about practicality, including politics, reproduction, and inheritance rights. In that culture, Song represents a refreshing and unique voice. If we can transport ourselves to that time, when romance was not over-done as it is in our time, perhaps we can gain new appreciation for such sensual love poetry as well as better understanding life in biblical times. Could Song put romance in a new perspective for us, something other than the overstated sap we find in many films and television shows? As opposed to such gaudy representations, Song instead

---

187. The film *Sweet Land* dramatizes this issue when a Minnesota Lutheran pastor during the time of World War I refuses to bless the union of one of his Norwegian parishioners and a German woman, Inge. She eventually declares that they are married in their hearts.

fairly hides in the canon; it is literature of subtle images, offering a gleam of intense passion amid stolid societal rules.

A final reason that Song absolutely deserves a place in the study and proclamation of faith communities relates to the other three books in this volume. Song, along with the other three biblical books in this commentary, undermines the oft-repeated falsehood that women in the Hebrew Bible had no voice, no power, and no place in society. As one of the very few biblical books that prominently feature a woman's voice, Song illustrates that a female presence in religion cannot be pinned only on the twentieth-century's women's movement. The ancient compilations of sacred books legitimated and even celebrated women's voices, in this case, one that proclaims love and sexuality with no shame. Should contemporary faith communities do any less?

FOUR

Judith

Introduction

THE BOOK OF JUDITH is a wartime tale of a people struggling against an enemy that outmatches them by far. The audience must wait for half the book as the odds stack against this underdog people, until finally we meet the story's heroine and namesake, Judith. This most unlikely liberator, a pious widow, takes on the seemingly hopeless situation with tenacity. With her people's permission to undertake a secret plan, Judith transforms herself into an alluring refugee, willing to offer strategic information to the enemy commander. While the general is in the midst of seducing Judith, she takes advantage of his vulnerability and assassinates him, conquering the enemy from the top.

The book raises questions about what means justify what end, how fluid gender roles can constitute strategy, and where God stands amid wartime deceit and violence. It also challenges us to consider what makes a book canonical or not, as we reflect on its pervasive influence over the centuries.

In the commentary below, the translations are from the New Revised Standard Version, unless otherwise indicated.

Outline

1) Assyria vs. Israel (1:1—7:32)
    a) Nebuchadnezzar's Offensive (1:1—3:10)
        i) Intro: sets the stage (1:1–16)

(1) Nebuchadnezzar's offensive against King Arphaxad of the Medes in Ecbatana (1:1–6)

(2) Nebuchadnezzar calls on other nations, but they ignored and humiliated him (1:7–11)

(3) Five years after he began warring against Arphaxad, he won a summary victory against Arphaxad and Ecbatana (1:12–16)

ii) Discussion in Nebuchadnezzar's palace sending Holofernes to take revenge on the whole region (2:1–13)

iii) Holofernes puts down the rebellion (2:14–27)

iv) Surrender (2:28—3:7)

v) Holofernes destroys the peoples' gods anyway, according to orders (3:8)

vi) Holofernes and his army arrive outside Judea (3:9–10)

b) Cut to Israel (4:1–15)

i) Background; historical context: "recently returned from exile" (4:1–3)

ii) Israel's defenses (4:4–15)

(1) Military strategy: hilltops, food stores, mountain passes (4:4–8)

(2) Entreating God for help (4:9–15)

c) Cut to Holofernes (5:1—6:13)

i) Holofernes learns about Israel's preparations and asks for more information (5:1–4)

ii) Achior of Ammon tells more about Israel and its history (5:5—6:11)

(1) Introduction (5:5)

(2) History of Israel (5:6–19)

(3) Summary: if Israel is unfaithful, they are vulnerable; if they are faithful, Holofernes has no hope (5:20–21)

iii) Holofernes gets defensive (5:22—6:4)

iv) Holofernes punishes Achior (6:5–13)

d) Cut to the Israelites (6:14–21)

i) Israelites rescue Achior; he gives them information about Holofernes' intent (6:12–17)

ii) The Israelites are afraid and entreat God again (6:18–21)

e) Battle preparations against Bethulia (7:1–32)

i)   Holofernes' troops get into position (7:1–3)

ii)   Israelites are afraid (7:4–5)

iii)   Holofernes' troops strategize and further prepare for the battle (7:6–18)

iv)   Israelites are afraid, and getting thirsty (7:19–32)

(1)   The Israelites beg God for help in their dire situation (7:19–22)

(2)   The Israelites beg Uzziah to surrender (7:23–29)

(3)   Uzziah agrees, after the people wait five more days (7:30–32)

2)   Judith saves Israel; defeats Assyria (8:1—16:25)

a)   Introduction of Judith (8:1–8)

b)   Judith has a better plan (8:9–36)

i)   Judith protests against Uzziah and the people's plan, and calls them to courage, faith and thankfulness (8:9–27)

ii)   Uzziah praises her wisdom, defends the people's idea, and asks for Judith's help (8:28–31)

iii)   Judith offers her help through a secret plan (8:32–36)

c)   Judith prepares herself to enact her plan (9:1—10:10)

i)   Prayer (9:1–14)

ii)   Getting on her disguise; packing a bag with food and dishes (10:1–5)

iii)   Taking her leave (10:6–10)

d)   Judith enacts her plan (10:11—13:9a)

i)   Judith and her maid are "captured"—she says they are "fleeing" and that she has valuable info for Holofernes; the captors notice her "beauty" (10:11–17)

ii)   Judith at Holofernes' camp (10:18—13:9a)

(1)   Guards' banter (10:18–19)

(2)   At Holofernes' tent (10:20—12:4)

(a)   Description of the scene (10:20–23)

(b)   Holofernes reassures Judith (11:1–4)

(c)   Judith reassures Holofernes; offers herself as Holofernes' spy and tip-off (11:5–19)

(d)   Holofernes is enamored with Judith and her message (11:20–23)

(e)   Holofernes offers Judith food; she refuses (12:1–4)

          (3) Judith is faithful to prayer and purification (12:5–9)

          (4) The banquet (12:10—13:9a)

              (a) Holofernes invites Judith to a banquet intended to seduce her (12:10–15)

              (b) Judith prepares for and attends the banquet, at which Holofernes drinks himself into a stupor (12:16–20)

              (c) The act (13:1–9a)

                  (i) The attendants leave Judith and drunken, passed-out Holofernes alone (13:1–4a)

                  (ii) Judith prays about what to do (13:4b–5)

                  (iii) Judith beheads Holofernes and hides the body (13:6–9a)

e) Back to Bethulia (13:9b–20)

    i) Judith and her maid flee (13:9b–10)

    ii) Judith and her maid announce themselves to the people of Bethulia; a celebration of God who worked through Judith ensues (13:11–20)

f) The final battle: setup and completion (14:1—15:7)

    i) Judith's instructions for the final battle (14:1–5)

    ii) Retelling the story to Achior, who converts (14:6–10)

    iii) Defeating the Assyrians (14:11—15:8)

        (1) Preparations (14:11–12)

        (2) The Assyrians find Holofernes headless (14:13–16)

        (3) They realize what Judith did (14:17–19)

        (4) Confusion ensues among the Assyrians (15:1–3a)

        (5) Israelites are widely triumphant (15:3b–7)

g) Judith the Victor (15:8—16:20)

    i) Judith receives widespread praise (15:8–10)

    ii) Judith receives the booty taken from Holofernes (15:11)

    iii) Judith leads a celebration (15:12—16:20)

        (1) The women dance; the men parade behind (15:12–13)

        (2) Judith leads everyone in a thanksgiving song to God (15:14—16:17)

        (3) More worship and celebration, including an offering (16:18–20)

h) And they all lived happily ever after (16:21–25)

Date and Setting

The book of Judith opens as many biblical books do, referring to the time in which the story took place as measured by the date of the reigning king (cf. Isa 1:1; Jer 1:2–3). The historical problem with Judith is that it names Nebuchadnezzar as the king of Assyria, although the historical King Nebuchadnezzar was king of Babylon (ca. 605–562 BCE), not Assyria. In fact Assyria was no longer a player in the ancient world when Nebuchadnezzar was king. In 722 BCE Assyria's King Shalamaneser V conquered the northern kingdom of Israel (2 Kgs 17:1–6); more than a century later Babylon's King Nebuchadnezzar II exiled the Judeans and destroyed the holy city of Jerusalem (597 and 586 BCE, respectively; 2 Kgs 24:1—25:30).

Thus when the book of Judith names "Nebuchadnezzar, who ruled over the Assyrians" (1:1), it essentially refers to two historically despicable enemies of Israel, depicting the enemy as an ultra-evil empire. Because these enemies are separated by such a large amount of time, it also makes this story blatantly nonhistorical. It would be like starting out a story in today's USA with the introduction, "when Hitler was king of Iraq . . ." Both the location and the leader are known as enemies, though in different time periods and places, so it would obviously be a fictional story involving a horrible adversary.

Like Nebuchadnezzar of Assyria, Arphaxad (Αρφαξαδ; ar-FOX-ad) of the Medes in Ecbatana (1:1) was an ahistorical figure. In ancient geography, Media took up varying portions of what we now know as Iran, from the Zagros mountains northeast to the Caspian Sea and down to the Persian Gulf. In the seventh century, Media joined Babylon in the coalition that eventually brought down Assyria—an ironic fact in light of the fact that Assyrians are referred to as the aggressors against the Medes in Judith. Media later became a Persian province; witness the Persian "Darius the Mede" from Dan 5:31 and Esth 1:3.[1] Ecbatana was east and slightly south of Nineveh; there may have been a settlement of Jews established there at the time of the Assyrian exile.[2] If that is the case, it heightens the extent to which Jews are the victims in this story—not only does Nebuchadnezzar target them in their homeland of Bethulia, but also in their diaspora homes.

---

1. VanZant, "Medes, Media," 4:6–8.
2. Perkins, "Ecbatana," 2:270–71.

Not until 4:6 does the text introduce Bethulia, the home city of Judith and her people, where the story's plot ultimately originates and returns. The text sets the town "near Dothan" (4:6) in the hill country of Samaria north of Jerusalem, with an advantageous location on a mountain, surrounded by mountain passes and strategically located for the protection of Judea (6:11; 13:10). However, we do not find any other references to this town in the Bible or elsewhere. It appears to be one more aspect of the book's fictive setting. This is all the more the case because we can translate the Hebrew word *betulah* in several different significant ways: "Virgin" or "young woman";[3] "house of God";[4] "house of ascent."[5] All of these would be evocative names for the central location in this story.

So far, the narrative only undermines the purported historical information provided in the book of Judith. Ultimately, we cannot know for sure the actual time in which the book was written or the story first told. Because it names both Assyria and Nebuchadnezzar as threats, we can at least date it after the events that they represent. Thus the book is at least post-exilic, though that leaves quite a bit of room for speculation.

One theory about the date of Judith is that because the book sets a conciliatory tone in terms of foreigners (other than the threatening enemy), perhaps Judith arose during the reconstruction period. This time follows the end of the exile in 539 BCE and is roughly equivalent to the Persian period, lasting until about 332 BCE with the rise of Alexander the Great. The era was marked in part by conflicting groups of Israelites. While one faction thought they should reject foreigners because their influence had helped lead to Israel's downfall, another faction advocated for the inclusion of at least some foreigners based on their loyalty to Israel and its God. André LaCocque makes the case that Judith belongs to this time period, with Achior of Ammon as a foreigner figure analogous to Ruth.[6] While LaCocque has a point that the book fits that rhetorical setting through its openness to the other, it does not fit so well in terms of its central plot line about taking down an ominous enemy. During the time of the reconstruction the Israelites tended to be more concerned about their internal interactions than those with outside rulers. For the

---

3. From the Hebrew בתולה *betulah*; *BDB*, 143b; Newman, "Bethulia," 1:449.

4. From בית לוה *beyt lewh*, Moore, *Judith*, 150.

5. From בית עליה (*beyt 'lyh*), Moore, *Judith*, 150; Craven, *Judith*, 73 n. 25.

6. See above Ruth chapter section on Moab and LaCocque, *Feminine*, 39–40.

most part, they viewed the Persians as a friendly distant government. A tale about violently overthrowing a tyrannical overlord does not seem appropriate for that time.

It does fit better, however, in the late Hellenistic period, particularly during and after the time of Antiochus IV Epiphanes (175–164 BCE). His despotic rule of persecution and torture of Jews (1 Macc 1:10–64; 2 Macc 6–7) led to an armed Jewish uprising called the Maccabean Revolt, beginning in 168 BCE (2 Macc 8; 10:14—12:28). In that conflict, a group of Jews successfully defended themselves against Greek troops when they determined to retake and reconsecrate their temple in 164 BCE. Their subsequent reign reinstated Jewish rule of Judea for the first time since the exile, lasting until 63 BCE (2 Macc 8; 10:14—12:28). The Hasmonean period, named for the dynasty that followed the uprising's leader, Judas Maccabeus, was unique not only because of renewed self-rule, but also for the fact that some Jewish leaders of this time imposed conversion on non-Jews.[7] The context of a community that suffers under a tyrannical foreign government and then successfully ousts it certainly fits the storyline of Judith. Thus the rule of Antiochus IV in the late Hellenistic era, or the Maccabean era immediately following it fit as a reasonable date for the book, or at least for part of it.

Reference to the specifically Greek "garlands" in 3:7 and 15:12–13 also locate the book in the Hellenistic era, as does a king demanding that his subjects worship him as a god (3:8).[8] Yet various theories exist to establish the date more specifically. For instance, Tal Ilan argues that Judith, along with Esther and Susanna, served as propaganda for the reign of the Jewish Hasmonean Queen Shelamzion, who reigned from 76–67 BCE. Ilan identifies several features that these three stories have in common: their dates, their promotion of a female leader and heroine, and their attentiveness to gender issues within societal hierarchy.[9] In addition, none of these texts are present among the Dead Sea Scrolls, which could accord with the hypothesis that the Qumran community rejected Hasmonean rule.[10] Ilan asserts that Judith's unique role in supporting a Jewish queen was to specify the proper conditions for such rule: other (male) leadership had failed, the people were facing disas-

7 Josephus, *Ant.*, 13.318–19; Wills, *The Jewish Novel*, 99.

8. See commentary on these passages below and Wills, *Judith*, 3:1123.

9. Ilan, *Integrating Women*, 127–53; Ilan, *Silencing the Queen*, 1.

10. Ilan, *Integrating Women*, 141.

ter, and there were no other options. This was the case at the start of
Shelamzion's reign, when she took on a floundering administration from
her late husband Alexander Yannai, and subsequently enacted strategies drastically differing from his.[11] This argument is plausible, but along
with other hypotheses about the date of Judith, it cannot be definitively
confirmed.

The book of Judith does apparently show evidence of other
Maccabean events paralleled in the text. For instance, one important
Hasmonean policy was to annex and reform Samaria, capital of the former northern kingdom Israel. The Hasmonean rulers John Hyrcanus
and Alexander Jannaeus (135–104; 103–78 BCE) both worked to accomplish these ends. Since Assyria had conquered Samaria in 722 BCE
and resettled foreigners there to mix with the Samaritans who remained
(2 Kgs 17:5–41), the inhabitants of the southern kingdom Judea viewed
their neighbors to the north as heretical idol worshippers, contaminated
by foreign beliefs and gods. The northern location of fictional Bethulia
(Jdt 4:6) could have been an anachronistic way for later Jews to assert
original ownership of the controversial Samaritan sanctuary in that region.[12] In addition, the "gods made with hands," referred to as a part of
Israel's way distant past in 8:18 could indicate Maccabean superiority to
the Samaritans by mentioning the idols of the northern sanctuary.[13]

Other arguments for placing the book in the Maccabean period
include reference to re-consecrating the temple in 4:3. The leadership
of a high priest without a king may also hint at the Maccabean period,
when we see this type of rule (1 Macc 12:6).[14] The name of the General
Holofernes' eunuch was Bagoas, which would have been familiar during this time.[15] Holofernes himself has a parallel figure in Maccabean
history; Antiochus IV Epiphanes' General Nicanor was beheaded by
Maccabean fighters. Like the Bethulians, they displayed his head as part
of their victory celebration.[16] Furthermore, Judith's age of 105 at her

---

11. Ibid., 150–51, who cites Josephus, *War* 1.110–2; *Ant.* 13.405–9.

12. Newman, "Bethulia," 1:449; White, "Bethulia," 1:715–16.

13. Wills, *Judith*, 3:1078.

14. Ibid., 3:1114; see commentary on 4:6–7 below.

15. See commentary below on 12:11.

16. See commentary below on 14:1.

death (16:23) correlates to the length of the Maccabean period (168–63 BCE).[17]

The core storyline of the book strikes me as more appropriate to a people who were suffering under despotism than to a people who had already overthrown such a ruler.[18] A tale of an unlikely hero who miraculously defeats a powerful ruler would have been life-giving when a people were longing for such an outcome. Having caught on though, such a story could have continued to circulate, receiving editorial additions from a later time once liberation from that leader had been attained. Perhaps the basic plotline arose during the time of Antiochus IV Epiphanes, and, having become popular, the story was then molded with relevant details into the Maccabean period for the sake of that audience. Such a process would fit into what we know about the development of the Jewish novel, which may well have begun with an oral story.[19] Thus I will settle on a date for the final form of the book in the early to middle Maccabean reign, around 135–95 BCE.[20]

Language, Text, and Canonicity

The text of Judith only remains in Greek and Latin, but scholars agree that it was probably originally written in Hebrew. The Greek shows clear signs of a translation from biblical Hebrew. In various places throughout the Greek manuscript appear peculiar uses of the Greek in phraseology and vocabulary. These oddities can be logically explained by assuming they translate certain Hebrew expressions and even grammar.[21] It is likely that the Hebrew Judith was translated into Greek along with other late books of the Hebrew Bible, and included in the books we identify now as the Septuagint. When Rabbis made their final decisions about what would be included in the canon, for some reason they did not accept Judith. Christians however, who relied on the Septuagint as a starting point for their canon, did retain Judith. Many Christians still today have the book in their Bibles as part of the deuterocanonical books ("sec-

17. Moore, *Judith*, 50.

18. See Wills, *Judith,* 3:1079.

19. See ibid., 3:1080 and below section on genre.

20. For additional discussion on the date of Judith, see Moore, *Judith,* 49–52; 67–71; and Wills, *Judith,* 3:1076–79.

21. See Moore, *Judith,* 66–67 for detailed analysis.

ond canon"). This includes Roman Catholic and Orthodox Christians. Protestants do not count Judith in their Bibles because when that movement arose in the sixteenth century, they deemed only the books of the Jewish (Hebrew) Bible as canonical, and the others they identified as the Apocrypha. The compelling and important question of why Judith was excluded from the canon by the early Rabbis remains. We do not know why Judith was not canonized any more than we know for sure the date of the book. In general, we only have minimal information about why the Rabbis deemed some books acceptable and others not. Criteria for those decisions included a book's authorship, holiness, its interpretation within the community, and finally its date.

The book of Judith has no superscription attributing it to an important figure such as Solomon, like we see in Ecclesiastes (1:1) and Song of Songs (1:1).[22] Those references, though they are likely editorial additions, may well have helped get those relatively late books canonized.[23] It is puzzling to many Bible readers that Judith was not included, since it is so like Esther, which was. There is certainly enough piety in Judith; most of what Judith does is attributed to God, and the fact that God can work through a mere woman seems to give even greater glory to God (13:15–16). In contrast, the canonical Hebrew Esther does not so much as mention God's name throughout. Yet the much more pious Greek Esther resides among the Deuterocanonical books as well. Though Jewish communities in the Middle Ages apparently appreciated Judith as a Maccabean hero for Hanukkah, as far as we know she did not enjoy that status in earlier centuries.[24] Archaeologists discovered no fragments from the book of Judith among the Dead Sea Scrolls, so it apparently did not hold sway with that group. As we saw above, at least one author argues that its absence from the Dead Sea library, along with Esther, may point to that community's disdain for Hasmonean rule.[25] The fact that Judith does not appear among those texts may mean nothing, since Esther was also missing and it was canonized. On the other hand, it

22. See "Structure and Outline" and "Purpose" sections in Song of Songs chapter, above.

23. See Canonization section in chapter 3, above.

24. Judith is enjoying a resurgence of popularity in contemporary Jewish circles; see the Judith Conclusion, below.

25. Ilan, *Integrating Women*, 141, and see above section on Date in Song Introduction.

could mean that Judith was not popular enough to have been considered as part of that community's sacred texts.

All of this leaves us with the date of Judith as a primary suspect for its omission from the canon. It seems likely that the perceived date of a given book had a great deal to do with its inclusion in the canon, perhaps because they would not have had time to gain legitimacy in the community. Books deemed older tended to be included, while books apparently identified as very late were excluded. The fact that the book is flagrantly fictional may also have had something to do with its omission from the canon. The community could not even pretend to assert the story was historical, as it could with the final form of Daniel, which was also probably written in the time of Antiochus IV Epiphanes, but poses as a book from a much earlier period. Thus Judith may well have been omitted from the canon because it was an obviously non-historical book written at a relatively late date.

Genre

As the above history section details, Judith belongs in the broad category of fiction. Beyond that, we can consider a number of other relevant genres for the book. In considering the genre of Judith, it is helpful to compare it to similar biblical books. Judith's story has much in common with other biblical hero tales, such as the Joseph story, Esther, and Daniel. A number of commentators have drawn comparisons between Judith and Esther, particularly Greek Esther. They are both Jewish women whose sexuality plays a part in their efforts to save their people, and they both express disdain for that part of their role (Jdt 13:16; Add Esth 14:15). They both lead their people to militarily defeat their enemies (Jdt 15:1–7; Esth 9:1–17). Furthermore, Esther and Judith both have transformative costume-change scenes (Jdt 10:3–4; Esth 2:12–14). Indeed, we could include Ruth in that comparison as well (Ruth 3:3), though hers is not so much a hero story. André LaCocque points out that the narratives of both Esther and Judith take quite a while to introduce their namesake, and that the Qumran texts included neither of these books.[26] More to the point of their genre, LaCocque furthermore describes these both as stories of Jewish survival with women as the heroes. He describes how

26. LaCocque, *Feminine*, 67–68. He also dates the two books to a similar time frame (67).

gender issues are in the foreground of both books.[27] In addition, the villain in both Esther and Judith meets his death in a way he had intended for others—Haman on his own gallows (Esth 7:10) and Holofernes by his own sword (Jdt 13:6–8).[28] Thus the books have numerous similarities as hero stories told for the sake of a community in need of encouragement, sustenance, and even celebration.

For further comparison to Esther, we saw that Esther contained features of the early Jewish and Greek novel.[29] Judith fits this description also. Lawrence Wills draws out the details of this designation. He explains that short Jewish novels preceded the Greek novels, and that the current form of the text may have originated with an oral tale.[30] That kind of development would fit with my proposal above that the core hero story arose during the persecutions of Antiochus IV Epiphanes, and later editors included features specific to the Maccabean era.

Nebuchadnezzar's Offensive (1:1—3:10)

The story opens with the war-mongering King Nebuchadnezzar of Assyria. In 1:1–6 this utterly evil but completely fictitious ruler (see Judith Introduction, above) targets the Medes, ruled by the similarly fabricated King Arphaxad. Ecbatana was known as the capital of the Medes in what today is Iran. It became the capital of the Persian province of Media after the Persian King Cyrus captured it in the sixth century.[31] Arphaxad was no underprepared king, with a garrisoned city that would give any invading army a run for their money. The measurements of the walls, given in cubits, would translate approximately to hewn stones of 5 by 10 feet; walls 119 feet high and 85 feet wide (1:2); and gates 170 feet high and 70 feet wide, to accommodate troops (1:3–4). That this fortification and a significantly powerful ancient city did not scare off Nebuchadnezzar illustrates how terribly powerful he and his troops were (1:5). In addition, many other peoples came to Nebuchadnezzar's aid (1:6), which further highlights his control in the region. Oddly, the text does not give a motive for Nebuchadnezzar's war against Ecbatana.

---

27. Ibid., 71–74.

28. Ibid., 74.

29. See Esther chapter, above.

30. Wills, *Judith*, 3:1079–81.

31. Newman, "Ecbatana," 2:178.

It only implies that he was trying to amass more subjects, land, troops—or all of the above (1:6). Like most villains, he was power hungry with an insatiable appetite.

Unfortunately for Nebuchadnezzar, not enough cities were fearful of him. Some of the peoples he summoned refused to comply (1:7–11). This list includes Samaria and Jerusalem, which would have jumped out at Israelite audiences as significant. The story will telescope in on those cities as it slowly leads us to its main characters and central events (4:1–15). Nebuchadnezzar was so infuriated by the rebelliousness of these nations that he planned to attack all of them (1:12). First, he went back to attack Ecbatana. It takes all of three verses to describe how that great city fell to Nebuchadnezzar (1:13–15). The text notes that he attacked Ecbatana "in the seventeenth year" (1:13), which may refer to the chronology of events in the life of the historical Nebuchadnezzar II. He attacked Jerusalem in his eighteenth year as king (Jer 32:1–2); therefore this comment may have struck its ancient audience as a foreshadowed indication of the impending threat to Jerusalem as the story of Judith unfolds.

Chapters 1–3 serve to show how utterly terrified Judeans would have been of this malevolent king. Although Nebuchadnezzar had not inspired fear in all the nations he threatened, he was clearly a mighty ruler with a skilled military to have taken down Ecbatana. If the audience had any doubt about the wickedness of this fictional King Nebuchadnezzar of Assyria, chapter two would have prepared them for the ugly acts of a terrible villain. Yet by repeating the nonsensical pairing of Nebuchadnezzar and Assyria for the fourth time in 2:1 (cf. 1:1, 7, 11), the narrator reminds the audience that this is a fantastical story. At the beginning of chapter two, the king sells his plan of revenge on those who would not join his earlier war parties to his higher-ups (2:1–2; cf. 1:11). The Greek of 2:2b is ambiguous; we cannot be sure if the king is characterizing those other nations as disobedient (NRSV), or if he is advocating for their destruction (NAB).[32]

The narrator introduces a key character in the book in 2:4: The king's general Holofernes. We do not learn much about Holofernes in this section, but rather we read his orders from the king, who is aggrandized with the appellation "the Great King, the lord of the whole earth" (2:5a). He is to assemble a massive army and go on a huge campaign

---

32. The NRSV seems to more accurately render the problematic Greek. See Moore, *Judith*, 132.

of death, destruction, and domination (2:5b–8). The demanded offerings of "earth and water" in 2:7 refers to a Persian sign of willingness to obediently agree to a treaty.[33] Aside from the dead, which are described graphically (2:8), Holofernes will take captives and accept only surrender (2:9–11). These statements surely remind Judith's audiences of the various captivities of the Jews during their history, particularly the Assyrian exile in 722, indicated by the aggressing nation Assyria, and the Babylonian exile in 587, indicated by the name Nebuchadnezzar.[34] The king's final flourish is to warn his commander to follow his instructions precisely (2:12–13). After all that preceded these orders, Holofernes is in no position to disobey.

While Holofernes is every bit as much fictional as the king in this story, his name and to some extent his role may have roots in Artaxerxes III Ochus' commander Holofernes (ca. 341 BCE; also spelled Olofernes). Another possible historical parallel to this figure is the Greek Commander under Antiochus IV Epiphanes, Nicanor (d. ca. 160 BCE). He met a similar fate as Holofernes in Judith 13:8, being decapitated after his defeat by Judas and the Maccabees (1 Macc 7:43–47; 2 Macc 15:30–35).[35]

In 2:14–20 Holofernes sets off amply supplied with troops, weaponry, provisions, and riches galore, all to support their military campaign. The battalion headed west from Nineveh all the way to the Mediterranean, preceding the king. Verse 20 contains three familiar biblical images to describe the mass of people who were with Holofernes and his troops. The "mixed crowd" in 2:20 translates πολὺς [ὁ] ἐπίμικτος (*polus epimiktos*). This is the same Greek phrase as in LXX of Exod 12:38, where it refers to those who joined the Israelites in their exit from Egypt. The "locusts" in 2:20 (ἀκρίς *akris*) recall Israel's enemies, particularly when they were great in number (Judg 6:5; 7:12; Joel 1:4; 2:25; Nah 3:15), but also one of the plagues sent against Egypt (Exod 10:12–19). Finally, NRSV's "dust of the earth" (literally "sand of the earth," ἄμμος τῆς γῆς *ammos tēs gēs*) is the phrase found in LXX for the Lord's promise of numerous descendents to Jacob (Gen 28:14).[36] These three

33. Herodotus, *Hist.* 6:48; Wills, *Judith*, 3:1102; Moore, *Judith*, 133.

34. Wills, *Judith*, 3:1102.

35. Wills, *Judith*, 3:1101; Moore, *Judith*, 132–33; Newman, "Holofernes," 2:846; Pietersma, "Holofernes," 3:257; Cousland, "Nicanor," 4:269; Rappaport, "Nicanor," 4:1105.

36. Crawford, *Judith*, 1383.

references were effective ways of expressing the size of Holofernes' regiment while also placing Judith in the wider context of the Hebrew Bible. It seems possible that since two of the images recall victorious images for the Israelites ("mixed crowd" and "sand of the earth"), the author may have been using these metaphors to foreshadow Israel's ultimate victory in this story.

The travelogue that details Holofernes' victories (2:19–27) entails an impossible, certainly fictional geography. While we can identify some of the locations and peoples listed (Upper Cilicia [2:21], in present-day southern Turkey), others are completely unknown (Bectileth [2:21], Rassisites and Chelleans [2:23]), while others lie in a pattern that would barely be attainable by such a mass of people, even if they all had horses (from Nineveh to north of Upper Cilicia in 2:21, which is around four hundred miles in three days). Nonetheless, this section effectively asserts that Holofernes conquered most of the known world, and was now a serious threat to the remaining areas on the Mediterranean coast (2:28: Sidon, Tyre, Jamnia, Azotus, Ascalon; Sur and Ocina are otherwise unknown). A Judean audience would surely have noticed that the story's ruthless commander was nearing their holy land.

By the end of chapter 3 it is clear what a terrible situation the Judeans are facing. Holofernes has conquered the peoples to their north (2:21), south (2:23), east (1:6, 14) and even west (2:28—3:8). And his most recent actions of aggression made clear that he would not tolerate a friendly takeover. Based on his actions toward the coastal peoples (3:8), he would require a most egregious punishment particularly for Judeans— that they transgress their covenant to have no god but the Lord (Exod 20:3; 34:14; Deut 5:7) and worship this heinous leader Nebuchadnezzar instead. When Holofernes finally stops to rest and re-supply, he and his forces are a serious threat to the Israelites. The locations named in 3:9–10 allow for some ambiguity, though not because they are unknown. This list of places could indicate that Holofernes' troops were camped in an ominous though inexact spot north of Samaria. The wide swath of locations named here may alternatively suggest an unreasonably large encampment stretching up to twenty miles across (if Geba is near Mt. Carmel and Scythopolis is at Beth-shean).[37] Either way, this placed the enemy about forty miles north of Jerusalem. Furthermore, they were nearing the city of Bethulia, which will become the story's central loca-

37. Moore, *Judith*, 143–44.

tion soon enough. It was close to Dothan, north of Samaria and a key location for securing Jerusalem (4:6–7). This was a suspenseful story from the beginning, but the stakes keep getting higher.

Cut to Israel (4:1–15)

In chapter 4 the action suddenly shifts from Holofernes and his troops to the Israelites in Judea. This change is the first step in a gradual move focusing in on the Israelites, Judea, and specifically the people of Bethulia, who will be the central places and players in this story. All of the action up to this point bodes miserably for the Israelites. They do not simply fear Holofernes as a ruthless general, but as yet another villain who threatens their holy Jerusalem Temple (4:1–2) as well as their very survival. The narrator helps us empathize with the Israelites in 4:3 by explaining that they have not been home long since the exile, and the Temple was newly rebuilt and rededicated for its holy purposes. In light of Holofernes' record, detailed in the previous chapters, we can imagine how truly terrified such a people would have been. With fresh memories of a razed Temple (2 Kgs 25:1–10), leaders who were tortured and killed (2 Kgs 25:4–7, 19–21), a mournful time spent in a foreign land (Ps 137), and the great efforts required for rebuilding (Ezra 1:1–11; 3:1—6:18), they would have been desperately motivated to evade this menace. Though this newly-post-exile setting does much to set the stakes in the story, it presents yet another historical problem in the book. If Nebuchadnezzar were king or if there were a kingdom of Assyria (1:1), this story would not fit in a postexilic setting. As I pointed out in the Judith Introduction, Nebuchadnezzar ruled from ca. 605 to 562 BCE, and the Assyrian capital Nineveh fell to Babylon in 612 BCE, while the exilic period began in 587 BCE. Nonetheless, this ahistorical setting makes the point: The Israelites have suffered at the hands of tyrannical nations enough to know that they have much to fear in Holofernes.

The Israelites therefore enact a three-pronged military strategy to secure hilltops, food stores and mountain passes (4:4–8). They receive quick cooperation from their neighbors to protect the whole area, from the region of Samaria where Holofernes' troops camped, to Beth-horon and the valley of Salem on the way up to Jerusalem. More unknown cities, as we have seen throughout the book, punctuate 4:4–5: Belmain, Choba, and Aesora. There is something appropriate about these fictional locations accompanying the scenario of teamwork among Israelites from north to south in 4:4–7. Such unified cooperation was something rarely if ever recorded in ancient Israel's history. Indeed, the southern region of Judea was historically at odds with northern Samaria. That animosity went all the way back to 928 BCE when David's united kingdom divided (1 Kgs 12:16–33), and it got worse when Assyria conquered the north in 722 BCE, taking Samaraia's leaders into exile and resettling the city with other captives. This made for a mixed pool of people who the Judeans of the south viewed as disobedient to the covenant for worshiping in their own ways at their own sanctuary (2 Kgs 17:1–41).

Finally the narrator presents the story's key fictional location Bethulia, which acted on orders from their high priest Joakim and elders (NRSV: "senate"; γερουσία *gerousia*) to secure Judea by shutting down the narrow mountain passes that led to it (4:6–7). First Esdras 5:5 names Joakim as a Davidic high priest who returned from Babylon to Jerusalem. Like numerous other references in Judith, that priest would not make historical sense in this context, but it does point to a setting in which a high priest was in charge of Jerusalem, apparently without a king. This would coincide with the time of the Maccabees, when the high priest Jonathan ruled with the elders (1 Macc 12:6, also *gerousia*),[38] thus adding corroboration to the historical setting I proposed in the Judith Introduction. Another possible reference to the Maccabean period in this passage is 4:3, in which the reconsecration of the temple could suggest the Maccabean rededication of temple in 164 BCE after the "desolating sacrilege" of Antiochus IV Epiphanes (1 Macc 1:54; 4:36–61; 2 Macc 10:1–9).[39]

Having taken the logical military steps to protect themselves, the Israelites enact their final defense tactic and implore God for help. They pray, fast, wear sackcloth, prostrate themselves, put ashes on their heads, and lament their impending doom (4:9–12). It is appropriate to speculate about whether the cattle wearing sackcloth (4:10) is humorous, satirical, or hyperbole.[40] While it does have a humorous effect like in Jonah 3:8, and fits with the book's fictional setting, it most importantly expresses the desperation crucial to this part of the story. The text graphically de-

---

38. Wills, *Judith*, 3:1114.

39. Ibid., 3:1112; Moore, *Judith*, 147–48.

40. Wills, *Judith*, 3:1114, discusses both humor and satire, concluding with Craven that it is humorous (*Artistry*, 115).

tails the people's feared worst-case scenario, that their babies would be kidnapped, their wives would become trophies, and that their homeland and holy Temple would be burned (4:12). All this again recalls both Assyria's capture of the northern kingdom in 722 BCE, as well as the Babylonian exile, as we saw in 4:2. In addition to the people, who make fervent prayers, the priests continue with supplications in their own appropriate ways (4:14–15). Oddly sandwiched between the entreaties of the people and of the priests lies a crucial verse of reassurance, 4:13. It affirms the efficacy of these nonmilitary strategies, and unflinchingly states that "The Lord heard their prayers and had regard for their distress." This not only attests to the faithfulness of the people and the mercy of the Lord, it also foreshadows the outcome of the story. The Lord will help the people to survive and even prevail over Nebuchadnezzar and Holofernes. While the reader knows this, the people of Bethulia do not, creating marvelous dramatic irony.[41] The Bethulians will have to rely on their own hope in divine assistance through some very difficult times before the story is over.

Cut to Holofernes (5:1—6:11)

The next shift in action moves us from the Israelites to Holofernes and his troops. When the general learns that this one region of hill-dwellers has not submitted to him, he becomes enraged, and seeks an explanation (5:1–4). Among those he asks are Moabites and Ammonites, notable enemies of the Israelites (Num 21:21–35//Deut 2:26–3:17; Num 22; Judg 3:12–30; Judg 10:7—12:4; 1 Sam 10:27—11:11; 14:47; 2 Sam 10:6–14; 11:1; 1 Chr 19:1—20:3; 2 Chr 20:10, 22–23; 27:1–5; Neh 4:7; Ps 83:6–7; Jer 49:2; Ezek 25:1–11; Amos 1:13; Zeph 2:8–11; perhaps relevant to the historical setting of the Judith story is 1 Macc 5:6–7).[42] The "governors of the coastland" (5:2) likely referred to Holofernes' recent conquests in 3:6. The answer to Holofernes' question about Bethulia's defiance comes in a particularly odd scenario. One of these historic enemies of the Israelites, the Ammonite foreigner Achior, steps in to offer an explanation (5:5–21). We find out by the end of this section that he did so at great risk to his life (5:22–6:13).

---

41. Wills, *Judith*, 3:1115.

42. Also see the section on Moab in Ruth chapter, above.

Achior's truthful report (5:5) stands as an outstanding summary of Israel's history, complete with appropriate theological insights. The Hebrew Bible includes historical reviews on a number of occasions (Deut 11:2–7; 26:5–9; Josh 24:2–13; Neh 9:6–31; Ps 106:4–46; Ps 136); never do those come from the lips of a non-Israelite except for a brief reference by Balaam in Num 24:8. Thus this strange scene with Achior may well have seemed humorous to the early audiences of Judith, yet it may also have been a way to express the triumphant mood of the story: Even foreigner-enemies understand the workings of the Israelites' God. Achior's account begins with the early generations, beginning with Abram, his place of origin, and the place where God called him to be (5:5–9; see Gen 11:26–29, 31; 12:1–7; 13:2–5). He tells about Joseph and the Hebrews both in Egypt and liberated from it (5:10–13; see Gen 45:8–11; 47:1–6; Exod 1:7–14; 2:23–25; 7:15—12:33; 14:21–22, 29; 15:19), their sojourn in the desert (5:14–15a; see Exod 19:1–2; 32:8; Num 21:13–34; Deut 2:30–35; 9:23), and their conquest and settlement of Canaan (5:15b–16; see Josh 3:10; 4:1–24; 10:40; 12:8; 24:11). He concludes with a theological statement posed as an historical fact: When these people obeyed their God, all was well with them; when they disobeyed, they suffered at the hands of foreign nations (5:17–18). The latter he details with a description of the Babylonian Exile (5:18b; see 2 Kgs 25:8–9). We see the retribution theology he articulates in much of the Hebrew Bible, though it did not go unquestioned.

As evidenced by the biblical citations above, Achior gives a fairly accurate telling of Israelite history, mostly in line with the pentateuchal narrative and the Deuteronomistic historian. He only deviates from the biblical telling of this history in a few places. One of the strangest things in Achior's telling of Israel's history is his apparent need to explain why Abram and his family left their ancestral home of Ur (5:7–8). He attributes it to their unwillingness to worship the gods of the Chaldeans (another name for Babylonians) instead of "the God of heaven" (5:8), thus painting the Chaldeans as religiously hostile.[43] Yet the biblical text offers no such account. It is understandable why Achior would fill in this narrative gap. It is logical to wonder why Abram would have left his ancestral home, other than the fact that the Lord made him ful-

---

43. "The God of heaven" appears elsewhere in Judith (6:19; 11:17) was a common Persian term, as found in 2 Chr 36:23; Ezra 1:2; 5:11, 12; Dan 2:37; Tob 10:11–12, and Elephantine Papyri, according to Moore, *Judith*, 159.

some promises after telling him to do it (Gen 12:1–7). It could be that in Judith's setting, after the Babylonian exile, it made sense to villainize Chaldeans all the way back to Israel's ancestral origins. Whatever the explanation for Achior's addition to Israelite history in 5:7–8, this is not the only place it appears. Josephus writes of a similar scenario for Abram in his *Antiquities of the Jews* (1.7.1).[44]

Other digressions from Hebrew Bible history appear in Achior's telling as well. He, like the book of Joshua, overlooks the comment in Judges that the Jebusites remained in Jerusalem after the Israelites infiltrated the land (5:7–8; see Judg 1:21; cf. 2 Sam 5:6–10). He also erroneously mentions Shechemites in 5:16 as some of the peoples Israel drove out of Canaan; they are included in Moses and Eliezar's census as part of the Israelite congregation (Num 26:31). That may be an anachronistic comment from a Hellenistic author antagonistic to Shechem, or it could refer to the Shechemite villains in the Dinah story (Genesis 34) to which Judith refers in 9:2–4.[45] The historically accurate reference to the destruction of Jerusalem and Babylonian exile in 5:18 again betrays the author's disregard for the book's purported setting. If either Nebuchadnezzar or Assyria were threats to these people, they would not be able to report the events of 5:18, which had yet to occur. Achior's final statement about Israel's history tells of a gathering-in of the scattered Israelites (5:19), something that never entirely came to pass. Achior follows his historical narrative with a conclusion that was unwelcome advice for the General Holofernes (5:20–21). The Deuteronomist had made clear that YHVH would bring defeat to a disobedient Israel (5:20; see Deut 32:1–25). Within this same retributive system, the Lord would defend the Israelites, if they had been following YHVH's laws (5:21; see Deut 28:1–2, 7).

All of these references to Israel's historic enemies (5:1–4, particularly Holofernes' "Canaanites" in v. 3) and events throughout the centuries (5:5–19) continue the fictionalization of the book, not only because they are inaccurate but because they draw the audience into a wholly separate time, one might say "the olden days." This historical background sets up Holofernes to meet Judith in 10:23. It will make him eager to accept an

44. Moore, *Judith*, 159.

45. Shechem was one of the conquests of the Maccabean ruler John Hyrcanus I (*Ant* 13.9.1). That takeover may have represented widespread Jewish animosity against the city (Moore, *Judith*, 160; Wills, *Judith*, 3:1119).

apparent defector of this people who "refused to come out and meet me" (5:4; 11:1–4), it corroborates her telling of Israel's ability (or inability) to defend itself against him (11:9–16), and it explains her religious obedience (11:17). In the scheme of the narrative, Achior's speech ultimately prepares Holofernes to welcome Judith as his spy—or so he thinks—and even considers her as his religious leader, because he purportedly understands her situation and her motives (11:18–23). Achior's long answer (5:5–19) to Holofernes' question, "what people is this?" (5:3) asserts that no one puts up such a desperate or clever defense as a people who have been repeatedly victimized, even if they have theological reasons to explain their suffering. Arguably, Haman and the Persians learned this from Esther as well. Achior's closing statement of advice to the General (5:20–21) almost make him sound like a devotee of Israel's God. Not only does he give a truthful report of Israel's history, he seems to believe its theological veracity. This serves as foreshadowing for the Ammonite's later triumphant conversion (14:10).

Achior's keen insights about Israel's history, reported as a service to Holofernes and his followers, earn him a death sentence. The general does not act on the first suggestion he receives, to dismember this volunteer spy (5:22), but instead orders that he be left at the story's central Israelite town, Bethulia (6:10), presumably to be killed along with the rest of that city's inhabitants (6:5–8). Holofernes' response to Achior's report highlights the general's devotion to King Nebuchadnezzar as his god (6:2–4). Both the Israelites and the Assyrians understand this as a supernatural war: The Israelites will win if they are obedient to their God (5:17–21); the Assyrians cannot accept that because their king Nebuchadnezzar is the only god (6:2). As far as Holofernes was concerned, Achior's telling of Israel's history with an ending that placed YHVH above Nebuchadnezzar signaled Achior's loyalty to Israel. Despite Holofernes' death plans for Achior, he is surprisingly saved at the last minute. In the process of getting Achior to the Bethulians, Holofernes' men got a taste of the military strength of this little hilltop town (6:12). Thus the soldiers were compelled to leave Achior tied up at the bottom of the hill outside Bethulia, and to flee back to their general (6:13).

Cut to the Israelites (6:14–21)

At this point the action returns to the Israelites in Bethulia. We caught a brief but impressive glimpse of them in 6:12, as they fought off the Assyrians who wanted to leave Achior with them. The people of Bethulia rescued him, taking him in as a God-sent spy rather than prisoner, finding out what to expect from Holofernes and his troops. Achior appeared before the town leaders in order to give his report about the Assyrians, and was even welcomed to a banquet at Uzziah's home (6:14–17, 21). Interestingly, and in contrast to what we will see go on in Holofernes' tent, that banquet was not simply a party: The attendees spent the night petitioning God in light of what they now knew was a dire situation (6:21b; 12:10–20).

Bethulia's elders, Uzziah, Chabris and Charmis (6:15; 8:10; 10:6) are fictional—or at least otherwise unknown. Nonetheless, their names and genealogies imparted some meaning to the original audiences. The name Uzziah means "my strength is YHVH," and though there is more than one biblical figure bearing the name, he was best known as a Judean king. Several prophets proclaimed their messages during his reign, including Isaiah (1:1; 6:1; 7:1), Hosea (1:1) and Amos (1:1). Though he was not entirely noncontroversial (2 Chr 26:16–23), the Deuteronomist gave him a favorable evaluation (2 Kgs 15:34). The identification of Uzziah as being "of the tribe of Simeon" associated him with the conquerors of the city Shechem, which is significant in the horrific episode involving Dinah that Judith later invokes (Genesis 34; Jdt 9:2–4 and commentary on those verses below) and may have been a location against which Judith's audience held great animosity (see above commentary on 5:16).[46] These three figures, but especially Uzziah, play an important role in the book of Judith. Uzziah functions like the king of Bethulia even though he is not; he is the one behind the important actions and decisions in the city (Jdt 6:15, 21; 7:23, 30; 8:9, 28, 35; 10:6; 13:18; 14:6; 15:4). The meaning of his name and the reputation of the Judean King Uzziah prepare the reader for a wise, obedient and mighty leader—though imperfect. The Uzziah we meet in Judith fits this description fairly well. He certainly desires to submit to God, though he does have his limits (6:18–21; 7:30).[47] Nonetheless, he is not too egotistical a man to allow Judith to save the day (8:10–35; 10:6).

46. Moore, *Judith*, 168.
47. Contra Moore, *Judith*, 167.

Battle Preparations against Bethulia (7:1–32)

Again, the scene moves back to Holofernes, but only for a short time. Chapter seven offers images of the Assyrians and the Israelites alternatively, which effectively draws us into the impending crisis. In the first scene Holofernes' troops are preparing to take Bethulia. The text describes his army and those from the surrounding regions as an astonishingly mighty force of almost two hundred thousand fighters (7:2). The narrative reads as though they had strategically moved their camp into position (7:3). Though some of the locations are unknown (Balbaim and Cyamon), the description sounds as though they are in the same place as where they first settled in 3:9–10.

The narrative shifts back to the Israelites in 7:4–5 just long enough to show how fearful they are. They articulate their distress in a noteworthy way, focusing on the decimation of the land (7:4b). Later they do worry about their personal well being, and that of their families (7:27), but here they lament about a land that the enemy will "strip clean," and that "cannot bear their weight." While contemporary people seem relatively uninterested in the ecological catastrophes that their wars trigger, this was the primary concern that came to mind for our ancient author. In fact it maintains the prominence of the land that we find throughout the Hebrew Bible. Despite their great concern, the Israelites show no sign of surrender at this point. They rallied for war with all their military resources (7:5).

When the story line moves back to Holofernes and his troops, he and his cavalry are investigating the environs of Bethulia (7:6–7). They particularly scrutinize the in-roads to the city and its water sources. Upon returning to camp, he apparently gives a report of his findings—though the text does not specifically indicate that. In any case, his return brings military advice from the foreign military leaders who are working with him (7:8–9). Notably, these voices include Israel's historic enemies the Edomites (1 Sam 14:47; 2 Sam 8:13; 1 Kgs 11:15–16; 2 Kgs 14:7–10) and Moabites.[48] In the time the story was written, Edom may have been viewed as even more significant than what we read elsewhere in the Hebrew Bible. During the time of the Maccabees, the peoples from this area were referred to as the Idumeans; Judas Hyrcanus and his followers forced some of them to convert to Judaism.[49] Regardless of the identity

---

48. Dearman, "Edom," 2:188–91; also see section on "Moab" in Ruth chapter, above.

49. Wills, *Judith*, 3:1127.

of these foreign nations, their willingness to take sides against Israel would have been cause for much disdain, as was the case in previous military struggles in their history (Ps 137:7; Amos 1:3–15; Obadiah). They instructed him simply to cut off Bethulia's water supply (7:9–14), an idea that Holofernes appreciated and enacted (7:16–17). Surrounding an embattled city until they ran out of water was no new military strategy in the ancient world. In fact, one of ancient Israel's most remarkable feats of engineering was the Siloam Tunnel, constructed as quickly as possible under King Hezekiah's reign while the real Assyrian army threatened Jerusalem (2 Kgs 20:20). This aqueduct allowed the waters from the Gihon Spring to flow into the city so that the inhabitants could survive barricaded there during a long siege from the enemy.[50] In contrast, this passage about Holofernes and his troops ends with Bethulia's water supply effectively curtailed. Furthermore, the hilltop city seems to be ominously surrounded by enemy troops, though it is a bit difficult to know for sure since their encampments are obscure locations, like so many others in Judith (Chusi, Egrebeh, Wadi Mochmur; 7:17–18).

The flow of the text gives the impression that the enemy's water-cutoff strategy had immediate effects: The narrator takes us directly from the surrounding troops (7:18) to the despairing Israelites (7:19). Yet in 7:20 we find that it actually took thirty-four days for Bethulia to run out of water. Unlike 7:4–5, where the Israelites begged God for help but then rallied their forces, here they beg God for help with no recourse of their own, because they are dying of thirst (7:19–22). They quickly turn to the only option that seems possible: surrender (7:26). They blame their leader Uzziah for not doing this sooner (7:24), and they blame God for their circumstances (7:25). In the spirit of the Hebrews newly freed from Egypt, they justify this conclusion on the basis that it would be better to be slaves than to watch their families slowly die of thirst (7:27 cf. Exod 14:11–12).[51] In the spirit of the Deuteronomist (Deut 4:26; 30:19; 31:28), they invoke their retributive God, heaven and earth, and their ancestors to back their plea to Uzziah (7:28). With this shift from themselves to God, they go on to petition God for help (7:29).

Uzziah has his own theological agenda, which is to remain obedient to God even in the face of impending death. Even that faithfulness has its limits, however, and that apparently numbers five days. Those

---

50. Ehrlich, "Siloam," 5:255–57.

51. Wills, *Judith*, 3:1129.

five days, plus the day of the conversation and the thirty-four days the people have already been under siege, make for a biblically-significant forty day wait for divine mercy (e.g., Gen 8:6–7; Exod 16:35; 24:18; 1 Sam 17:16; 1 Kgs 19:8; Jonah 3:4). Uzziah boldly declares that God will send help within that time (7:30), but if not he will assent to their pleas for surrender (7:31). It is an ultimatum for God (7:30) and a test to these miserable people (7:32). Ultimately, it becomes the challenge that brings our heroine to the forefront of the story.

Introduction of Judith (8:1–8)

When my students read Judith, they often report that they wonder when they will ever meet the namesake of the story. She finally appears in 8:1, halfway through the book. This delay provides more than just suspense, as the previous seven chapters have been crucial in setting the stage for what happens when Judith does finally appear. Without that part of the narrative we would not know the dire consequences Judith and her people face; we would not know how badly they need help, nor would we know the astonishing heroism of her deeds. The narrator spends eight verses introducing Judith. All we know of her relevance to the story during that time is that she "heard about these things." In many ways she was just the hero Israel needed: Came from a good family line (8:1); more than faithful to Israel's laws and customs (8:5–6, 8); wealthy and hardworking (8:7b), admired by all and God-fearing (8:8). Yet she could not exactly be viewed as the new Moses. She was after all female, and a widow. The narrator makes up for this in all the right ways, by describing her as both "beautiful" and "lovely" (8:7a).[52] Like the "worthy woman" of Prov 31:10–31, Judith possessed everything she needed to become a superheroine in her own time. She will even have the obligatory costume change in chapter 10.

It is highly unusual to find a genealogy for a woman in the Hebrew Bible, and unheard of to see such a long and apparently prestigious one as Judith's in 8:1. Yet, similar to the geography and history in Judith, this genealogy presents some difficulties compared to other biblical ancestor lists. The narrator traces Judith's line all the way back to Israel (Jacob). Yet the genealogy erroneously lists Sarasadai as Jacob's son.

---

52. Wills notes that Judith bears beauty and wealth, the two great features of the Greek novels' heroine (*Judith*, 3:1132).

Sarasadai was the father of Salamiel ("Zurishaddai" and "Shelumiel" in Num 10:19), who was the leader of the Simeonites. The Simeonite ancestry will become important later in the Judith story, in 9:2. Many of the other names in the list are linked improperly to father and son in Judith: Joseph, Oziel ("Uzziel," a Kohathite in Exod 6:18 and elsewhere), Hilkiah, Ahitub, Eliab (Oholiab, a Danite in Exod 31:6). In these cases the text simply skips several generations between the names, using "son of" quite loosely.[53] Other names of interest in her genealogy include Ox ("Uz" in Gen 22:21), Merari (a son of Levi; Gen 46:11), Gideon (Judg 6:11—8:36), and Elijah (1 Kings 17–18). In all of this we see Judith connected to Jacob himself, as well as to significant priestly and prophetic leaders. Furthermore, the narrator certainly made a point with Judith's name itself, as it is related to "Judean," means "Jewess," and possibly alludes to Judas Maccabeus.[54] The cumulative effect of the genealogy is to validate Judith as a Jew of outstanding lineage, even if it didn't remove her from the realm of fiction.

Judith would have been viewed as utterly devoted in her mourning practices (8:4–6), which went way beyond the expected observances of a widow. To some extent, that may be attributed to the fact that as an apparently childless widow, she was the (or at least a) beneficiary of her deceased husband's estate. In most biblical texts, it goes without saying that widows were impoverished (Exod 22:21–22; Deut 24:19–21; Ps 146:9; Isa 1:17; 4:1; Jer 7:6–7; Ezek 22:7; Mal 3:5). Thus, unlike most childless widows, Judith could afford to remain in mourning and not avail herself of the custom of levirate marriage (see section on Levirate Marriage in Ruth Introduction, above). While it was not unheard of for a widow to inherit from her deceased husband (Ruth 4:3–9), it was quite an oddity. A wife inheriting her deceased husband's estate was certainly not assumed like it is today. It makes Judith a rarity among women in her time, a wealthy and independent figure, perfectly positioned to solve the problems facing Israel. Again, she was just the heroine they needed.

---

53. Moore, *Judith*, 187.

54. Wills, *Judith*, 3:1131; LaCocque writes that Judith "is Judas Maccabee in the feminine; her very name says as much (cf. 1 Macc. 3:1–9). At the time of the composition of Judith, it was surely not a trivial feat to feminize the hero of the day!" (*Feminine*, 39).

Judith Has a Better Plan (8:9–36)

In this section our newly introduced heroine Judith does not describe a new plan so much as shame Bethulia's leaders for the pact they had made with the people. From 8:9 to 8:27, Judith authoritatively pleads and preaches to the city elders. Her articulate message has a neat rhetorical flow in which she makes her case (8:11b–17), justifies it (8:18–23), and presents a closing argument complete with historical reminder and theological rationale (8:24–27). Uzziah's response to her in 8:28–31 paints Judith as the heroine the text has already foreshadowed in 8:1–8. While he acknowledges her great wisdom (8:28–29), he defends his own actions (8:30), and admits he needs her intervention (8:31, 35–36), which he will find comes not as rain like he requests (8:31), but in the form of a secret plan (8:32–34).

In 8:10 we meet another new and important character in this story, Judith's "maid," or "favorite slave" (ἄβραν *abran*). Though the narrator does not tell us her name, she does have a prominent role in the events yet to unfold. We get a sense of that from the fact that she "was in charge of all [Judith] possessed," and we know from 8:7b this was a significant task of estate management. Furthermore, her representation of Judith apparently indicated serious clout, as she was able to "summon" the three town elders to Judith (8:10).

In her long speech to these men, Judith accuses the city leaders of testing the Lord with their five-day ultimatum (8:11–13). The language is loaded here, as the word for "test" (πειράζω *peirazō*) appears in the same lexical form in some momentous biblical scenes, particularly Exod 17:2, where Moses accused the Israelites of testing YHVH. At that time, the Israelites were thirsty wandering in the wilderness, like the people of Bethulia are thirsty here.[55] In fact, several other places in the biblical text refer back to this testing incident in Exodus (Num 14:22; Deut 33:8; Ps 106:14 [MT 105:14]), and yet other passages warn against testing God (Wisd 1:2; Sir 18:23). Passover Haggadot from the sixteenth century made this connection explicit by including Judith in their illustrations.[56]

---

55. Jan Willem van Henten makes a more elaborate comparison of Judith and Exod 17:1–7, starting with the Bethulians' complaints in 7:23–28. Additionally, van Henten makes a broader comparison to the Exodus story, comparing the forty days the Bethulians had to wait for help to the forty years the Israelites had to wander in the wilderness ("Judith," 232–38).

56. Stone, "Judith," 82–83.

Judith the biblical theologian becomes Judith the sage in 8:14–16. Her sentiments echo those of the wisdom writings in Job, Proverbs, Ecclesiastes, Wisdom, and Sirach (Job 11:7; 28:12–13, 20–23; Prov 1:28; Eccl 3:11; 7:24; 8:17; Wis 1:2; Sir 23:19). Between these connections and her similarities to the wise woman in Proverbs 31 (see above on 8:1–8), Judith is a wise woman to be sure; it is unlikely the book's early audiences would have missed that based on her comments here. Judith ends her description of the divine character in 8:14–16 by instructing her people to bring God genuine petitions for assistance, coupled with an attitude that God will do what God sees fit, not necessarily what the people want (8:17). Her speech moves back to biblical history and theology in 8:18, reminding the elders of the first commandment (8:18, 20) and the past and future consequences of violating it (8:19, 21–23): The people have the responsibility and opportunity to protect the temple (8:21, 24). Wills points out that this comment about no more idol worship (8:18) may relate to the eradication of idols and distant sanctuaries under Hasmonean rule.[57] Her final admonition is for her leaders to have gratitude for God (8:25–27). In so doing, she returns to her language about testing (πειράζω *peirazō*; 8:12) and reverses it. Rather than chastising the people for testing God as she did in 8:12, she asserts that God is testing them. This too is a common biblical scene, and Judith offers some examples of it in 8:26, from the episode with Abraham about to sacrifice his son Isaac (Gen 22:1) to Jacob's many years of trying service to his uncle Laban (Genesis 28–31). She concludes that God's testing is beneficial discipline (8:27, cf. Dan 12:10; Wis 3:5; 4 Macc 9:7).

When Uzziah responds, he acknowledges Judith's sage-like words (8:29) with vocabulary that echoes classic Wisdom phrases: "wisdom" (σοφία *sophia*) and "understanding" (σύνεσις *sunesis*) (some notable verses that include both Greek words in LXX include Prov 1:7; 2:2, 6; Job 12:13; 28:20; Sir 1:4, 18–19; 14:20; 15:3; 44:4; 50:27). Uzziah then apparently tries to explain his side of the story (8:30). In so doing, he describes a situation that does not quite fit with what the narrator has previously reported. Yes, the people were thirsty and remain so, but he exaggerates the extent to which they forced the elders to make the ultimatum to God (7:28–31).

He goes on to ask for her prayers, assuming that they will be more efficacious than anyone else's. This serves as an additional possible

---

57. Wills, *Judith*, 3:1137.

parallel to the Exodus story; this time she could be filling the role of Moses, who was especially able to intervene to God on behalf of the people (8:31cf. Exod 20:19; 32:11, 30). Uzziah has a specific prayer request in mind: rain to relieve the people's thirst. Judith, however, has a better idea.

Finally in 8:32–34, the elders and the readers get a glimpse of the events yet to come. Whatever Judith has in mind, it will make history (8:32), and it will have her acting as an agent for God (8:33b). The phrase "by my hand" (ἐν χειρί μου *en keiri mou*), indicating that she will be God's instrument in order to save the day, repeats again in 9:9 and 12:4. Notably, her big plan is a secret (8:34), yet she nonetheless receives the full blessing of the city leaders, who apparently place their trust in her as their only option (8:35). All they—and the audience—can do from here is find a good place to wait and see what happens (8:36). What better set-up could there be for a superhero to save the day at the last minute, with the audience eagerly anticipating every detail?

Judith Prepares Herself to Enact Her Plan (9:1—10:10)

Judith's prayer in 9:1–14 stands out as one of the most remarkable in the Hebrew Bible. It compares to the prayers of Hannah (1 Sam 2:1–10), Daniel (2:20–23; 9:4–19), Judas Maccabeus (1 Macc 4:30–33), Manasseh (Pr Man 1–15) and of course many of the Psalms. More to the point, Wills points out that it correlates to other women's prayers in Jewish novels of the time, including Susanna (1:42–43), Sarah (Tob 3:11–15), Additions of Esther (14:1–19), and Aseneth (*Jos. Asen.* 17:10; 21:10–21; 26:7; 27:10).[58] Before Judith's plan goes into action, the narrator keeps us waiting with this chapter-long petition and spiritual preparation from our heroine. Much of the prayer consists of remembrance and reminders of God's previous interventions in Israelite history. It is a bold, honest, and eloquent prayer, and appropriately sets the stage for Judith's coming actions. Without this prayer, the events of chapters 10–13 would give quite a different impression, as would the character of Judith.

Judith's prayer begins with a few details to emphasize just how pious she was, including her pose of prostration, the ashes on her head, and the fact that she "uncovered" her sackcloth, suggesting that she had it on underneath her other mourning garments (8:5). The tim-

58. Wills, *Judith*, 3:1141.

ing of her prayer coincides with the evening incense offering in the Jerusalem Temple (9:1), a possible indication that the author was celebrating renewed Jewish control and ritual observance there during the Maccabean era.

One remarkable feature of Judith's prayer in 9:1–14 is the number of epithets she uses for God. Some are familiar; others are completely unique. She opens addressing the divinity as "O Lord God of my ancestor Simeon . . ." (9:2). Simeon was one of Leah and Jacob's sons (Gen 29:33). In Gen 33:18–20, Jacob and his family were all camped in the Canaanite city Shechem, where he had bought land and set up an altar. While there, Simeon's sister Dinah was raped by the son of the region's prince, who was himself named Shechem. The narrator in Gen 34:7b clearly condemned that act saying "It [raping Dinah] shall not be done." Judith quotes that judgment directly from LXX in Jdt 9:2 as she recounts the Genesis story. Simeon and his brother Levi later took revenge on the Shechemites for the rape by demanding that they be circumcised if they were to marry among them, which is what Shechem wanted with Dinah, but then the brothers massacred them while they were still recovering from the procedure. Their father Jacob chastised Simeon and Levi for making such enemies in the land (Gen 34:30) and for their violent anger (Gen 49:5–7; also see 4 Macc 2:19). Thus Judith's address invoking Simeon would have been a bizarre way to start a prayer not only because the epithet appears nowhere else, but also because the episode about Simeon and the Shechemites receives nothing but negative assessments elsewhere in the biblical text.

This sorted history of Simeon nonetheless makes him appropriate for the scenario about to unfold in Judith. For one thing, the book of Judith has already foreshadowed the reference to Simeon several times with a comment about conquering the Shechemites (5:16) and by including Simeonite ancestors for Uzziah (6:15) and Judith, who here makes perfectly clear that she comes from his line (8:1). Furthermore, Simeon used deceit for what he and his brothers deemed fitting and necessary revenge (Gen 34:13); Judith will ultimately pray to use her deceit in order to accomplish God's ends (9:10). Judith's condensed reference to the story of Dinah and Simeon also makes God a more active force than what we see in Genesis 34 (9:2–4). As Judith reports it in her prayer, God used Simeon's actions to punish the Shechemites. That is not at all how Genesis 34 portrays the event. It reports no divine judgment on it either positively or negatively, even though Jacob condemned it. It could be that Judith's mention of this event as a divinely guided model for her own actions arises from the book's historical setting. If the book hails from the time of the Maccabean revolt, perhaps the reference to the Shechemites, who were taken advantage of while healing from mass circumcision (Gen 34:18–24), relates to the forced circumcisions of Judas Maccabeus' enemies (1 Macc 2:46). Some of the details of Jdt 9:2–4 could serve as explanation or justification of thoses events, for instance despising the uncleanness they incurred by spilling blood (Jdt 9:4).

Verses 5–6 of Judith's prayer move her from invoking the Simeon episode to her petition for victory over the Assyrians (9:7–14). These verses highlight her trust in God's guidance of events both in the past and in the future. Beginning with 9:7 she introduces the ominous Assyrian army, though she undermines their threat with a reassuring claim that includes her second epithet in this prayer, "They do not know that you are the Lord who crushes wars." In this statement she wholeheartedly expects God to undo the Assyrian threat, and that the enemy will be completely surprised by the outcome. It is a triumphant way to articulate a prayer, especially because it is the exact divine appellation used by the poet in the Song of the Sea (Exod 15:3 LXX //Jdt 9:7 κύριος συντρίβων πολέμους *kyriōs syntribōn polemoys*), rejoicing in the Exodus victory.[59] As Moore has shown, further parallels to the Exodus text appear in this section of Judith's prayer, adding to those earlier in the book.[60] In 9:7, Judith speaks of the Assyrians' "horses and riders" (ἵππῳ καὶ ἀναβάτη *hippō kai anabatē*); both words also appear in LXX Exod 14:23 and 15:1, referring to the Egyptians. We will see one more connection between the texts in 9:9, where Judith asks God to "send your wrath" in crushing the Assyrians. They are the same Greek words and tense as in the Song of the Sea, which praises God for victory over the Egyptians (ἀπέστειλας τὴν ὀργήν *apesteilas tēn orgēn*; Exod 15:7 LXX//ἀπόστειλον . . . *aposteilon* . . . ; Jdt 9:9), despite slight differences in the English translations. This, like so many episodes in Israel's history, will be a new exodus, orchestrated by Israel's powerful and victorious God, here with Judith as God's Moses-like leader.

59. Moore, *Judith*, 192.
60. See commentary above on Jdt 2:20; 5:10–15; 7:27; 8:11–13, 30.

Judith articulates some specific requests in 9:8. There a three-line parallelism outlines her concern for the temple amid her petition to conquer the Assyrians, whom she fears will:

> defile your sanctuary
> pollute the tabernacle
> break off the horns of your altar.

This makes clear what is at stake. Next we learn the length to which Judith will go to protect the temple. As she continues to pray for God's help (9:9a) her plan begins to unfold. She personally needs God's assistance to conquer the enemy through dishonesty (9:9b–10). This will be a war between the Assyrians and Judith, with Judith fighting on behalf of God, armed with a sword of divinely inspired deceitful words. As Judith herself points out three times in the book, hers is not just any hand that will defeat the enemy; it is "the hand of a woman," or more precisely, a "female" (Jdt 9:10; 13:15; 16:5 ἐν χειρὶ θηλείας *en cheiri thēleias*).[61] Female warriors appear in the Bible just enough to know that one would not want the notoriety of having been killed by one (Jdg 9:51–54), and that they are nonetheless effective (Jdg 4:4–15, 21; 5:24–25).

In 9:11 Judith enlists the oft-used prayer strategy of the Psalmists by reminding God of the divine character. The verse first describes what God is not (9:11a),[62] and then provides a parallel positive portrayal (9:11b). In this latter part of the verse, we hear the third divine epithet of Judith's prayer, "You are the God of the lowly, helper of the oppressed, upholder of the weak, protector of the forsaken, savior of those without hope." The phrase "God of the lowly" does not appear anywhere else in the canonical or even deuterocanonical texts. Though there are multiple places in the Bible that focus on God's concern for the "lowly" and the oppressed of all kinds (comparable verses that also use ταπεινός *tapeinos* in LXX include Ps 82:3; 10:17; 138:6; Prov 3:34; Job 5:11; Amos 2:7; 8:6; Isa 66:2; Add Esth 11:11; Sir 35:21), Judith's unique use of this epithet is only one of numerous reasons to consider her a liberation figure.[63]

The next divine name in Judith's prayer invokes the ancestry of Judith and of Israel itself, and supplements that with God's role as cre-

---

61. Moore, *Judith*, 193.

62. Moore compares the vocabulary here to that in 2 Sam 17:45–47; 2 Chr 16:8–9; Jdg 7:2; Exod 15:2 (Moore, *Judith*, 193).

63. See the Judith Conclusion for more on this.

ator (9:12): "God of my father, God of the heritage of Israel, Lord of heaven and earth, Creator of the waters, King of all your creation." We might wonder if her specific mention of God as "Creator of the waters" has something to do with the significance of water in Judith's story (the Greek ὕδωρ *hudōr* for "water" appears not only here in 9:12, but also in Jdt 2:7; 7:7, 12, 17 twice, 20, 21; 8:9; 9:12; 10:3; 11:12; 12:7 and 16:15). It would be difficult to conclude this with certainty, as water plays such a central role in the biblical creation texts anyway (Gen 1:2, 6–10, 20–22; Ps 103:3, 6, 10; 136:6, all LXX citations that also use ὕδωρ *hudōr*). Judith closes her prayer by again asking for help with her plan of deceit for the sake of the holy city (9:13), and then using her fifth and final divine epithet. This time "God of all power and might" (9:14; cf. 1 Chr 29:12; 2 Chr. 20:6; Esth 10:2) highlights the Lord as the one and only God, who will therefore be victorious for Israel.

With this, Judith closes her prayer and begins to enact her secret plan. First, she moves from her place of prayer and mourning (presumably her rooftop tent) to the place where she would go on those occasions when Jewish law required her to break her rigorous grief rituals (8:5–6; 10:2). Preceding Sidney Bristow and Clark Kent by centuries, Judith then commences the ever-important costume change.[64] After removing her mourning garb, she does an astonishing—but easy to miss—thing. Judith washes "with water" in 10:3, which perhaps appeared scandalous in light of the fact that her whole city was dying of thirst (7:7, 12–13, 20–22). While it could be that Judith simply kept a small amount of used and ostensibly undrinkable wash water for this purpose, the narrator's specific mention of the water may signal her bath as a shocking act. She follows the bath with perfume, hairstyle and jewelry, notably the kind of thing she had worn for her husband (10:3–4a). Judith's superhero costume is in many ways a disguise, covering up her true identity as a pious, devoted widow of over three years.[65] Though we do not yet know

64. Sidney Bristow is the heroine of the 2001–2006 television series *Alias*, about a brilliant, righteous, gorgeous spy, highly skilled in martial arts and arms use, even while wearing heels. Clark Kent is the less contemporary, classic superhero Superman, who typically does his costume change in a phone booth. Moore offers an insightful and in-depth analysis of Judith as undergoing a rite of passage based on Arnold van Gennep and Victor Turner's research, and as a hero figure according to the work of Joseph Campbell (*Judith*, 1141–49).

65. Wills shows that her disguise is the complete antithesis of expected attire for a pious Jewish woman. See Esth Add 14:1–2 and Isa 3:16–24 (*Judith*, 3:1147).

the details of Judith's plan, the narrator has dictated our expectation that it will involve seduction (10:4b) and not warfare—perhaps even more scandalous than her use of water for a bath. In fact the bath itself, as well as the other physical preparations, sets up the audience to anticipate a sex scene, as in the Bathsheba, Susanna, Esther, Song of Songs and Ruth texts (2 Sam 11:2–4; Sus 1:16–26; Esth 2:3, 9, 12–18; Song 5:3–6; Ruth 3:3).[66] The last detail of preparation involves Judith's provisions (10:5). She may have concealed her identity as a grieving widow, but not as a Jew. The fact that she packs her own food and table service shows that though she will not fast, she will be obedient to the Jewish dietary code, like Daniel (1:8–16), Tobit (1:10–11), Judas Maccabeus (2 Macc 5:27) and Greek Esther (14:17), but unlike Hebrew Esther (2:9).[67]

Suitably prepared, Judith takes her leave from the city just as she predicted (8:33), with her favorite slave by her side—just like any superhero's trusty sidekick—and the city elders bidding her farewell (10:6). Just as we would expect, these men notice her stunning appearance, but they do an odd thing in response—ask for God's blessing on her (10:7–8). Wills helpfully points out that recognition of the heroine's beauty is a standard trope in the Greek novel.[68] The comment about her beauty may also be foreshadowing on the author's part, as it highlights what will become Judith's very means of victory over Holofernes. Finally, the superhero and sidekick dramatically exited the city gate and faded into the distance, leaving the townspeople and the readers to wonder what she would do to save her people, her city, and her God's temple (10:9–10).

Judith Enacts Her Plan (10:11—13:9a), and Back to Bethulia (13:9b–20)

This long section contains the crucial episode of the story. It begins with Judith and her servant, having faded out of view of Bethulia, being immediately captured by the Assyrian army. To an audience exposed to the story for the first time, this opening action may seem like more of an ominous downturn in events than part of the plan (10:11–12a). But before long the narrator makes clear that all is in keeping with Judith's

---

66. Amy-Jill Levine compares this aspect of the Susanna, Bathsheba, Judith, and Esther texts in "Hemmed," 1:183–84. Also see LaCocque, *Feminine*.

67. Wills, *Judith*, 3:1158.

68. Ibid., 3:1148.

plan, based on her half-lie in 10:12b. While the reader knows that she is not running away from her people, there is some truth her statement that "they are about to be handed over to you to be devoured." First, Judith knows that her people were on the verge of handing themselves over to the Assyrians (7:23–31). Second, according to the deuteronomistic theology cited by Achior and then Judith, their impending surrender would signal a lack of trust in God, earning them destruction (5:20–21; 8:9–27). It will be interesting to reflect on the shades of truth and deceit in Judith's words throughout this scene.

Judith's final words to these soldiers include an offer that characterizes her as more spy than refugee (10:13). Pausing only to reflect on her irresistible beauty, the guards are quick to accept her proposal to act as a Bethulian informant to the Assyrians (10:14–15). They send her on to their commander having attempted to assuage her fear (10:16). The mention of Judith's fear by Holofernes' men also serves as irony. As we and they will see, Judith is the one to fear. Enough guards accompany her with such attention to suggest they are actually intimidated by this Hebrew woman (10:17). We discover quickly enough, however, that the intrigue with her has more to do with lust than fear (10:19). In fact, the patrol of Holofernes' men foreshadows their weakness in their rationalization that they must now kill all Israelite men, assuming that will neutralize these "beguiling" women. Yet ironically, what they have most to fear is "the hand of a woman" (9:10; 13:15; 16:5) named Judith, who has incidentally had no husband for years. This scene humorously makes what is a larger point throughout the book: Gender stereotypes will be the downfall of the Assyrian army, from the soldiers to their commander.

The narrator has Judith make a grand entrance into the rich setting of Holofernes' tent, with a note about the general's bed to further heighten the sexual tension and invoke the nature and setting of the events yet to unfold (10:20–21). We might wonder how early audiences of Judith felt at this point, whether they were scandalized, titillated, or fearful amid the suspense at this point in the story. Holofernes comes to meet Judith with a grand entrance (10:22), but she quickly becomes the focus of attention (10:23a). Here she bows to him—jarringly reminiscent of her bow to God in 10:8 (both προσκυνέω *proskyneō*)—though Holofernes' attendants remove her from this position of subservience (10:23b). The commander, like his soldiers in 10:16, assumes Judith is afraid and comforts her using the same words, "do not fear in your heart" (10:16//11:1; μὴ φοβηθῇς τῇ καρδίᾳ σου *mē phobēthēs tē kardia sou*; my translation). And, like his soldiers, this comment in Holofernes' mouth serves as an ironic setup since he is the one who should be afraid. He continues to assure Judith of her security with him (11:3b–4) after outlining his terms that loyalty to Nebuchadnezzar creates peace for all. Only briefly amid this welcome speech to Judith does Holofernes inquire as to the reason for her presence (11:3a). He is seemingly too caught up in his own apparently paternalistic and macho assumptions about her to make that a big priority.

In answering Holofernes' question (11:3a), Judith does not miss the opportunity to further enact her plan. She answers him with more half-truths and full-blown lies, as well as some completely true statements. She characterizes herself as an Israelite traitor who has abandoned her people just prior to their demise, and offers herself as Holofernes' spy and a loyalist to Nebuchadnezzar in order to pass on information that will help them conquer Israel. Now that the general has reassured Judith of her safety (11:1, 3b–4), she reassures him of her truthfulness (11:5), and follows that closely with a statement that would come true: With Judith's guidance, Holofernes would be an integral part of a divine plan (11:6)! He of course does not guess that will involve his own death. One way that Judith walks the line between truth and lie is by repeatedly using "my lord" (κύριός μου *kurios moy*) as a "double entendre."[69] In stating "I will say nothing false to my lord this night" (11:5), and "my lord will not fail to achieve his purposes" (11:6), Judith retains her allegiance to God as well as a level of sincerity. At the same time, she lets Holofernes think her loyalties now reside with him and Nebuchadnezzar. Judith heightens that false impression by swearing her truthfulness on the life of *his* lord, Nebuchadnezzar. She further compliments Holofernes by declaring his excellence as a commander saying that he is the reason for Nebuchadnezzar's success (11:7–8).

Our heroine next invokes a name that would have surely caught Holofernes' attention, Achior the Ammonite, who so angered the general with his insights about the people of Israel in 5:5–21. Judith returns to telling the truth, as she assures Holofernes that Achior was in fact correct in his report about Israel and their God. If they disobey divine law, they

---

69. Levine identifies this in 11:5, 6, 11; 12:14; Levine, "Sacrifice and Salvation," 23; Wills, *Judith*, 3:1153.

cannot prevail against Assyria or anyone (11:9–10). In her next statements, however, we do not know enough to assess whether Judith was
giving an accurate description of the Israelites' situation. She explains
that the Israelites were on the verge of breaking their own laws—and
thus losing God's protection—by eating sacred and non-kosher foods to
prevent their starvation (11:11–13). They were waiting only for guidance
from their elders to proceed with this desperate plan, at which point
they would be defeated by Assyria (11:14–15). There was certainly some
truth to Judith's statements about the unlawfulness of eating holy and
unclean foods (Jdt 11:13; Exod 23:19; 34:26; Lev 23:10, 17, 20; Deut 18:4;
Num 18:21; Deut 12:17). More than one commentator has explained
that these issues would have been of interest to an audience with priestly
concerns, though no foreign enemy would have cared about such detail.[70] Nonetheless, there were loopholes in these laws, exceptions that
would have been known to Judith's audience but not to Holofernes. For
instance, David and his men eat bread consecrated for only the priests in
1 Sam 21:3–6, with the unprecedented rationale that they were celibate
during their time of warfare. The Gospel of Matthew has Jesus cite this
as a precedent for his own legal justification for picking grain on the
Sabbath (Matt 12:1–4). An audience in the Maccabean period may also
have been familiar with Mattathias' determination that it was better to
break the Sabbath law than to be exterminated by the enemy (1 Macc
2:29–41). Thus the explanation Judith provides to Holofernes about her
people in 11:11–15 is a half-truth. The rules she cites had exceptions.
Furthermore, if these were indeed the survival plans of the Israelites, we
readers knew nothing of it until this time. That leaves us wondering if
Judith has fabricated the whole thing, or if it was an unspoken part of
her concern when she protested to Uzziah about the people's ultimatum
to God (8:9–13). Whether true or false, her insider's information for
Holofernes is that her people were about to do the very thing that would
leave them vulnerable to the Assyrian army: Disobey God (11:14–15).

In 11:16 Judith opens with another blatant lie in saying for the second time that she ran away from Bethulia (cf. 10:12). Yet she also repeats
for the second time her true claim that God is using her and Holofernes
to accomplish extraordinary, world-renowned ends (cf. 11:6). Her loyal-

---

70. Wills, *Judith*, 3:1154; Craven explores Judith's comments here not only as priestly concerns but more precisely as those of particular Jewish groups in this time period
including the Zealots, Pharisees and Sadducees (Craven, *Artistry*, 118–21).

ties get even more complicated in 11:17–19, and she again abandons the truth when she promises to do prayer-based reconnaissance for the general until he has easily conquered even Jerusalem. Judith attributes her strategy to "foreknowledge" (11:19), something she attributed to God in her prayer of preparation (9:6). While foreknowledge may have sincerely directed her tactics against the Assyrians, she certainly was not using it to help attack Jerusalem. Somehow Holofernes does not balk at the absurdity of her proposal that the Israelite God will help him defeat the Israelite people due to their transgressions. Since that theology was a standard of the Deuteronomist, it certainly comes as no surprise to those familiar with the Hebrew Bible, either then or now (see Jdt 5:20 and Deut 32:1–25).

Despite the fact that she told him the same thing that caused him to leave Achior to his fate, Holofernes responds quite positively to Judith's speech in 11:20–23. Perhaps her looks (11:21b, 23) and her promise of his victory (11:14–15, 18–19) made him deaf to that bad news (11:9–10). In their glowing response to Judith, Holofernes and his men paint her in similar terms as Uzziah did in chapter 8. Even they see her as a Wise Woman, which is clear from the wisdom language they like Uzziah applied to her (σοφία, *sophia*, "wisdom," 8:29//11:20; συνέσει *synesei*, "understanding," 8:29//11:21; ἀγαθὴ *agathē*, "good," 8:28–29//11:23). Their admiration of her wisdom also contains humor; as Wills points out, what they read as wisdom "consists in cleverness," which will be their downfall.[71]

Following these proclamations about Judith, Holofernes goes on to pledge that her successful proposal will result—amazingly—in his conversion. His words echo those of none other than Ruth the Moabite: "your God shall be my God" (11:23//Ruth 1:16, using nearly identical Greek phrases). Ironically, Judith's efforts to save her people at the expense of Holofernes are perceived by him as worthy of conversion. In addition, his promise anticipates the ultimate conversion of Achior the Ammonite, the informant Holofernes rejected and left for dead. This is a significant pledge in light of Nebuchadnezzar's earlier identification of himself as "lord of the whole earth" (2:5). Yet based on his final offer to Judith of residence in Nebuchadnezzar's palace and fame throughout the world—reminiscent of Esther's rise to power in King Ahasuerus' court—perhaps this statement serves as yet another double entendre.

---

71. Wills, *Judith*, 3:1155.

Maybe, rather than pledging his own conversion with "your God shall be my God," Holofernes assumes Judith's.[72] In the end, he will be the fool when it comes to Judith's renown and the reasons for it.

Improving on his flattering words to Judith, Holofernes invites her to his luxuriant table—perhaps as a first date (12:1)! In fact, this is an opportunity by the author to highlight Judith's piety and purity, not Holofernes' hospitality. Judith explains that she cannot share his table or food but has brought her own supply—plenty to last until "the Lord carries out by my hand what he has determined" (12:2, 4). Holofernes shows concern for Judith in asking where she can replenish her food stores, assuming they would have to come from her people (12:3). Were he a very logical or thoughtful character, this would have raised his suspicions. As far as he knows, Judith has fled from her people, who are on the brink of destruction (10:12; 11:16). As he has posed it in 12:3b, she would have no options for acquiring more kosher food other than Israel's triumph and his own defeat.

Though she refuses his food and table, Judith does sleep in Holofernes' tent part of the night, until she receives his permission to leave for her nightly ritual of prayer and purification. That she asks for this consent and that he gives it illustrates both Judith's vulnerability as a prisoner of war, and Holofernes' trust in this captivating captive (12:5b–7a). Judith's nightly baths in the nearby spring are referred to with the verb βαπτίζω (*baptizō*; Jdt 12:7b), which has a distinctly ritual meaning (we see the same verb in LXX 2 Kgs 5:14; Sir 34:25; Mark 7:4; Col 2:12; Heb 6:2; 9:10), in contrast to her washing in preparation for this mission (περικλύζομαι, *periklyzomai*; 10:3). Nonetheless, her ritual cleanness here ironically recalls that first bath as a set-up for a sexually charged scene; it may well serve in both ways here. For a pious Jewish audience it may illustrate Judith's innocence, while at the same time foreshadowing the erotic scene that Holofernes awaits.[73]

The book of Judith comes to its climax in the next scene, set at a banquet in Holofernes' tent and ending with our superhero's act of victory (12:10–13:9a). The narrator builds the suspense by reminding us that this is "the fourth day" (12:10) on a five-day deadline (7:30). Holofernes sends his eunuch Bagoas to bring Judith to his banquet with an arrogant and crude line befitting the stereotypical boys' club: "it would be a dis-

---

72. Ibid., 3:1155.

73. Wills, *Judith*, 3:1158. Also see discussion related to 10:3, above.

grace if we let such a woman go without having intercourse with her. If we do not seduce her, she will laugh at us" (12:12). This NRSV translation retains some ambiguity with its rendering "having intercourse with her." The range of meaning of the Greek ὁμιλέω (*homileō*) includes social conversation, business dealings, and marriage, much like the literal but infrequently used English meaning of "have intercourse with."[74] Paired with the Greek ἐπισπασώμεθα (*epispasōmetha*), which means "draw to oneself," the likely intent of the verse becomes clearer, hence NRSV's "seduce her."[75] This astonishing line would likely have cued the audience to laugh. In particular, it seems forebodingly comical as well as shocking for women throughout history who have heard and experienced all too much similar machismo. For many women in wartime this sad and terrifying statement reflects one of many justifications of rape. We will see soon enough who gets the last laugh at the end of this banquet, when the only "intercourse" Holofernes has is with his own sword.

Interestingly, Holofernes' attendant Bagoas (Jdt 12:11, 13, 15; 13:1, 3; 14:14) bears a name that would have been familiar to audiences in the Maccabean period. We find the same name referred to in Josephus (*Ant* 11.7.1), where this man was one of Artaxerxes' generals who desecrated the temple and contributed to the corruption of the priesthood. In Diodorus Siculus (17, 5.3–6), Bagoas was a eunuch like in Judith, though in this case he was a court official who carried out numerous assassinations in order to manipulate the throne. He finally met his demise when his scheme to poison one king backfired.[76] In any case, the name of this eunuch in Judith may well have caused early audiences of Judith to fear greatly for their heroine, thinking he would be a conniving and villainous character. Furthermore, his identity as a eunuch—whether or not that meant he was as castrate—may have suggested his and Holofernes' assumption that Judith was being integrated into Holofernes' harem, since overseeing the harem was usually the job of a eunuch.[77]

The narrator has Bagoas use carefully chosen words of invitation to Judith in 12:13, complimenting her looks, and suggesting that she "drink wine with us and become today like one of the Assyrian women who serve in the palace of Nebuchadnezzar." These latter comments

74. *LSJ*, BibleWorks, v.8, 30520.

75. Ibid., v.8. 16863.

76. Kuhrt, *The Persian Empire*, 424–25; Moore, *Judith*, 223.

77. See discussion on eunuchs in Esther chapter, above; Wills, *Judith*, 3:1158.

may have raised eyebrows among early audiences, since they suggest she might break her kosher regimen by drinking something unclean, and that she might stray from her pious widowhood not only by having sex, but with someone uncircumcised. Her obliging verbal and physical responses in 12:14–15 would have had the audience in some range of horror, titillation and laughter with the suspense of what would happen next. Her eagerness to please in 12:14 is yet one more instance of her ability to tell the truth and lie at the same time. She will indeed accommodate Holofernes in a way that will bring her happiness the rest of her life, but because she does not say what exactly that will entail, Holofernes assumes she is offering her sexual services, while Judith has something very different in mind. She is playing with him. As the banquet commences, the narrator takes time to mention how Holofernes was burning with desire for Judith, and apparently eager to get her drunk for the sake of his conquest (12:16–17). Perhaps in his own lustful stupor he does not notice that when she accepts his invitation to drink, she partakes of her own supply of kosher wine (12:18–19). In any case, the general becomes the victim of his own designs, drinking "more than he had ever drunk in any one day since he was born" (12:20b). Presumably, that was enough to make him the vulnerable party at this party.

Finally, at the beginning of chapter 13, we discover the much-awaited core of Judith's plan. While we may have thought only a few verses ago that Judith would be the victim of a sex-crazed Holofernes, instead Judith turns the tables and beats the general at his own game, ending his life and conquering Assyria in one fell swoop. Holofernes' slaves took their leave after a long night of partying, leaving their master alone—though passed out—with his presumed conquest (13:1–2). Unlike what many artists have portrayed of the scene, in which Judith's slave stands at her side or even helps while she decapitates Holofernes, in 13:3 our heroine's most trusted companion waits outside of the commander's tent.[78] With Judith's slave is Bagoas; Judith had reminded them that she would come out for her evening prayers, like on every other night (13:3). That comment becomes a narrative segue for a prayer. This prayer of Judith most closely resembles that of Judas Maccabeus, in praying to conquer his enemies (1 Macc 4:30–33), and falls into the tra-

---

78. In Artemisia Gentileschi's two *Judith Beheading Holofernes* paintings, the maid-servant helps hold Holofernes down while Judith chops off his head; in Caravaggio's work of the same name, she stands behind her, holding the food bag.

dition of the imprecations in the psalms (such as Pss 41:5–10; 137:8–9). Judith, standing over the stone-cold-drunk Holofernes, prays that God would make her deed glorify Jerusalem by conquering its enemy. Then, mid-prayer, she takes the commander's own sword from his bedpost (13:6). With that in one hand, and his hair in the other, she resumes her prayer in a most unusual posture, this time petitioning God for strength (13:7). Her prayer is apparently answered, because with only two chops she severs his head at the neck (13:8). Her final acts in this scene are to take the headless corpse from Holofernes' place of comfort, bring down the bejeweled finery from above his bed (10:21), and place his head in the food bag that her slave was holding outside of the tent (13:9–10a). The text is not explicit as to whether Judith's slave knew what would happen while her master was in the tent with the enemy. We can infer she has some idea since the narrator records no surprise on her part, only that she "placed [Holofernes' head] in her food bag" (13:10a). Not only is this scene full of action, it is suffused with meaning. Judith's beheading of Holofernes symbolizes the destruction of all he represented: Assyria; Nebuchadnezzar; uncleanness; luxury at the expense of oppression; the threat of war and all that it entails, including rape; and ultimately any foreign domination of the Jews.

Since Judith was expected to leave the camp for her evening prayers, and to take her food bag along, nothing at all seemed amiss to Bagoas as the two women exited this scandalous scene. Neither he nor any of Holofernes' other men would have reason to think the women would do anything other than to return to what the Assyrians believed was their safe haven from a soon-to-be destroyed people. Instead they return home with good news in a bag to their people, who are dying of thirst in Bethulia. As Judith announces herself at the city gate, she proclaims a statement of faith: God has not abandoned them but has saved them through her actions (13:10b–11, 14). The peoples' response is astonishment not so much at her message, but that she had returned at all (13:13). That points to one subtle but remarkable success in Judith's plan, that the people remained patiently faithful to God and to Judith while they wasted away waiting for those five days to pass. Finally she showed the people her evidence, the lavish canopy from Holofernes' bed, and his severed head. Their greedy, wicked enemy was dead, attributing his demise to God and her own deceitful seduction and quick sword-wielding hand (13:15–16). Her boast here, that she cut off his head to defeat him, *and* that she did not have sex with him to do it, has surely been the prayer of many women who have determined that their sexuality was the only way to accomplish some life-saving end. They have prayed that they could somehow use seduction without having to follow through with sex. Now that the Bethulians have the physical evidence, they join Judith's celebration and praise of God (13:17). Uzziah goes on to bestow an effusive blessing on Judith, confirmed by all the people (13:18–20). Comparable blessings include Abram in Gen 12:2 and 14:19, Jael in Judg 5:24, Ruth in 2:12; 3:10, Boaz in Ruth 2:20, and Abigail in 1 Sam 25:33–34, all of which use the Greek εὐλογητός *eylogētos* or εὐλογέω *eylogeō*.

The Final Battle: Setup and Completion (14:1—15:7)

Upon her return, Judith moves beyond her role as hero into one of military commander. Her opening instruction to hang Holofernes' head on the city wall is the gruesome touch of a victorious warrior (14:1; cf. 1 Sam 17:51–54; 31:9–10), an act quite unexpected of a pious widow. By now, Judith has effectively transitioned from one to the other.[79] Additionally, this act provides another parallel between Judith and Judas Maccabeus, who along with his troops decapitated the dead Nicanor and used his head to rally the Jerusalemites (1 Macc 7:47; 2 Macc 15:30–35).[80] She gives orders to the people of Bethulia and the troops, in light of her own decisive actions of the previous scene. Her strategy is to take down the enemy Assyrians while they are in shock over the assassination of their commander, before they have had time to regroup (14:2–4).

Surprisingly, Judith thinks there is a more pressing task than that. She asks to see Achior in order to show him the dead and decapitated face of his would-be killer, Holofernes (14:5). Her encounter with the Ammonite becomes her platform to tell the whole community the details of the story that readers know, but the Bethulians did not (14:8). The community responds in 14:9 with their second unison affirmation of Judith's actions, much like their cries of "Amen" in 13:20. Achior's first reaction was to faint, apparently at the sight of Holofernes' severed

79. See Wills' relevant insights on Judith in a state of liminality and the book as depicting her journey through a rite of passage (*Judith*, 3:1142, 1159).

80. Wills makes the additional connection that the Jews' celebration over Nicanor's death (1 Macc 7:48–50; 2 Macc 15:35–36) parallels the Bethulians' festivities in Judith's honor (13:19–20; 16:23), *Judith*, 3:1167. Also see discussion above on Judith and Judas in the commentary on 8:1.

head (14:6b), something the narrator notably does not report of either Judith or her slave. Perhaps it was such a horrid sight and he was rather squeamish, or maybe he was simply shocked at the implication that the Assyrians had been conquered at the top by this Bethulian widow. His ultimate reaction however, was neither of shock or dismay but of reverence to Judith (14:7), and finally to the God of Israel (14:10). This in fact becomes the occasion of his conversion, a significant act for an Ammonite in light of Deut 23:3–6 (echoed in Neh 13:1–2), and in fact for any foreigner during this time in history. Achior does mention other foreigners in 14:7b but assumes they will be inspired to fear Judith rather than to follow her God. Having heard his theologically astute recounting of Israelite history however (5:5–19), this narrative has prepared the audience for this event.

Based on his conversion, Achior compares to the Moabite Ruth, who similarly claims the God of Israel in Ruth 1:16–17. This aspect of Judith arguably places it in conversation with other Second Temple period biblical literature that engages the controversial issue of who belongs in the Jewish community and how they attain such membership.[81] Other relevant texts include Ezra 6:21; 9:1–10:44, Isa 56:4, 6, and perhaps even Jonah, which offers a theological view of an Israelite's foray into enemy territory. Judith is likely from a later time than these texts; it points to the fact that debate about who was a Jew continued for at least centuries. Notably, Achior does not attribute his conversion to Judith's actions *per se*, but to the deeds of Israel's God (14:10a). We find a similar explanation of YHVH's mighty acts preceding and including the Exodus (for instance Exod 10:2; 14:4; Deut 29:6 [Heb: v. 5]): "The Lord did those things so that both Israelite and Egyptian would "know that I am the LORD."

In 14:11—15:8, the action moves back to the Assyrians, who do not yet know what the Bethulians know. The battle scene ensues with the Bethulians carrying out Judith's order to hang Holofernes' head high on the city wall (14:11; cf. 14:1). With that symbolic act as their starting point, they descend on the Assyrian camp in battle formation. The Assyrians welcome their invasion, feeling sure it was simply an invitation to destroy these hold-out rebels (14:13b). Of course, the surprise was theirs when Judith's plan unfolded to the detail. Rather than finding the great commander in a lovers' embrace with the Bethulian woman,

---

81. See Date and Purpose, in Ruth chapter, above.

Bagoas found Holofernes' body decapitated on the floor, and responded with appropriate anguish (14:14–16). It did not take him long to figure out what happened: their ravishing volunteer spy was in fact an assassin (14:17–18). Bagoas' exclamation in v. 18 repeats the narrator's specific description of the scene in v. 15, "Holofernes is lying on the ground, and his head is missing!" This literary feature comes off as odd or even humorous. While we might expect him simply to shout, "That woman killed the general," instead he responds with this comically pedantic line. With that cry, Bagoas' alarm spreads to the whole encampment of Assyrians, and ultimately turns into group panic, just as Judith had predicted (14:9—15:2; cf. 14:3). If only all military commanders could call the shots of their opponents as well as Judith! Paradoxically, the Assyrians both "do not wait for one another" and act "with one impulse," the outcome of which is their total yet unorganized abandon of the territory, not to mention the military campaign (15:2). In short order the Israelites invade and force the Assyrians to retreat to the furthest reaches of the land, according to Judith's perfectly-unfolding plan (15:3b–8). At this point Uzziah functions as Judith's lieutenant (15:4). This is not an entirely new role for him, as he and Bethulia's other leaders essentially made her their commander in 8:35, at the start of her plan. The Israelites, unlike the Assyrians, act here "with one accord" (15:5 cf. 15:2).

The three locations named in 15:4–5a, like so many places in Judith, likely do not exist anywhere other than in the author's fabricated geography. They do not appear anywhere outside of Judith, though various commentators have suggested associating them with known locations that have similar names. Betomasthaim also appears in Jdt 4:6 as Betomesthaim. That citation suggests that it, like Bethulia was strategically located for guarding the mountain passes into Judea. Judith 4:4 also mentions Choba; there it is one of the Israelite cities that received warning to prepare for the Assyrian invasion. Judith 15:5 seems to indicate that it lay on one of Israel's borders. The point is that Israelite warriors from throughout the whole land join the Bethulians, including some from known locations like "Jerusalem and all the hill country," and those to the north and northeast, Galilee and Gilead (15:5). They bring the Assyrians to their end "with great slaughter." The narrator even mentions the absurd detail that Israelites chased this foe "beyond Damascus," far beyond their borders and into Syria (15:5). It was a way of saying the Israelites chased the Assyrians part-way home to Nineveh.

Israelites throughout the land benefitted from the booty that warriors raided from the Assyrians' huge abandoned encampment (15:6–7). This poses another point of comparison to Esther, as the Greek version unapologetically describes the Jews' acquisition of booty from their enemies (Add Esth 9:10). In contrast, the Hebrew version of Esther does not allow for anything but the strict rules of "the ban," or *herem* (חרם), requiring total destruction of the enemy and all their material goods so that no one and nothing could lure them to worship foreign gods (Esther 9:10, 16; see Deut 13:6–19; 20:16–18; Josh 6:18; Jdg 8:22–27; 1 Sam 15:1–35). It could be that the later Hellenistic context of Greek Esther and Judith was more tolerant of the secular warfare practice of plunder. For instance, Wills notes a similar scene of the Hasmonean victory over Nicanor in 1 Macc 7:43–47.[82]

Amid this battle scene in 15:3b–7, we could easily overlook the fact that the Israelites were pursuing an army that had voluntarily withdrawn (15:1–3a). Based on this section alone (15:3b–7) readers would not think the Bethulians were ever the underdogs. This may pose an ethical dilemma reminiscent of what we read in Esther, where the Jews who had barely escaped extermination killed the enemy—and then some (Esth 9:5–16).[83]

Judith the Victor (15:8—16:20)

This section contains grand praise for Judith, and encompasses a magnificent hymn lauding her deeds. The first to speak is the high priest, Joakim, and the Jerusalem elders (15:8). This high priest also appears earlier in Judith (4:8, 14), and Neh 12:12 lists a high priest of the same name. Though the role of high priest purportedly existed through much of Israel's history (Lev 21:10–15; Num 35:25–32), it had particular significance during the Second Temple Period, in which the high priest ruled along with a governor for much of the time, so the position gained in political clout (Neh 3:1; Hag 1:12; 2:4; Zech 3:8). It was a highly vied-for office during the Hasmonean era, and was subject to corruption and power-plays (Sir 50:1; 1 Macc 7:1–9; 10:15–38; 12:3–10, 20; 2 Macc 3:1–4:10).[84]

---

82. Wills, *Judith*, 3:1171.

83. See the Judith Conclusion for further discussion on this topic.

84. It is debatable whether pentateuchal citations truly represent a pre-exilic high priesthood. Rehm, "Levites," 4:309; Kugler, "Priests," 3:610–12.

Like Uzziah before them (13:18–20), Joakim and the Jerusalem elders praise God, pay tribute to Judith, and receive enthusiastic assent for their words from the people in the form of "Amen" (15:8–10). In 15:9 we find profuse and poetic commendation for Judith in the form of a three-line parallelism:

> You are the glory of Jerusalem,
> You are the great boast of Israel,
> You are the great pride of our nation!

They could hardly gush more. They end their words by asking for God's blessing on Judith, but in 10a they notably attribute her success not to the Lord, but to Judith's "own hand." Furthermore, they do not even marvel here that these deeds were accomplished by the "hand of a woman," like we find in Jdt 9:10; 13:15; 16:5.

The Israelite raiding of the Assyrians from 15:6–7 resumes in v. 11, where we learn that the Assyrian encampment apparently had enough provisions and riches to sustain thirty days of raiding! The narrator notes that the warriors awarded Judith all of Holofernes' riches, which was surely the best of the loot. Though someone else collected her reward, Judith herself readies her pack animals and loads these items. It seems fitting that as a prelude to a huge celebration in her honor (15:12—16:20), led by women (15:12), Judith packs her own moving van (15:11b).

The women of Israel pay tribute to Judith in a rather elaborate way, including greenery to dance with and to place on their heads (15:12–13). This women's victory celebration is not unique to Judith. We find similar festivities with song and dance led by Miriam following the Exodus (Exod 15:20–21), and by Deborah after she led Israel to rout the Canaanites (Judg 5:1–31). The men join in on the singing; they too are bedecked with flora as well as their weapons. This joyous scene stands in ironic contrast to that of 3:7 in which the peoples who were terrified of Holofernes welcomed him with "dance" and "garlands." Parallels in vocabulary here (15:13) highlight the beloved Judith as a comparably skilled leader.[85] The three final verses of chapter fifteen effectively assemble the parade of those who will "loudly" (15:14) join with Judith in her magnificent closing hymn (16:1–20).

This grand finale has much in common with the victory hymn following the exodus (15:1–21), and that following Deborah, Barak, and

---

85. Wills, *Judith*, 3:1108.

Jael's military successes against the Canaanites (Judg 5:1–31).[86] The scene also recalls similar celebrations for welcoming home victorious war parties, down to the detail of the same musical instruments. In Jdg 11:34, Jepthah's daughter receives her father this way; in 1 Sam 18:6 the people celebrate Saul and David, following David's successful contest against Goliath the Philistine, and in 2 Sam 6:5 (//1 Chr 13:8), the community rejoices at the return of the ark, led by David dancing. Judith's song follows the basic pattern of a song of praise, such as we find in the Psalms. It begins with an "opening invitation to praise" (16:1), moves on to "reasons for praise," which begins as usual with "for" (כִּי *ki* in the Psalms; in Jdt 16:2 this is ὅτι *hoti*), and closes with a "recapitulation of the invitation" (16:13–17).[87] The psalm opens with Judith leading the people in praise for the Lord (16:1–2). She uses the same divine appellation as in her prayer of 9:7, "a God who crushes wars." As we saw there, that title is a repetition from the Song of the Sea (Exod 15:3). Thus Judith invokes Israel's war-crushing God before and after taking down the Assyrian General, reminding the audience that this event rivals that of their formative victory against Egypt. In 16:2, Judith also emphasizes God's presence with her assertion "he sets up his camp among his people," as opposed to the Assyrians whose king was not on the battlefield with them, and whose commander had been unceremoniously removed from power, right in the middle of his camp.

Judith's song moves to talk about the enemy that God crushed, recalling the details of their size and their fearsome threats (16:3–4). Verse 4 gives the sense that God, rather than Judith is speaking in the first person ("my territory . . . my young men . . . my infants . . . my children . . . my virgins"). This poses the battle as one between Holofernes and the Lord. The hymn resolves in 16:5 with a refrain familiar from her prayer in 9:10 and from her victorious return to Bethulia in 13:15: The Lord's work was accomplished in this case "by the hand of a woman." This underhanded compliment only works as a rhetorical device if the audience assumes a woman would ordinarily be unable to accomplish something like this. Thus, the statement introduces a section of the hymn consisting of praise particularly for Judith (16:6–10). This section will focus on her physical appearance—we might say her "feminine wiles"—apparently her greatest weapon as a woman.

86. See White, "In the Steps."
87. McCann, "Psalms," 4:648.

The rhetoric moves to comparison in 16:6, which invokes more standard superheroes, "the sons of the Titans" and "tall giants." This probably did not refer to the Titans of Greek mythology, but is simply a way to translate two originally Hebrew terms into Greek. "Titans" (τιτάνων titanōn) similarly translates רפאים *rephaim* in 2 Sam 5:18, 22 LXX, while "giants" (γίγαντες) translates *nephilim* נפלים in Gen 6:4; Num 13:33 LXX and *rephaim* in 1 Chr 20:8; Job 26:5; Isa 13:3; 14:9 and Isa 13:3 LXX. Sidnie Ann White suggests that the LXX translator had to find a Greek synonym for "giants" in order to accommodate the Hebrew poetic parallelism, which was likely originally *rephaim* and *nephilim*. "Titans" sufficed, but should not be interpreted as detracting from Judith's piety by referring to Greek gods.[88] While Titans and giants would surely be able warriors, and would probably fulfill most people's choices for such an ominous situation, Judith surpasses them using good looks, perfume, and alluring clothing to fell this great enemy (16:7–9).

Verse 7 describes a remarkable reversal, in that Judith "put away her widow's clothing to exalt the oppressed." As we saw above, a widow would herself be categorized as the oppressed in ancient Israel.[89] It is remarkable that she could go from being oppressed herself to being a champion of the oppressed, signified through a clothing change. In v. 9 we find another significant poetic feature in this portion of the hymn, where a three-line parallelism compares aspects of Judith's "arsenal" (her "sandal," "beauty," and "sword") with parts of Holofernes' body (his "eyes," "mind," and "neck"). The third line of this poetic device has a surprise ending that catches the audience's attention in a similar way that it caught Holofernes off-guard! While he—and we—were thinking of Judith's appearance, she had something else entirely planned. In fact, if we include vv. 7–8 as laying four lines of groundwork for this marvelous parallelism in v. 9, the total comes to six synonymous lines, culminating in 9b.[90] The end of this section of praise for Judith points to the Persians and Medes as impressed by Judith's prowess (16:10). This reference serves as something of an inclusio, as it recalls the opening battle in which Nebuchadnezzar attacks Media (1:1–6). The hymn goes on to recall the people's response to Judith's victory. Verses 11 and 12 emphasize Judith's role as a liberator through repetition that stresses her

88. White, "Titans," 6:578.

89. See above commentary on 8:4–6.

90. Wills, *Judith*, 3:1177.

people's lowliness (see Judith's prayer in 9:1–14 and related commentary, above). The "oppressed," "weak," and "sons of slave girls" constituted the "army of my Lord" and thus became the winners in this war, rather than the victims of the Assyrians.

The final section in Judith's song (16:13–17) evokes the opening invitation to praise about singing to God (16:1; 13–14a), and includes additional reasons for praise (vv. 14b–16) as well as a woe statement (v. 17), more frequently seen in laments. These five verses use familiar scriptural tropes to clearly establish the book in the wider context of the Hebrew Bible. Judith sings refrains familiar as opening statements of praise in the Psalms, particularly, "I will sing to my God a new song" (see Ps 33:3; 96:1; 98:1; 144:9; 149:1).[91] Verse 14 refers to Gen 1:1—2:4, invoking God's creation through speech. The phrase "the rocks melt like wax" (v. 15) translates the same Greek phrase in the praise Psalm 97:5. It may sound like Judith belittles offerings in v. 16, but we can see that is not entirely the case in 18–19. Instead, the intent in v. 16 is to place fear of the Lord above all else, like we see the Wisdom literature among other places (1 Sam 12:14; Job 28:28; Ps 34:11 [Heb 34:12]; 111:10; Prov 1:7; 2:1–5; 9:10–12; 10:27; 14:26–27; 16:6; 19:23; 22:4), and to emphasize like some of the prophets that ritual itself is not God's greatest desire (Hos 9:1–4; Amos 5:21–24). The woe statement in v. 17, as well as the preceding four verses, focuses on the greatness and power of God, and reminds the reader that Judith was not the sole actor in the events narrated in the book. As Wills points out, this line is a contradiction to Nebuchadnezzar's insistence that he was "lord of all the earth" (2:5).[92]

Immediately following Judith's hymn, the text describes the people's ritual activities upon returning from battle (16:18–20). They gather at Jerusalem for worship and purification, to present offerings and share in celebratory meals. The narrator notes that Judith does not keep the booty that had been awarded to her (15:11), but offered it all to the Lord, including the bejeweled canopy from Holofernes' bed, in which she had wrapped his body after beheading him (16:19). This comment keeps Judith's piety intact, whereas the earlier impression that she might have kept this booty placed her in a questionable light. After all, such was the demise of King Saul (1 Sam 15:1–35).

91. The Greek in Jdt 16:13 reads ὕμνον καινόν *humnon kainon*, while the Psalms LXX have ᾆσμα καινόν *asma kainon*. The similarity in meaning is notable nonetheless.

92. Wills, *Judith*, 3:1179.

The ending of this story consists of a hero's epilogue. The people return home as though there had never been a time of starvation and misery within their city's walls; there is no mention of things having to get back to normal (16:21a). We learn that Judith chooses to remain unmarried, despite numerous offers of marriage (v. 22). This status invites yet further feminist reflection on the character Judith. Nowhere in this book does a male voice or figure take over for her, as it does in Ruth and Esther. She is a strong, independent woman—liberated financially and personally from patriarchy, save for her connection to her deceased husband Manasseh in her old age and even death (v. 23). In her latter days she extended the role she had begun as liberator (9:11; 16:11–12) by emancipating her favorite slave—the one who had after all been at her side on her heroic journey to defeat the Assyrians (v. 23). This feature compares to the happy ending of Job, where he gave a bequest even to his daughters along with his sons, though women would normally not receive an inheritance (42:15). Adding to the many ways that Judith transgressed traditional gender roles, she took on the customary male role of bequeathing her riches to her own family and that of her husband (v. 24b). The people honor her death with a significantly holy seven days of mourning (v. 24a). The final verse of Judith constitutes the ultimate happy ending, and the utmost praise (25). Her very presence on earth safeguarded her people, even for some time after her death. In this way, the book ends as it began, with a clear indication of it as a fantastical story.

Conclusion

The book of Judith arose as a Jewish hero tale in Hebrew, with a story line and protagonist much like Joseph, Esther, and Daniel. Whether due to its date or its content, its community of origin did not remain its home. Instead, the book found popularity among early Christian readers, who eventually accorded it some level of canonicity. While the book of Judith has always captured the imaginations of its readers, in recent decades it has enjoyed resurgent popularity. From shifting gender roles to deceit for the sake of survival, the book raises many issues of contemporary relevance.

One place we can see Judith's influence is in the art of the renaissance, and contemporary discussions of that. Caravaggio made a famous painting of Judith beheading Holofernes, and numerous other artists of his era chose this warrior woman as the basis of their sculptures, paintings, and music, from Michelangelo to Vivaldi. Another notable painter of Judith was Artemisia Gentileschi. Born in Rome in 1593, she stood out in that landscape because few women were permitted to learn or create art in the formal marketplace. In the style of Caravaggio and her artist father Orazio, Gentileschi created numerous paintings based on the Judith story, from the gory beheading scene to one in which Judith and her slave stand ready to leave the Assyrian camp with Holofernes' severed head in a basket.[93] With her unique role as a female baroque painter, Gentileschi has gained recognition among contemporary feminist art critics, historians and biblical scholars in recent decades. An oft-discussed aspect of her life is the rape she suffered at the hands of her tutor, Agostino Tassi, who apparently promised to marry her following the rape, but did not fulfill that vow. Tassi was a colleague of Gentileschi's father, whom he may have appointed to give her some instruction. Though Tassi was convicted, he spent less than nine months in prison. Because Italian transcripts exist of this rape trial in May 1611, this incident has received much attention among commentators, particularly the ways it may have affected Gentileschi's depictions of Judith. A controversial film depicting the life of young Artemisia further increased her popularity. The 1997 film directed by Agnès Merlet relies on numerous untruths about Gentileschi's life, and depicts the artist having an erotic love affair with Tassi.[94] However, the film rightly points out that the rape trial had to do with the legalities of the day—that a man who stole a girl's virginity would dishonor her and her family unless he married her—rather than whether or not this young woman wanted to have sex with her tutor.[95]

With a more scholarly eye, the notable art historian Mary Garrard uses Gentileschi's life as a lens for interpreting her gruesome and bloody paintings of Judith and Holofernes. "Many writers have interpreted the gory decapitation shown in Artemisia's Uffizi *Judith* in psychosexual terms, as an expression of imagined revenge against her rapist Agostino Tassi. The evidence for this interpretation resides simultaneously in the

93. See the marvelous descriptive analysis of Gentileschi's Judiths by Ciletti, "Gran Macchina è Bellezza," 63–105.

94. *Artemisia*.

95. Pollock, "Feminist Dilemmas," 190–201.

image of the executioner-heroine—for some, a presumed self-portrait of the artist—and in an equation that is both biblical and Freudian, between decapitation and castration: the just punishment for rape in an eye-for-an-eye tradition."[96] As we will see, this analysis is pertinent not only to Gentileschi,[97] but also to Judith. Judith too had every reason to fear her own rape and the widespread violation of her people, all of which motivated her to kill Holofernes. Because both Gentileschi and Judith had their own significant power as well as vulnerability, their stories become a fascinating dialogue about gender and violence.

For all the attention Gentileschi has received for good and for ill, Judith in turn has found a renewed place in the spotlight. A much more contemporary artist than Gentileschi, Judy Chicago, has similarly drawn attention to Judith. Chicago honored Judith with her own place setting in her massive and intricate installation work *The Dinner Party*. Originally unveiled in 1979, this triangular table with personalized space for each guest welcomes thirty-eight women, including Judith and Artemisia Gentileschi. Chicago deemed these the most outstanding women in history. The table runner at Judith's place includes her name in Hebrew characters; a sword crosses the first letter of the script "Judith" across the front.[98] Artists such as Chicago and Gentileschi have aroused much interest to the story of Judith from audiences that would know little or nothing of her otherwise. On several occasions when I have taught the story of Judith, persons who know of the artwork on Judith express excitement to finally know the story on which the art is based.

Both of these women artists capitalize on the ways in which Judith challenges traditional gender roles. The text emphasizes this by repeating three times that the Israelites' victory was achieved at "the hand of a woman," or more precisely, a "female" (Jdt 9:10; 13:15; 16:5 ἐν χειρὶ θηλείας *en cheiri thēleias*).[99] The threefold repetition of "the hand of a woman" in reference to Judith the conqueror plays on the derogatory assumptions that a woman who defeated the enemy would be surprising to all and utterly dishonorable to the losers. This paradox of the female victor—that because of her sex she shames the men she kills, and yet

96. Garrard, *Artemisia*, 278.

97. Contra Pollock, "Feminist Dilemmas, 201.

98. Brine, "Judith," 4. Photos and a description of the Judith place setting appear online: http://www.brooklynmuseum.org/eascfa/dinner_party/place_settings/judith.php.

99. Moore, *Judith*, 193.

she has killed them—creates a quandary especially for feminist readers. While they may appreciate Judith's unique take on gender roles, they most likely reject the idea that a woman is such an unlikely conqueror— Deborah and Jael are noteworthy examples of the conquering woman warrior.

Additionally, Judith's method of killing Holofernes invites its own gender speculation, which has much in common with analyses of Gentileschi's work. It does not take an elaborate Freudian analysis to see what has subconsciously occurred in 13:8 when Judith decapitates Holofernes. Judith uses Holofernes' own phallic symbol (his sword) to perpetrate against him the rape that he would have committed against her and her people. She then symbolically castrates him by chopping off his head, rendering him worse than impotent. To this extent, the book of Judith becomes the epitome of a women's triumph story—the *Thelma and Louise* or *Extremities* of its time—though Judith is portrayed as more dominant than even those women.[100] What Judith accomplished in her narrative is what Gentileschi seemingly fantasized about in her paintings. She is a figure for women to hold up and aspire to as their protectress and model for self-preservation and revenge. Craven offers this powerful reflection on the potential impact of Judith on women and their wider communities: "Imagine what life would be like if women were free to chastise the leading men of their communities, if they dared to act independently in the face of traumas, if they refused to marry, and if they had money and servants of their own. Indeed if they, like Judith, hired women to manage their households, what would become of all the Eliezers of the world? I suspect that the sages would have judged that their communities simply could not bear too many women like Judith."[101] As we know, Judith went on to singlehandedly assassinate one of the most powerful men of her day. It is worth considering whether our contemporary communities reject, tolerate, or embrace women like Judith. Such women have long been the building blocks of many cultures, though that does not ensure their acceptance.

Besides inspiring artistic renderings and gender analyses, Judith has not surprisingly had great influence among religious people because

100. *Extremities* was first a play by William Mastrosime, and was made into a film in 1986. Thanks to Scott Griessell, who suggested *Extremities* as we discussed contemporary comparisons to the story of Judith.

101. Craven, *Artistry*, 117–18.

she is a biblical figure, canonical in at least some circles. In the 1970s and 80s Rigoberta Menchú and her movement of indigenous Guatemalans identified with Judith as a biblical figure who used violence to triumph righteously over her peoples' oppressors. Menchú specifically identified Judith as someone for the women in her community to emulate, along with Moses and David (against Goliath) for the men.[102] More broadly, Menchú spoke of the Bible as a primary weapon in her community's efforts at self-defense.[103]

In some circles of contemporary Judaism, the book of Judith has regained its status as a significant Hanukkah story alongside that of Judas Maccabeus.[104] At least one contemporary Rabbi has revived Judith's story for Hanukkah not only because it adds another gripping tale to that struggle, but also because hers adds a female character to the list of Jewish champions.[105]

These depictions and interpretations of Judith, separated by centuries and continents, constitute a small sampling of the ways in which this Bethulian superhero has captured the imaginations of readers.[106] The artistic depictions in particular remind us that we all bring our own life experiences, including cultural assumptions, values, and beliefs, along with us to our interpretations of the text. In Artemisia Gentileschi's art and Rigoberta Menchú's struggle, we can see that the Bible—in this case Judith—may accompany a reader through her suffering and even triumphs.

Thus Judith reminds us, like Esther, that the biblical text can be an outlet for fantasies of self-defense or revenge. The act of telling, hearing, and enjoying such stories does not require us to carry out such acts, but it may originally have served as a release valve for those emotions. This does however raise the troubling possibility that a book like Judith may provoke actual violence for the purpose of carrying out God's plan and protecting God's people. This matter has created a dilemma for people of

102. Menchú, *I, Rigoberta*, 155.

103. Ibid., 159.

104. For early references to the use of Judith in Hanukkah, see Gera, "Jewish," 23–40, especially her Appendix of Judith Hanukkah texts, 38–39; also Susan Weingarten, "Food," 97–126.

105. Frucht, "Letter," 16–21.

106. For an exhaustive analysis of Judith's influence in Western culture see Stocker, *Judith*. The book includes numerous color and black-and-white illustrations of Judith art.

faith through the centuries, from Judith herself to Dietrich Bonheoffer, and scores in between. Indeed, arguments about just war theory and its applicability to contemporary wars in Iraq and Afghanistan persist, even if they are generally eclipsed by debate about tactics, budget, and how many lives "we" lost. This discussion also exposes a troubling aspect of liberation theology: If God is on the side of the oppressed, what happens if the oppressed rise up and become the oppressors themselves?

Related to this, several ethical dilemmas arise in Judith. A central problem in the book for people of faith is the matter of violence, from Judith's assassination of Holofernes (13:8) to the Israelites' pursuit and decimation of a retreating and leaderless army (15:5–6). We can explain this as part of an obviously fictional story told by a people who longed for justice from and dreamed of revenge against their enemies. Yet in Judith's historical setting, the scene raises questions of greater concern. If the book arose during the Hasmonean reign, this aspect of the story may have reflected not only a self-defense fantasy of an oppressed people, but the triumphalist narrative of the victor. That would make this a rather uncomfortable read for those who do not want to side with the oppressor. Nonetheless, we must acknowledge that this is one of very few times in the Israelites' history that they held the role of conqueror, and even the Maccabean victory was never as absolute as that of the Bethulians. History continues to illustrate that the oppressed can and often do become the oppressor. Perhaps when a people know firsthand the fear of being victimized, they may become overzealous in fighting against anyone who might tyrannize them again.

In addition to the matter of violence, the book raises the ethical problem of deceit. The number of lies Judith tells in this book is difficult to tally. After all, several of her untruths count as double entendre in which her veracity depends on the interpretation.[107] The book of Judith itself and its main character show some self-consciousness about these issues. We see this particularly in Judith's prayers, though her concern is not so much for the morality of the assassination she will carry out and the lies she will tell, but that her motive will be for the sake of the Lord and the people of Israel (9:13–14; 13:4). This should not be overly surprising since she does after all compare her impending actions to victories over Israel's oppressors in other situations, particularly the Exodus

107. See commentary above on 11:6 and 23.

and the revenge against the Simeonites.[108] Because Judith prays for help with her deceit and violent victory, does that make God complicit in her acts? Surely this is not a new theological dilemma in the scheme of the biblical text, evidenced again by the Exodus, among other scenarios. Yet for many persons of faith, this problem of God as aggressor persists, even for the sake of defending God's vulnerable people.

Alongside these dilemmas, we must acknowledge that Judith is an extraordinary character. Her story arouses suspense and victory cheers; it invites deep ethical and theological reflection. Yet too many people base their knowledge of Judith—if they have any knowledge of her—on those secondary interpretations, and not on an actual reading of the text. As I conclude this chapter and this book, I advocate not only reading Judith, but studying and even preaching on her story. She may not have made it into all of the canons, but her compelling story is well worth our attention.

108. See commentary above on 9:2 and 9:7.

Bibliography

Abrams, J. J., producer. *Alias*. ABC Television. September 30, 2001—May 22, 2006.

Adamson Andrew, and Vicky Jenson, directors. *Shrek*. Screenplay by Ted Elliott. Glendale, CA: Dreamworks, 2001.

Bal, Mieke. "Heroism and Proper Names, or the Fruits of Analogy." In *A Feminist Companion to Ruth*, edited by Athalya Brenner, 42–69. FCB 3. Sheffield: Sheffield Academic, 2001.

Batoni, Pompeo Girolamo. *Esther before Ahasuerus*. 1738–1740.

Beauvoir, Simone de. *The Second Sex*. Translated by H. M. Parshley. New York: Knopf, 1993.

Berg, Sandra Beth. *The Book of Esther: Motifs, Themes and Structure*. SBLDS 44. Missoula, MT: Scholars, 1979.

Berlin, Adele. *Esther*. Jewish Publication Society Commentary Series. Philadelphia: Jewish Publication Society, 2001.

Bernard, of Clairvaux, Saint. *The Works of Bernard of Clairvaux*. Vol 12, *Song of Songs 1: Sermons 1–20*. Translated by Kilian Walsh. Kalamazoo: Cistercian, 1971.

Bickerman, Elias J. "The Colophon of the Greek Book of Esther." In *Studies in the Book of Esther*, edited by Carey A. Moore, 225–45. Library of Biblical Studies. New York: Ktav, 1982.

———. *Four Strange Books of the Bible: Jonah, Daniel, Koheleth, Ester*. New York: Schocken, 1984.

Black, Fiona C. "Beauty or the Beast? The Grotesque Body in the Song of Songs." *BibInt* 8 (2000) 302–23.

Bledstein, Adrien J. "Female Companionships: If the Book of Ruth Were Written by a Woman . . ." In *A Feminist Companion to Ruth*, edited by Athalya Brenner, 116–33. FCB 3. Sheffield: Sheffield Academic, 2001.

Botterweck, G. Johannes. "יוֹנָה." In *TDOT* 6:37–39.

Brenner, Athalya. "Come Back, Come Back the Shulammite" in *A Feminist Companion to the Song of Songs*, edited by Athalya Brenner, 234–57. FCB 1. Sheffield: Sheffield Academic, 1993.

———. "The Food of Love: Gendered Food and Food Imagery in the Song of Songs." *Semeia* 86 (1999) 101–12.

Brown, S. Kent. "Egypt, History of (Greco-Roman)." In *ABD* 2:370–71.

Burton, Tim, director. *Edward Scissorhands*. Screenplay by Caroline Thompson. Starring Johnny Depp, Winona Ryder, Dianne Wiest and Anthony Michael Hall. Twentieth Century Fox, 1990.

Campbell, Edward F., Jr. *Ruth*. AB 7. Garden City, NY: Doubleday, 1975.

Caravaggio, Michelangelo Merisi da. *Judith Beheading Holofernes* 1599–1600, Palazzo Barberini, Rome, Italy.

Carr, David M. "Gender and the Shaping of Desire in the Song of Songs and Its Interpretation." *JBL* 119 (2000) 233–48.

Chittester, Joan A. *The Story of Ruth: Twelve Moments in Every Woman's Life*. Grand Rapids: Eerdmans, 2007.

Ciletti, Elena. "*Gran Macchina è Bellezza*: Looking at the Gentileschi Judiths." In *The Artemisia Files: Artemisia Gentileschi for Feminists and Other Thinking People*, edited by Mieke Bal, 63–105. Chicago: University of Chicago Press, 2005.

Claeissens, Anthuenis. *Esther before King Ahasuerus with Haman being sent to the Gallows*. 1577.

Clausen, René. *Set Me as a Seal*. Champaign, IL: Fostco Music Press, 1989.

Clines, David J. A. *The Esther Scroll: The Story of the Story*. Sheffield: JSOT Press, 1984.

———. "Mordecai." In *ABD* 4:902–4.

Collins, John J. *Introduction to the Hebrew Bible*. Minneapolis: Fortress, 2004.

Conrad, Leipzig J. "כלה." In *TDOT* 7:166.

Cousland, J. R. C. "Nicanor." In *NIDB* 4:269.

Craven, Toni. *Artistry and Faith in the Book of Judith*. SBLDS 70. Chico, CA: Scholars, 1983.

———. "The Book of Judith in the Context of Twentieth-Century Studies of the Apocryphal/Deuterocanonical Books." *CBR* 1 (2003) 187–229.

Crawford, Sidnie W. "Esther." In *NIB* 3:853–972.

———. "Judith." In *NISB* 1379–1400.

Day, Linda M. *Esther*. AOTC. Nashville: Abingdon, 2005.

Dearman, J. Andrew. "Edom." In *NIDB* 2:188–91.

De Troyer, Kristin. "An Oriental Beauty Parlor: An Analysis of Esther 2:8–18 in the Hebrew, the Septuagint and the Second Greek Text." In *A Feminist Companion to Esther, Judith and Susanna*, edited by Athalya Brenner, 47–70. FCB 7. Sheffield: Sheffield Academic, 1995.

Dobbs-Allsopp, F. W. "The Delight of Beauty and Song of Songs 4:1–7." *Interpretation* 59 (2005) 260–77.

Driver, Samuel Rolles. *An Introduction to the Literature of the Old Testament*. New York: Scribner, 1914.

Duran, Nicole Wilkinson. "Bougaean." In *NIDB* 1:494.

———. *Having Men for Dinner: Biblical Women's Deadly Banquets*. Cleveland: Pilgrim, 2006.

Ehrlich, Carl S. "Siloam." In *NIDB* 5:255–57.

Exum, J. Cheryl. *Song of Songs*. Old Testament Library. Louisville: Westminster John Knox, 2005.

Fabry, H. J. "שׁוב." In *TDOT* 14:487–89.

Falk, Marcia. *The Song of Songs: Love Lyrics from the Bible*. Sheffield: Almond, 1982.

Farmer, Kathleen A. "Ruth." In *NIB* 2:889–946.

———. "Ruth." In *NISB*, 383–90.

Fox, Michael V. *Character and Ideology in the Book of Esther*. Studies on Personalities of the Old Testament. Columbia: University of South Carolina Press, 1991.

———. *Qohelet and His Contradictions*. JSOTSup 71. Sheffield: Almond, 1989.

———. *The Song of Songs and the Ancient Egyptian Love Songs*. Madison: University of Wisconsin Press, 1985.

———. *A Time to Tear Down and a Time to Build Up: A Rereading of Ecclesiastes*. Grand Rapids: Eerdmans, 1999.

Frucht, Leora Eren. "Letter from Modi'in: Hanukka with Two Genders." *Hadassah Magazine* December 2009/January 2010, 16–21.

Garrard, Mary D. *Artemisia Gentileschi around 1622: The Shaping and Reshaping of an Artistic Identity*. Princeton: Princeton University Press. 1991.

Garrett, Duane A., and Paul R. House. *Song of Songs/Lamentations*. Nashville: Nelson, 2004.

Artemisia Gentileschi. *Judith Beheading Holofernes*. 1612–1613, Capodimonte Museum, Naples, Italy

Gera, Deborah Levine. "The Jewish Textual Traditions." In *The Sword of Judith: Judith Studies across the Disciplines*, edited by Kevin R. Brine et al., 23–40. Cambridge: OpenBook, 2010.

Greenspoon, Leonard, and Sidnie W. Crawford. *The Book of Esther in Modern Research*. JSOTSup 380. London: JSOT Press, 2009.

Halfants, M. Corneille. "Introduction." In *The Works of Bernard of Clairvaux*, Vol. 12, *Song of Songs 1: Sermons 1–20*. Translated by Kilian Walsh. Kalamazoo, MI: Cistercian, 1971.

Hamilton, Jeffries M. "En-Gedi." In *ABD* 2:502.

Henten, Jan Willem van. "Judith as Alternative Leader: A Rereading of Judith 7–13." In *A Feminist Companion to Esther, Judith and Susanna*, edited by Athalya Brenner, 232–38. FCB 7. Sheffield: Sheffield Academic, 1995.

Hess, Richard. *Song of Songs*. Baker Commentary of the Old Testament. Grand Rapids: Baker Academic, 2005.

Herodotus. *Histories*. Translated by A. D. Godley. 4 vols. LCL. Cambridge: Harvard University Press, 1920.

Ilan, Tal. *Integrating Women into Second Temple History*. 1999. Peabody, MA: Hendrickson, 2001.

———. *Silencing the Queen: The Literary Histories of Shelamzion and Other Jewish Women*. Texts & Studies in Ancient Judaism 115. Tübingen: Mohr/Siebeck, 2006.

James, Carolyn Custis. *The Gospel of Ruth: Loving God Enough to Break the Rules*. Grand Rapids: Zondervan, 2008.

Johnson, Jeffrey A., and Joel Gregory. *The Song of Solomon: Love, Sex & Relationships*. Longwood, FL: Xulon, 2007.

Johnson, Niall, director. *Keeping Mum*. Screenplay by Richard Russo and Niall Johnson. Starring Rowan Atkinson, Kristin Scott Thomas, Maggie Smith, and Patrick Swayze. Summit Entertainment, 2005.

Jones, Norah. "Come Away with Me." *Come Away with Me*. CD. New York: Blue Note, 2005.

Josephus. *Antiquities*. In *Josephus, the Essential Works*, edited by Paul L. Maier. Grand Rapids: Kregel, 1988.

Judge, Mike, producer. *Beavis and Butthead*. Aired on MTV. 1993–1997.

Kates, Judith A. *Reading Ruth: Contemporary Women Reclaim a Sacred Story*. New York: Random House, 1994.

Keel, Othmar. *Song of Songs: A Continental Commentary*. CC. Translated by Frederick J. Gaiser. Minneapolis: Fortress, 1994.

Kidd, Sue Monk. "A Penguin Reader's Guide *to The Secret Life of Bees*." In *The Secret Life of Bees*. New York: Penguin, 2008.

Klein, Ralph W. "Artaxerxes." In *NIDB* 1:275.

Kugler, Robert. "Priests and Levites." In *NIDB* 3:610–12.

Kuhrt, Amélie. *The Persian Empire*. New York: Routledge, 2010.

LaBianca, Øystein S. "Heshbon." In *Eerdmans Dictionary of the Bible*, edited by David Noel Freedman, 585–86. Grand Rapids: Eerdmans, 2000.

LaCocque, Andre. *The Feminine Unconventional: Four Subversive Figures in Israel's Tradition*. Minneapolis: Fortress, 1990.

———. *Ruth*. CC. Minneapolis: Fortress, 1994.

———. *Romance, She Wrote: A Hermeneutical Essay on Song of Songs*. Harrisburg, PA: Trinity, 1998.

Llewellyn-Jones, Lloyd, and James Robson. *Ctesias' History of Persia: Tales of the Orient*. New York: Routledge, 2010.

Levenson, John D. *Esther*. OTL. Louisville: Westminster John Knox, 1997.

Levine, Amy-Jill. "Hemmed in on Every Side: Jews and Women in the Book of Susanna." In *Reading from this Place*. Vol. 1, *Social Location and Biblical Interpretation in the United States*, edited by Fernando F. Segovia and Mary Ann Tolbert, 175–90. 2 vols. Minneapolis: Fortress, 1995

———. "Sacrifice and Salvation: Otherness and Domestication in the Book of Judith." In *No One Spoke Ill of Her: Essays on Judith*, edited by James C. VanderKam, 17–30. Early Judaism and Its Literature 2. Atlanta: Scholars, 1992.

Lutzky, Harriet. "Shadday as a Goddess Epithet." *VT* 48 (1998) 15–36.

Mastrosime, William. *Extremities: A Play in Two Acts*. New York: French, 1984.

Mayer, Milton. *They Thought They Were Free: The Germans, 1933–45*. Chicago: University of Chicago Press, 1966.

McCann, J. Clinton. "Psalms—Introduction." In *NIB* 4:641–77.

McGeough, Kevin. "Esther the Hero: Going beyond 'Wisdom' in Heroic Narratives." *CBQ* 70 (2008) 44–65.

MacNaughton, Ian, and John Howard Davies. *Monty Python's Flying Circus*. DVD. Episode 3, Season 1. New York: New Video, 1969–1970.

McLachlan, Sarah. "Ice Cream." *Fumbling toward Ecstasy*. CD. Montreal: Nettwerk, 1992.

Menchú, Rigoberta. *I, Rigoberta Menchú: An Indian Woman in Guatemala*. Edited and Introduced by Elisabeth Burgos-Debray. Translated by Ann Wright. Brooklyn: Verso, 1984.

Merlet, Agnès, screenwriter and director. *Artemisia*. Starring Valentina Cervi, Michel Serrault, and Miki Manojlovic. Cinecittà Studios, 1998.

Meyers, Carol. *Discovering Eve: Ancient Israelite Women in Context*. New York: Oxford University Press, 1988.

———. "Returning Home: Ruth 1.8 and the Gendering of the Book of Ruth." In *A Feminist Companion to Ruth*, edited by Athalya Brenner, 85–114. FCB 3. Sheffield: Sheffield Academic, 2001.

Milton, John. *Paradise Lost*. Edited by Martin Evans. Cambridge: Cambridge University Press, 1973.

Miroschedji, Pierre de. "Susa." In *ABD* 6:244.

Moore, Carey A. *Esther*. AB 7B. Garden City, NY: Doubleday, 1971.

———. *Judith*. AB 40. Garden City, NY: Doubleday, 1985

Murphy, Roland E. *The Song of Songs*. Hermeneia. Minneapolis: Fortress, 1990.

———. *The Tree of Life: An Exploration of Biblical Wisdom Literature*. 3rd ed. Grand Rapids: Eerdmans, 2002.

Cukor, George, director. *My Fair Lady*. Screenplay by Alan Jay Lerner. Starring Audrey Hepburn, Rex Harrison, and Stanley Holloway. Warner Bros. Pictures, 1964.

Nelson, Tommy. *The Song of Solomon*. Dallas: Hudson, 1999.

Newman, Judith H. "Bethulia." In *NIDB* 1:449.

———. "Ecbatana." In *NIDB* 2:178.

———"Holofernes." In *NIDB* 2:846.

Niditch, Susan. "Esther: Folklore, Wisdom, Feminism and Authority." In *A Feminist Companion to Esther, Judith and Susanna,* edited by Athalya Brenner, 26–46. FCB 7. Sheffield: Sheffield Academic, 1995.

Niehr, H., and G. Steins, "שָׁדַד." In *TDOT* 14:424–46.

Nielsen, Kirsten. *Ruth.* OTL. Louisville: Westminster John Knox, 1997.

O'Collins, Gerald G. "Crucifixion." In *ABD* 1:1207–10.

Origen. *The Song of Songs, Commentaries and Homilies.* Translated by R. P. Lawrence. New York: Newman, 1957.

Onions, C. T. et al., editors. *Oxford Dictionary of English Etymology.* London: Clarendon, 1985.

Pa, Anna May Say. "Reading Ruth 3:1–5 from an Asian Woman's Perspective." In *Engaging the Bible in a Gendered World: An Introduction to Feminist Biblical Interpretation in Honor of Katharine Doob Sakenfeld* , edited by Linda Day and Carolyn Pressler, 47–59. Louisville: Westminster John Knox, 2006.

Perkins, L. "Ecbatana." In *ABD* 2:270–71.

Peterson, Eugene H. *The Message.* Colorado Springs: NavPress, 2002.

Pietersma, Albert. "Holofernes." In *ABD* 3:257

Pollock, Griselda. "Feminist Dilemmas with the Art/Life Problem." In *The Artemisia Files: Artemisia Gentileschi for Feminists and Other Thinking People,* edited by Mieke Bal, 169–206. Chicago: University of Chicago Press, 2006.

Pope, Marvin H. "Bible, Euphemism and Dysphemism in." In *ABD* 1:723.

———. *Song of Songs.* AB 7C. Garden City, NY: Doubleday, 1995.

Rappaport, Uriel. "Nicanor." In *ABD* 4:1105.

Rashkow, Ilona. "The Discourse of Power and the Power of Discourse." In *A Feminist Companion to Ruth,* edited by Athalya Brenner, 26–41. FCB 7. Sheffield: Sheffield Academic, 2001.

Rehm, Merlin D. "Levites and Priests." In *ABD* 4:309.

Ringgren, Helmer. "*nkr.*" In *TDOT* 9:423–32.

Rose, Martin. "Names of God in the OT." In *ABD* 4:1005.

Said, Edward W. *Orientalism.* New York: Random House, 1978.

Sajbel, Michael O. *One Night with the King.* Screenplay by Stephan Blinn. Starring Tiffany Dupont, Luke Goss, John Noble, and Omar Sharif. Hollywood: Gener8Xion Entertainment, 2006.

Sakenfeld, Katherine Doob. *The Meaning of* Hesed *in the Hebrew Bible: A New Inquiry.* HSM 17. Missoula: Scholars, 1978.

———. *Ruth.* Interpretation: A Bible Commentary for Teaching and Preaching. Louisville: John Knox, 1999.

Sanders, James A. "Adaptable for Life: The Nature and Function of Canon." In *Magnalia Dei, The Might Acts of God: Essays on the Bible and Archaeology in Memory of G. Ernest Wright,* edited by Frank Moore Cross et al., 531–60. Garden City, NY: Doubleday, 1976.

Sasson, Jack M. "Esther." In *The Literary Guide to the Bible,* edited by Robert Alter and Frank Kermode, 335–42. Cambridge: Belknap, 1987.

———. *Ruth: A New Translation with a Philological Commentary and a Formalist-Folklorist Interpretation.* JHNES. Baltimore: Johns Hopkins University Press, 1979.

Schmidt, Frederick W. "Bougaean." In *ABD* 1:773–74.

Scholem, Gershom. "Magen David." In *Encyclopedia Judaica,* edited by Fred Skolnik, 13:336–39. 22 vols. 2nd ed. Detroit: Macmillan Reference, 2007.

Selim, Ali, director and screenwriter. *Sweet Land*. Starring Elizabeth Reaser, Lois Smith and Patrick Heusinger. Beverly Hills, CA: Twentieth Century Fox, 2005. DVD.

Seow, Choon Leong. "God, Names of." In *NIDB* 2:593.

Smith-Christopher, Daniel L. "Xerxes." In *Eerdmans Dictionary of the Bible*, edited by David Noel Freedman, 1401. Grand Rapids: Eerdmans, 2000.

Soelle, Dorothee, and Joe H. Kirchberger. *Great Women of the Bible in Art and Literature*. Abridged ed. Minneapolis: Fortress, 2006.

Soulen, Richard N. "The *wasfs* of the Song of Songs and Heremeneutics." In *A Feminist Companion to the Song of Songs*, edited by Athalya Brenner, 234–57. FCB 1. Sheffield: Sheffield Academic, 1993.

Spencer, Scott. "Eunuch." In *NIDB* 2:355–56.

Stocker, Margarita. *Judith, Sexual Warrior: Women and Power in Western Culture*. New Haven: Yale University Press, 1998.

Stone, Nira. "Judith and Holofernes: Some Observations on the Development of the Scene in Art." In *No One Spoke Ill of Her: Essays on Judith*, edited by James C. VanderKam, 73–93. Early Judaism and Its Literature. Atlanta: Scholars, 1992.

Scott, Ridley, director. *Thelma and Louise*. Screenplay by Callie Khouri. Los Angeles: MGM, 1991.

Tapert, Robert, producer. *Xena: Warrior Princess*. Tapert and Raimi. MCA Television, 1995–2001. Television.

Thoreau, Henry David. *Walden: or, Life in the Woods*. Boston: Shambhala, 2004.

Trible, Phyllis. *God and the Rhetoric of Sexuality*. Overtures to Biblical Theology. Philadelphia: Fortress, 1978.

Van Dijk-Hemmes, Fokkelien. "Ruth: A Product of Women's Culture?" In *A Feminist Companion to Ruth*, edited by Athalya Brenner, 134–39. FCB 3. Sheffield: Sheffield Academic, 2001.

Van Wijk-Bos, Johanna W. H. *Ezra, Nehemiah, and Esther*. Westminster Bible Companion. Louisville: Wesminster John Knox, 1998.

VanZant, Michael G. "Medes, Media." In *NIDB* 4:6–8.

Waard, Jan de, and Eugene A Nida. *A Translator's Handbook on the Book of Ruth*. New York: United Bible Societies, 1973.

Weems, Renita. "Song of Songs." In *NIB*, 5:361–434.

———. *What Matters Most: Ten Lessons in Living Passionately from the Song of Solomon*. New York: Walk Worthy Press, 2004.

Weingarten, Susan. "Food, Sex, and Redemption in Megillat Yehudit (the 'Scroll of Judith')." In *The Sword of Judith: Judith Studies across the Disciplines*, edited by Kevin R. Brine et al., 97–126. Cambridge: Open Book, 2010.

White, Sidney Ann. "Bethulia." In *ABD* 1:715–16.

———. "In the Steps of Jael and Deborah: Judith as Heroine." In *No One Spoke Ill of Her: Essays on Judith*, edited by James C. VanderKam, 5–16. Early Judaism and Its Literature 2. Atlanta: Scholars, 1992.

———. "Titans." In *ABD* 6:578.

Whitehorne, John. "Cleopatra." In *ABD* 1:1064.

Wills, Lawrence Mitchell. *The Jew in the Court of the Foreign King: Ancient Jewish Court Legends*. HDR 26. Minneapolis: Fortress, 1990.

———. *The Jewish Novel in the Ancient World*. Myth and Poetics. Ithaca: Cornell University Press, 1995.

———. "Judith." In *NIB* 3:1073–1177.

Wittenburg Door. http://www.wittenburgdoor.com/newsletter/songofsolomon.jpg/.

Young, Robert M., director. *Extremities*. Screenplay by William Mastrosime. Starring Farrah Fawcett, James Russo, and Alfre Woodard. Atlantic Entertainment Group, 1986.

Zobel, H.J. "חסד." In *TDOT* 5:45–50.

Topical Index